Reading the World through Sports and Young Adult Literature

Reading the World through Sports and Young Adult Literature

Resources for the English Classroom

Luke Rodesiler
Purdue University Fort Wayne

Mark A. Lewis
James Madison University

Alan Brown
Wake Forest University

NCTE

National Council of Teachers of English
340 N. Neil St., Suite #104, Champaign, IL 61820
www.ncte.org

Staff Editor: Cynthia Gomez
Manuscript Editor: Michael Ryan
Interior Design: Jenny Jensen Greenleaf
Cover Design: Pat Mayer
Cover Image: iStock.com/PeopleImages and Dreamstime.com/Yuri Arcurs

ISBN 978-0-8141-0179-7; EPUB eISBN 978-0-8141-0180-3; PDF eISBN 978-0-8141-0181-0

It is the policy of NCTE in its journals and other publications to provide a forum for the open discussion of ideas concerning the content and the teaching of English and the language arts. Publicity accorded to any particular point of view does not imply endorsement by the Executive Committee, the Board of Directors, or the membership at large, except in announcements of policy, where such endorsement is clearly specified.

NCTE provides equal employment opportunity to all staff members and applicants for employment without regard to race, color, religion, sex, national origin, age, physical, mental or perceived handicap/disability, sexual orientation including gender identity or expression, ancestry, genetic information, marital status, military status, unfavorable discharge from military service, pregnancy, citizenship status, personal appearance, matriculation or political affiliation, or any other protected status under applicable federal, state, and local laws.

Every effort has been made to provide current URLs and email addresses, but, because of the rapidly changing nature of the web, some sites and addresses may no longer be accessible.

Library of Congress Control Number: 2023950915

To the teachers and students working to build a more humane world: Thank you.

–Luke

To my mother, Janet. She died from brain cancer while I was working on this book, and writing Chapter Eight was therapeutic for me. I hope the ideas we share in that chapter help teachers productively talk about grief with their students. My mom's favorite sport was soccer, and I miss sharing a game with her.

–Mark

To my family–Brandi, Finley, and Quinton–and to my current and former students and colleagues who are not afraid to grapple with the sociopolitical issues discussed in these chapters given their roles as learners, teachers, scholars, athletes, authors, and advocates.

–Alan

CONTENTS

FOREWORD

Sports touch all of our lives. Whether we're sports fans or not, the popularity and accessibility of sports means that their coverage is inescapable. So, too, are the real-world consequences of sports, both as a billion-dollar industry with material implications and as a cultural beacon that holds a mirror up to society and to ourselves. Despite growing calls in recent years to "stick to sports," the reality is that sports have never been just about what's happening on the field, wins and losses, or injury updates. With sports, as with literature, it's imperative to read between the lines.

In preparing to write this foreword, I thought about my own journey, both as a sports fan and a sports journalist whose career has been built on using sports as a lens to examine broader issues in society and the world. I thought about how useful it would have been to have had a book like *Reading the World through Sports and Young Adult Literature* during my formative years, to put me on the path to deeper, more critical thinking about these games and these athletes I love. It was, in fact, a class in college called "The Sociohistorical Foundations of American Sport" that ultimately shaped my approach to my coverage. This class opened my eyes to the various ways that sports go hand-in-hand with what's happening in the world. They always have.

I also thought about my high school English teachers, who not only helped me hone the craft of writing but of examining texts in historical and cultural context. I credit any success I've had to these teachers, who taught me how to read inquisitively and skeptically and to never stop asking questions. The educators who've put together this book have dedicated their lives to cultivating the next generation of critical thinkers and thought leaders. In the decades of experience among them, Luke Rodesiler, Mark Lewis, and Alan Brown have examined the ways to use popular culture and literature to reach diverse student bodies with a common goal: using our everyday interactions with the popular media that surrounds us to think more deeply about the state of the world and to challenge the status quo. The group of English teachers contributing to this book have done the same across the country. I guarantee every single one of them has former students who had experiences like mine, who can point to these teachers as pivotal figures in their paths to adulthood and citizenry.

In *Reading the World through Sports and Young Adult Literature*, you'll grapple with the various ways sports reflect our society, in ways both good and bad. You'll learn to question longstanding notions of toxic masculinity, misogyny, homophobia, gendered violence, mental health, physical health, ableism, substance abuse, a "win-at-all-costs" mentality, and peer pressure. Even the most cynical among us will learn the power that sports can hold in building confidence, unifying a locker room, overcoming hardship, working through personal battles, and what it means to be part of a team.

The reason sports can serve as this powerful lens is because they can be a great equalizer—people from all walks of life, from every socioeconomic and ethnic background, can come together around a beautiful game. At the same time, sports, like anything else, can be used to divide. They can bring out the most basic, tribal instincts among groups with different perspectives and different interests. The examination of these often-conflicting dynamics allows us to see and understand other sides more clearly, to avoid letting the superficial aspects of sports cloud the underlying truths of what's really going on, and to help you decide for yourself how to approach these issues.

There's a reason it seems that nowadays debates around sports grow evermore contentious: Sports have power. That power is deeply rooted when many of us develop our fandom—often in younger, more formative years when we're unconsciously shaping our identities. Just as two fans can watch the same football play and have completely opposite opinions about whether or not it was a catch, so, too, can two people experience sports with different perspectives on what those sports mean to their lives.

At a time when it seems the classroom itself is under attack, it remains the best place to examine these perspectives, a place to learn from each other and from worldviews we ourselves might not occupy. Books like this one are so important to combat complacency, not to shy away from hard realities but to grapple with ethical dilemmas even when those conversations are uncomfortable or uneasy.

And still, sports are about joy. When you strip away the money and the trophies and the bragging rights, they're about coming together for a common goal, learning and growing from mistakes, supporting those around you in success and in failure. My hope with this book is that it teaches you how to keep things in perspective. Sports aren't the most important thing in life, even though they're often given outsized importance. But because they matter to so many of us, it's critical to continue to question them and particularly those in authority with the power to shape our experiences from the top down.

A baseball player skipping a game to be present at his child's birth shouldn't be subjected to social media abuse because his team lost that day. That's a real conversation happening in sports circles as we more broadly debate the right to paid parental leave for workers in other industries. A football owner receiving billions of taxpayer dollars to build a new stadium should come under the same scrutiny we give companies benefiting from corporate welfare. A players' association striving for wage, healthcare, and retirement coverage for its workers deserves the same support as other labor unions fighting for fair workplace practices. A soccer player who checks herself into rehab for substance abuse is not "weak" but is battling a very real disease, as are the millions of Americans affected by the opioid crisis. A hockey player afraid to publicly come out for fear of bullying and harassment should be able to live as their authentic selves, as should the millions of LGBTQ+ youth who often find themselves among our most vulnerable. A tennis player has just as much right to use her platform to speak out against racial inequality and police brutality as you and I do.

I'm grateful for books like this one for helping to move these conversations forward at a time when many in power rush to stifle dissent. My hope is that you take these conversations outside the classroom, that you continue to learn and grow through the lens of sports, and that you pass these lessons down to future generations. When we love something, be it sports or our country, we have a duty to look at it critically for the purpose of making it better, to help it live up to its promise. We're not there yet. Never stop asking why.

Kavitha A. Davidson is a sportswriter based in New York. She most recently served as a correspondent on HBO's Real Sports with Bryant Gumbel, *for which she won a Sports Emmy Award. She also serves on the Board of Directors of the Yogi Berra Museum. She was previously a sports and culture writer for* The Athletic *and the host and editorial director of* The Lead, The Athletic's *flagship daily podcast, where she won an Edward R. Murrow Award, a Gracie Award, and a Webby Award. She was previously a columnist and feature writer for espnW and* ESPN The Magazine. *Before that, she wrote a daily sports column for Bloomberg with a heavy focus on the intersection of sports and business, culture, race, and gender. Her first book,* Loving Sports When They Don't Love You Back, *coauthored with Jessica Luther, was published in September 2020 by the University of Texas Press and was named one of the Best Books to Give by* The New York Times *in 2020. A native New Yorker, she attended Columbia University, where she was the sports editor of the* Columbia Daily Spectator.

ACKNOWLEDGMENTS

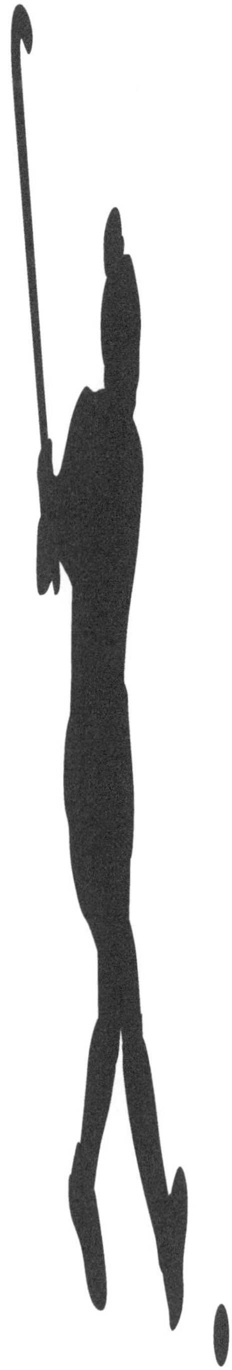

There are numerous people we must thank for helping us move this book project across the finish line. We start by thanking the talented educators who generously wrote the "Voices from the Field" entries that appear throughout the book: Crystal L. Beach, Guy Hill, Rick Joseph, Rachel Roloff, Mitchell Nobis, Shannon McLeod Mound, Erin Denby, Kristen M. Black, Olivia Anderson, Steven J. Arenas, and Kate Youngblood all drew from their unique classroom experiences to enrich the core chapters of this book. We are also incredibly grateful to journalist Kavitha Davidson for writing the foreword that sets the stage for the chapters that follow. Helping youth examine sports culture and our global society through a critical lens in much the way Davidson does with her work is one of our central aims with this book, so we appreciate her participation in the project. As well, we must recognize the colleagues nationwide who have advanced our thinking about the roles that sports culture can play in fostering literacy learning. At the NCTE Annual Convention and in other spaces, a growing cadre of teachers and teacher educators have helped us consider what is possible. Additionally, we thank Kurt Austin and the staff of the NCTE Books Program, their editorial board, and the reviewers they recruited to vet our original manuscript. Ultimately, their support positions us to reach teachers who seek to engage students in the critical study of pressing sociopolitical issues using accessible content that taps students' knowledge of, interests in, and experiences with sports culture. Finally, we appreciate all the students who have spent time talking to us about sports, fandom, literature, and sociopolitical issues throughout our years in secondary classrooms. Their passion for sports and their insights on what troubles our global society drive our work.

1

Sports, Sociopolitical Issues, and Young Adult Literature

The intersections of sports and sociopolitical issues are numerous, as elite, justice-minded athletes have consistently served as agents of social change. Jackie Robinson breaking Major League Baseball's color barrier in 1947; boxing champion Muhammad Ali refusing to be drafted into the United States (US) military and, subsequently, the Vietnam War in 1966; and tennis great Billie Jean King fighting for gender equity in the "Battle of the Sexes" in 1973 stand as celebrated historical examples.

More contemporary models abound as well. NFL quarterback Colin Kaepernick protesting systemic racism and police violence by kneeling during the US national anthem in 2016; members of the US women's national soccer team charging US Soccer with institutionalized gender discrimination in 2019; WNBA star Maya Moore putting her basketball career on hold to advocate for criminal justice reform in 2020; and racecar driver Darrell "Bubba" Wallace pushing NASCAR to ban the Confederate flag in the midst of protests following the May 2020 murder of George Floyd at the hands of a police officer are all high-profile illustrations.

While prominent athletes have been known to challenge societal ills, history shows that figures from collegiate and professional sports have also been known to perpetuate them. For example, in the summer of 2023 alone, Northwestern University fired head football coach Pat Fitzgerald following an investigation into allegations of hazing within the football program (Thamel, 2023); UFC fighter Sean Strickland unleashed a series of sexist and misogynistic comments at a pre-fight press conference (Audilet, 2023); and Glen Kuiper, a longtime announcer for MLB's Oakland A's, was fired for using a racist epithet during a broadcast (Kawahara, 2023). Unfortunately, we could identify several stories like these from any time period in contemporary US history.

Whether as activists or antagonists, high-profile sports figures have been entangled in their share of sociopolitical issues over time, but they are not alone in that regard. Teens who compete in school-sponsored athletics have also found their lives touched by issues that extend beyond the sports world, with some actively battling against societal ills and others contributing to them. For example, journalists have reported on stories about the following topics:

- teen athletes advocating for gender equality (Barton, 2022)
- teen athletes protesting racism (Slonaker, 2023)
- teen athletes challenging homophobic stereotypes (Jacobs, 2022)
- teen athletes with (dis)abilities fighting for the right to compete (DeVito, 2022)
- teen athletes suffering sports-related brain injuries (Ho, 2023)
- teen athletes facing rape charges (14 News Staff, 2023)
- teen athletes battling societal pressures regarding the ideal body image (Hawgood, 2022)
- teen athletes finding solace through sport when grieving a death (Woods, 2022)
- teen athletes bullying and hazing others (Davis, 2023)
- teen athletes dying from opioid abuse (Peetz, 2022).

With sports and sociopolitical issues colliding so routinely, sports culture offers a generative, familiar context for engaging students in the critical study of today's pressing matters.

Critical Literacy and Sports Culture

Organized efforts to ban books that invite discussion about sociopolitical issues such as race and racism, sexual orientation, and gender identity have dramatically increased in recent years (PEN America, 2022). But creating opportunities for middle and high school students to critically explore such matters, including intersectional concerns related to these issues, falls squarely in line with one primary goal for literacy instruction scholars have long established: offsetting inequities (Gere et al., 1992). When inviting students to interrogate sociopolitical issues, teachers position them to raise questions about the politics of daily life (Janks, 2010), to better understand the sociopolitical systems in which they live (O'Brien, 2001), and to challenge unequal power relations (Anderson & Irvine, 1993). Examining sociopolitical issues relevant to students' lives in ways that question the status quo and challenge inequities and injustices, as well as actively working to redesign our world for the better, is the work of critical literacy

(Morrell, 2005; Vasquez et al., 2019). There is not a single correct model of critical literacy, and the work can be done with any text, including those connected to sports culture.

In the English language arts classroom, sports-related texts can support teaching for critical literacy while also honoring the knowledge and experiences students bring with them to the classroom. "Focusing on sociopolitical issues" is a dimension of critical literacy Lewison et al. (2002) advanced and, as the historical and contemporary examples in the opening pages of this chapter suggest, sports and sociopolitical issues often intertwine. This intertwining is not lost on most students, especially those who are active in sports culture, whether they participate in interscholastic athletics, play sports recreationally, compete in fantasy sports, or otherwise immerse themselves in sports fandom to keep up with the latest developments involving their favorite teams and athletes, both in the arena and out. Students' knowledge of, experiences with, and critiques about sports culture, then, are assets for teaching and learning, providing valuable frames of reference when exploring sociopolitical issues of the present day. This is an argument advanced in *Developing Contemporary Literacies through Sports: A Guide for the English Classroom* (Brown & Rodesiler, 2016), and it is one we aim to build on with this book.

Scholars have described using various types of sports-related texts to help students explore sociopolitical issues arising in the milieu of contemporary sports culture and the world beyond. For example, scholars have suggested critically analyzing memes and other forms of popular media to problematize the rhetoric surrounding female athletes (Beach & Dredger, 2018); critically reading political cartoons to challenge the positioning of Native Americans as mascots (Rodesiler & Premont, 2018); and critically viewing major motion pictures to disrupt the White savior trope evident in select sports-related films (Garland, 2016). With this book, we turn our attention to exploring how teachers can use award-winning and recommended works of sports-related young adult literature (YAL) and various supplemental materials in ways that honor students' knowledge and experiences while also supporting them in critically reading contemporary sports culture and the greater world we inhabit.

Sports and Sociopolitical Issues in Young Adult Literature

The category of YAL—stories about young adults involved in relatable conflicts—is rich with award-winning and recommended works of contemporary realistic fiction that (a) are set against the backdrop of the athletic arena and (b) feature teen-athlete protagonists who find themselves entangled by sociopolitical issues relevant to the lives of today's youth. Moreover, the subcategory of sports-related YAL has a history dating back to the birth of YAL in the 1960s.

When recounting the origins of YAL, scholars such as Gallo (2006) and Simmons (2000) have credited a short list of novels published in the late 1960s with setting the foundation. Alongside S. E. Hinton's (1967) *The Outsiders* and Paul Zindel's (1968) *The Pigman*, a third novel commonly cited is Robert Lipsyte's (1967) *The Contender*, a story of self-discovery about a high school dropout who takes up boxing as refuge from the Harlem streets. According to scholars, then, a sports-related novel was there from the start, helping to pave the way for YAL as we know it today (Rodesiler & Lewis, 2020).

Following Lipsyte's first YA novel, fictional stories focused more on the athlete-protagonist coming-of-age and less on in-game action itself—those stories Crowe (2004) labeled "*sportlerroman*" (p. 38)—continued to emerge. These stories, including works published in the 1980s and 1990s by authors such as Walter Dean Myers, Chris Crutcher, Marie Lee, David Klass, and Jan Cheripko, are not focused as much on winning as they are on "the lessons characters learn from their involvement with athletics and with other people" (Crowe, 2004, p. 41).

Since the turn of the century, works of sports-related YAL dealing with sociopolitical issues have continued to garner critical acclaim. Novels in this subcategory have routinely appeared on book lists generated by the Young Adult Library Services Association (YALSA), a division of the American Library Association. For example, the annual YALSA Top Ten Quick Picks for Reluctant Readers has included titles such as *Exit, Pursued by a Bear* (Johnston, 2016), *All American Boys* (Reynolds & Kiely, 2015), *Black and White* (Volponi, 2005), and more recently, *Golden Arm* (Deuker, 2020), *The Passing Playbook* (Fitzsimons, 2021), and *Swim Team* (Christmas, 2022).

But sports-related YAL is not just for reluctant readers, and routine inclusion on the YALSA Top Ten Best Fiction for Young Adults list underscores that fact. Titles such as *Heroine* (McGinnis, 2019), *Winger* (Smith, 2014), *Leverage* (Cohen, 2011), and *Mexican WhiteBoy* (de la Peña, 2008) are just a few examples of sports-related YAL that have received the honor.

Still, it is not only critics who value sports-related YAL. Teen readers have also lauded select titles. The International Literacy Association's Young Adults' Choices reading lists (published by the Children's Book Council as the "Favorites Lists" since 2023), which were generated by middle- and secondary-level students themselves, often included sports-related YAL. Novels such as *Hit Count* (Lynch, 2015), *Swagger* (Deuker, 2013), and *Going for the Record* (Swanson, 2004) stand among the works of sports-related YAL highlighted by teens in the Young Adults' Choices reading lists since 2000. So, though not historically a staple of school curricula, sports-related YAL is routinely recognized as having literary merit by critics and teens alike.

Recognizing the value of sports-related YAL, scholars have presented ideas for incorporating it into the classroom in ways that engage students in the critical exploration of contemporary sociopolitical issues. These include gender norms (Glenn & King-Watkins, 2019), misogyny and transphobia (Cramer, 2021), bullying (Sieben, 2016), and racism (Zwillenberg & Gioia, 2017), among others. With this book, we aim to build on and extend such scholarship, giving teachers ideas for facilitating the meaningful exploration of sociopolitical issues via award-winning and/or recommended works of sports-related YAL.

Working with Challenging Texts

Some people might use the label "challenging texts" to describe many of the novels we promote in this book. We would concur with that assessment. According to Chisholm and Whitmore (2018), a challenging text is one that stirs feelings of "discomfort and uncertainty for teachers and for students" (p. 8) for various reasons, including the following: (a) it addresses a topic that is taboo in schools, such as death or sexual assault; (b) the teacher does not feel adequately prepared to address the content; and (c) the content can be emotionally painful for the teacher and/or students to process. First, teaching with and about challenging texts can be difficult, but that does not mean it should be avoided. Matters like racism, sexism, and bullying are unfortunate realities of the world in which we live. The prevalence of such issues is unlikely to change for the better if youth are never afforded structured opportunities to confront them and imagine alternative ways of being and interacting with others. Second, as described in the next section, we include in each chapter background information about the corresponding sociopolitical issue, both in relation to sports culture and to our broader society. It is our hope that this information helps teachers as they prepare to address challenging content. Finally, when it comes to the emotionally painful aspect of the content, we take a page from Chisholm and Whitmore. That is, we empathize with those who aim to protect youth (and themselves) from uncomfortable emotions, but we also recognize that taking a responsible risk is necessary if classrooms are to be places where youth explore difficult topics with a teacher's support.

In the chapters that follow, we present specific activities for classroom use, but at this point, we aim to highlight some general principles and practices associated with trauma-informed instruction that can be helpful when teaching with challenging texts. A trauma-informed approach to instruction requires first understanding that students may be affected by trauma in their lives and then striving to accommodate their needs while preventing further harm (Carello & Butler, 2015). Multiple principles can undergird this approach. These include recognizing students' emotional safety as a necessary condition for learning, dismissing romantic notions about students' traumatic experiences, and being prepared to refer students to counseling or emergency care providers if necessary (Carello & Butler, 2014). Further, when taking a trauma-informed approach to teaching with challenging texts, teachers might employ practices that include notifying students of forthcoming scenes that may evoke emotional responses, checking in with students to gauge how they are faring with the content and whether adjustments are warranted, and inviting (but never forcing) participation in discussions about sensitive topics (Carello & Butler, 2015). Accounting for principles and practices like these stands to support the exploration of sociopolitical issues in sports-related YAL.

Organization of This Book

In *Reading, Writing, and Rising Up*, Linda Christensen (2017) declared, "Literature should open conversations and dialogue, should move us all to a greater understanding of the world and humanity" (p. 182). With that statement in mind, we wrote this book to help practicing and prospective teachers design instruction that supports students in exploring contemporary sociopolitical issues through accessible sports-related YAL.

Each of the next 10 chapters begins with an overview of a sociopolitical issue that (a) is relevant to the lives of today's youth, (b) is evident in modern sports culture, and (c) can be explored through award-winning and/or recommended works of contemporary sports-related YAL. These overviews help to establish the significance of the issues in the world at large and their relevance to sports culture. We then provide a synopsis of a work of sports-related YAL in which a teen athlete, the story's protagonist, is entangled in or otherwise challenged by the corresponding sociopolitical issue. Further, we highlight critical reviews, recommendations, and awards the featured novel has garnered. These elements stand to help teachers make informed decisions and craft compelling arguments as they move to add the books in question to their curricula amid a climate where rationalizing text selection is of paramount importance.

Each core chapter also outlines instructional methods that teachers can apply immediately or adapt as necessary to help students in their unique contexts engage with the featured sociopolitical issue and corresponding anchor text. This section contains a host of relevant activities. The ideas we pitch are rooted in research and scholarship about effective literacy instruction. They include a range of methods intended for whole-class instruction that supports students in developing the six domains of language arts—reading, writing, speaking, listening, viewing, and visually representing—and growing as informed citizens of the world. We encourage readers to adapt activities suggested in one chapter for use with texts presented in other chapters as appropriate, and we point out some instances when such adaptations seem especially appropriate. Moreover, it is important to note that the methods and materials presented in subsequent chapters are viable not only for secondary sports literature courses like those profiled in *Bringing Sports Culture to the English Classroom: An Interest-Driven Approach to Literacy Instruction* (Rodesiler, 2022) but they are also viable for more traditional language arts classes as well.

Finally, each of the next 10 chapters also includes suggestions regarding additional resources teachers might use to help students explore the central sociopolitical issue. These suggested resources include other works of YAL that teachers might incorporate to support book clubs designed for exploring the sociopolitical issue in question, as well as viable options for film study. As we did with the instructional methods, we encourage teachers to consider their respective contexts when weighing how they could use the suggested resources to meet the needs of the students they serve.

In the book's twelfth and final chapter, we reiterate our intentions, recognize our limitations, and emphasize the work that remains. We highlight additional sociopolitical issues and resources that teachers might bring into the classroom and address the challenging times educators find themselves working in of late. We also make a push for teachers to advocate for students and support them in taking action on the issues they seek to address. Finally, we close by underscoring the intertwining of sports and society and the ways it supports literacy learning.

We dedicate the next 10 chapters to exploring 10 distinct works of sports-related YAL that teachers can use to spark important discussions and actions among students living in an increasingly complex world. The texts, ideas, and activities we present stand to help students develop critical literacy practices and build greater understandings of humanity—their own and others' as well. We believe that, through the intentional exploration of sociopolitical issues emerging against the backdrop of sports culture, students will be better prepared to tackle such issues in any realm of society, wherever life should take them.

Young Adult Literature

Christmas, J. (2022). *Swim team*. HarperAlley.

Cohen, J. C. (2011). *Leverage*. Dutton Books for Young Readers.

de la Peña, M. (2008). *Mexican whiteboy*. Delacorte.

Deuker, C. (2013). *Swagger*. Houghton Mifflin.

———. (2020). *Golden arm*. Clarion Books.

Fitzsimons, I. (2021). *The passing playbook*. Dial Books.

Hinton, S. E. (1967). *The outsiders*. Dell.

Johnston, E. K. (2016). *Exit, pursued by a bear*. Dutton Books for Young Readers.

Lipsyte, R. (1967/2018). *The contender*. HarperCollins.

Lynch, C. (2015). *Hit count*. Algonquin Young Readers.

McGinnis, M. (2019). *Heroine*. Katherine Tegen Books.

Reynolds, J., & Kiely, B. (2015). *All American boys*. Atheneum/Caitlyn Dlouhy.

Smith, A. (2013). *Winger*. Simon & Schuster.

Swanson, J. A. (2004). *Going for the record*. Eerdmans.

Volponi, P. (2005). *Black and white*. Viking Press.

Zindel, P. (1968). *The pigman*. Dell.

REFERENCES

14 News Staff. (2023, March 10). *Trial dates set for Central athlete facing rape charges*. https://www.14news.com/2023/03/10/trial-dates-set-central-athlete-facing-rape-charges

Anderson, G. L., & Irvine, P. (1993). Informing critical literacy with ethnography. In C. Lankshear & P. McLaren (Eds.), *Critical literacy: Politics, praxis, and the postmodern* (pp. 81–104). State University of New York Press.

Audilet, M. (2023, June 28). *Fans disturbed by UFC fighter's appalling comments on women*. The Spun. https://thespun.com/more/top-stories/fans-disturbed-by-ufc-fighters-appalling-comments-on-women

Barton, A. (2022, May 23). Burlington High soccer made national news for a yellow card. Why they are now in a museum. *Burlington Free Press*. https://www.burlingtonfreepress.com /story/news/2022/05/23/burlington-high-school-girls-soccer-team-equal-pay-womens-soccer-brighton-museum-exhibit/9890452002/

Beach, C. L., & Dredger, K. S. (2018). Sporty girls and tomboys: Negotiating the rhetoric surrounding female athletes. In I. Renga & C. Benedetti (Eds.), *Sports and K–12 education: Insights for teachers, coaches, and school leaders* (pp. 119–133). Rowman & Littlefield.

Bradbury, S. (2020, February 3). Judge considers barring public from hearing for former Fairview High School quarterback accused of sexual assault. *The Denver Post*. https://www.denverpost.com/2020/02/03/aidan-atkinson-sexual-assault-fairview-boulder-case

Brown, A., & Rodesiler, L. (Eds.). (2016). *Developing contemporary literacies through sports: A guide for the English classroom*. National Council of Teachers of English.

Carello, J., & Butler, L. D. (2014). Potentially perilous pedagogies: Teaching trauma is not the same as trauma-informed teaching. *Journal of Trauma & Dissociation, 15*(2), 153–168.

———. (2015). Practicing what we teach: Trauma-informed educational practice. *Journal of Teaching in Social Work, 35*(3), 262–278.

Chisholm, J. S., & Whitmore, K. F. (2018). *Reading challenging texts: Layering literacies through the arts*. Routledge; National Council of Teachers of English.

Christensen, L. (2017). *Reading, writing, and rising up: Teaching about social justice and the power of the written word* (2nd ed.). Rethinking Schools.

Cramer, K. M. (2021). Depictions of LGBTQ athletes in young adult literature that interrogate sport culture. *Language Arts Journal of Michigan, 36*(1), 43–50.

Crowe, C. (2004). *More than a game: Sports literature for young adults*. Scarecrow Press.

Davis, S. (2023, February 15). 22-page report details alleged hazing in Middleton football program. *Wisconsin State Journal*. https://madison.com/sports/high-school/football/22-page-report-details-alleged-hazing-in-middleton-football-program/article_734d494f-0902-5fb4-9cfd-b715e00883db.html

DeVito, M. (2022, May 28). Granville High School class of 2022: Persevering through challenges. *Newark Advocate*. https://www.newarkadvocate.com/story/news/2022/05/28/granville-high-school-class-2022-persevering-through-challenges/9731945002/

Gallo, D. R. (2006). The caring community of young adult literature. *The ALAN Review, 33*(2), 24–28. https://scholar.lib.vt.edu/ejournals/ALAN/v33n2/gallo.pdf

Garland, K. (2016). Exploring racial stereotypes through sports-related film. In A. Brown & L. Rodesiler (Eds.), *Developing contemporary literacies through sports: A guide for the English classroom* (pp. 167–172). National Council of Teachers of English.

Gere, A. R., Fairbanks, C., & Howes. A. (1992). *Language and reflection: An integrated approach to teaching English*. Macmillan.

Glenn, W., & King-Watkins, D. (2019). Fictional girls who play with the boys: Barriers to access in the transition to male-dominated sports teams. *Children's Literature in Education, 51*, 309–331.

Hawgood, A. (2022, March 5). What is 'bigorexia'? *The New York Times*. https://www.nytimes.com/2022/03/05/style/teen-bodybuilding-bigorexia-tiktok.html

Ho, M. (2023, January 26). Scary concussion left her unable to walk. Now, SLO County basketball star is thriving again. *The San Luis Obispo Tribune*. https://www.sanluisobispo.com/sports/high-school/article270785017.html

Jacobs, J. (2022, May 19). *This Connecticut high school valedictorian reimagined own legacy by fighting stereotypes*. CT Insider. https://www.ctinsider.com/gametimect/article/Jeff-Jacobs-This-Connecticut-high-school-17184981.php

Janks, H. (2010). *Literacy and power*. Routledge.

Lewison, M., Flint, A. S., & Van Sluys, K. (2002). Taking on critical literacy: The journey of newcomers and novices. *Language Arts*, *79*(5), 382–392.

Morrell, E. (2005). Critical English education. *English Education*, *37*(4), 312–321.

O'Brien, J. (2001). Children reading critically: A local history. In B. Comber & A. Simpson (Eds.), *Negotiating critical literacies in classrooms* (pp. 41–60). Lawrence Erlbaum.

Peetz, C. (2022, April 23). *After Whitman student's fentanyl overdose, family hopes awareness will prevent similar tragedy*. MoCo360. https://moco360.media/2022/04/23/after-whitman-students-fentanyl-overdose-family-hopes-awareness-will-prevent-similar-tragedy/

PEN America. (2022). *Banned in the USA: Rising school book bans threaten free expression and students' first amendment rights*. https://pen.org/banned-in-the-usa

Rodesiler, L. (2022). *Bringing sports culture to the English classroom: An interest-driven approach to literacy instruction*. Teachers College Press.

Rodesiler, L., & Lewis, M. A. (2020). From maven to mentor: The archetypal coaches of *The Contender*. In V. Malo-Juvera & C. Hill (Eds.), *Critical explorations of young adult literature: Identifying and critiquing the canon* (pp. 85–101). Routledge.

Rodesiler, L., & Premont, D. (2018). On second thought: Teaching for social justice through sports culture. *English Journal*, *107*(6), 82–88.

Sieben, N. (2016). Rewriting for justice: Breaking down bullying in *Openly Straight*. In A. Brown & L. Rodesiler (Eds.), *Developing contemporary literacies through sports: A guide for the English classroom* (pp. 186–194). National Council of Teachers of English.

Simmons, J. S. (2000). Middle schoolers and the right to read. *The ALAN Review*, *27*(3), 45–49. https://scholar.lib.vt.edu/ejournals/ALAN/spring00/simmons.html

Slonaker, T. (2023, February 7). *Burlington High girls' basketball team calls out 'culture of racism' in Vermont school sports*. VTDigger. https://vtdigger.org/2023/02/07/burlington-high-girls-basketball-team-calls-out-culture-of-racism-in-vermont-school-sports

Thamel, P. (2023, July 10). *Northwestern fires football coach Pat Fitzgerald amid hazing claims*. ESPN. https://www.espn.com/college-football/story/_/id/37991452/northwestern-fires-football-coach-pat-fitzgerald

Vasquez, V. M., Janks, H., & Comber, B. (2019). Critical literacy as a way of being and doing. *Language Arts*, *96*(5), 300–311.

Woods, D. (2022, June 23). *Grieving son transformed himself from mediocre discus thrower to state champion*. IndyStar. https://www.indystar.com/story/sports/high-school/2022/06/23/discus-thrower-found-therapy-sport-after-his-mothers-death/7543873001

Zwillenberg, J. G., & Gioia, D. (2017). Racism, privilege, and voice in *All American Boys*: A counter-narrative of resistance and hope. *The ALAN Review*, *45*(1), 57–71.

2

Combatting Sexism and Misogyny in Sports Culture

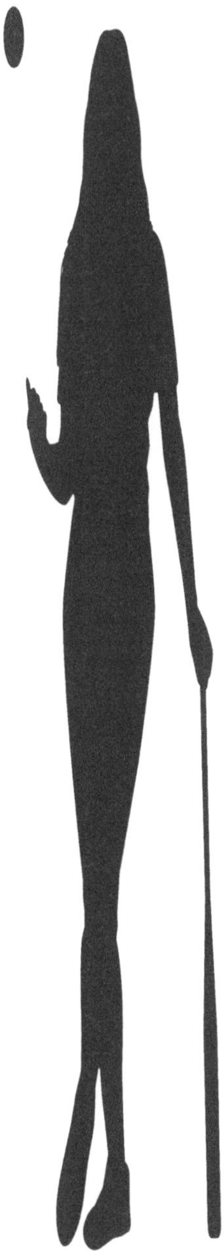

"They all want me to be this perfect role model," she said. "You know, the ideal of what a female baseball player is supposed to be. That I have to be *exemplary*, in every possible way. But I'm pretty sure that the person they want me to be is entirely sexless, and I think I'm in the habit of suppressing that whole part of myself, you know?"

—*Jill Cafferty,* A Season of Daring Greatly *(White, 2017, pp. 407–408, emphasis in original)*

Women have been fighting for equality throughout the history of sports, often represented as lesser athletes when compared to their male counterparts. Between the years 2000 and 2011, for instance, women appeared on just 4.9 percent of *Sports Illustrated* covers, and when included, they shared the spotlight with male athletes, were not identifiable as athletes, were portrayed in a sexually objectifiable manner, or were associated with gender-neutral sports (Weber & Carini, 2012). In a study of *Sports Illustrated* and *ESPN The Magazine*, Wasike (2017) found that men were likely to be viewed in more active and less sexualized poses. If this is the view of men and women in sport that students find in popular media, is it any wonder that girls or nonbinary youth may question their sense of belonging or that boys may believe the stereotypes often exacerbated by hypermasculinity, including toughness, misogyny, and homophobia (Fowler, 2021)?

Sexualized portrayals of women in any setting, including sports, can lead to self-objectification in young women, which can have lasting cognitive and emotional consequences, as well as mental and physical health risks (American Psychological Association, 2007). These portrayals may also negatively impact boys' and men's attitudes toward girls and women, and in more extreme cases they may potentially lead to instances of sexual harassment like the following:

- Students at Armstrong High School in Pennsylvania were banned from sporting events for shouting vulgarities and sexually charged chants at the visiting team's female goalie during a hockey game (Taranto, 2021).
- A former girls' basketball coach in the Riverside (CA) Unified School District was convicted after being accused of using offensive language and engaging in lewd conduct toward his team's players (Rokos, 2022).
- The Spanish soccer federation president, Luis Rubiales, was suspended by FIFA for unwantedly grabbing and kissing soccer player Jenni Hermoso on the lips after her team's 2023 Women's World Cup victory (Thomas, 2023).
- Female athletes were the target of 87 percent of abusive online posts during the 2020 Olympics in Tokyo, and 65 percent of these online posts included sexist, racist, transphobic, or homophobic comments, or baseless doping accusations (Bailey, 2021).

If sports are a microcosm of society, then these examples of sexual harassment and gender-based discrimination are, unfortunately, just a small selection of a larger confluence of societal factors that stem from and/or end with sexism and misogyny.

THE SOCIAL CONCERN OF SEXISM AND MISOGYNY

A study of gender discrimination in the United States by the National Library of Medicine found that discrimination and harassment are common experiences for women, particularly women who identify as racial or ethnic minorities or LGBTQ+ (SteelFisher et al., 2019). In their findings, SteelFisher et al. (2019) noted that 18 percent of women reported gender-based discrimination in healthcare; 41 percent in the workplace; 31 percent during the job application process; 20 percent in applying to or while attending college; 16 percent in home buying or rental; and 15 percent during interactions with the police.

Gender discrimination is more commonly found in the workplace than anywhere else. According to a 2017 Pew Research Center survey, about 42 percent of working women say they have faced workplace discrimination (Parker & Funk, 2017). A 2017 Marist poll also showed that 35 percent of women experienced sexual harassment on the job (Santhanam, 2017), while a 2018 Stop Street Harassment poll found that 81 percent of women have experienced sexual harassment during their lifetime, with 77 percent of women admitting to being verbally harassed, 51 percent facing unwelcome sexual touching, and 41 percent experiencing cybersexual harassment (Chatterjee, 2018). That same poll provided evidence that men are commonly the perpetrators.

These numbers are staggering, and while such forms of discrimination are excruciating enough for women, they are made worse by additional layers of systemic inequities. Over many years, the modern feminist movement has taken on legal and social issues around the world, including the women's suffrage movement; reproductive rights; domestic violence, marital rape, and divorce law; and sexual freedom (Srivastava et al., 2017). Historically, the need to protest for women's rights, which continues today with the overturning of *Roe v. Wade* and restricted access to abortion (Russell & Sasani, 2023; Sidik, 2022), is necessitated by systemic and institutional biases that produce sexism and misogyny, the latter considered more forceful because it refers to being reviled and hated simply for being a woman (Aron, 2019).

THE CONSTANT BATTLE FOR GENDER EQUALITY IN SPORTS

Institutionalized gender discrimination affects all aspects of women's sports, from slighted pay and medical care to lackluster training facilities and travel arrangements (Mervosh & Caron, 2019). Every day is a new battle, and, unfortunately, new battles can feel similar to the ones that preceded them. Consider the history of women in sports who have fought for equality despite the persecution they endured, including the following athletes noted by Mervosh and Caron (2019):

- Kathrine Switzer registered to run the Boston Marathon in 1967 under the name K. V. to hide her identity; she was the first woman to complete the race despite officials physically attempting to drag her off the course.
- Chris Ernst and her Yale University women's crew team protested in 1976 for not having adequate showering facilities, stripping to their waists to show Title IX spelled out across their chests and backs.
- Venus Williams wrote a 2007 op-ed titled "Wimbledon Has Sent Me a Message: I'm Only a Second-Class Champion" as part of a successful attempt to pressure the tennis tournament into awarding the same prize money to women and men.
- Bianca Valenti and other professional women surfers won a hard-fought victory in 2018 against the World Surf League to receive equal prize money and be allowed to compete in the Maverick's Challenge, which had previously been open only to men.

While these notable achievements offer glimpses of hope for future women in sports, there are too many other examples (e.g., Babe Didrikson Zaharis becoming the first female golfer in a PGA Tour event in 1938 with few women golfers following in her footsteps) to assume that these are simply isolated cases. Helping students better understand the demands on the women who break down barriers in sports, including recent pioneers, such as Becky Hammon (NBA coach), Sandra Douglass Morgan (NFL team president), Jennifer King and Lori Locust (NFL coaches), Kim Ng (MLB general manager), and Tori Miller (NBA G League general manager), is an endeavor worth exploring in the English language arts classroom.

Educators and scholars have begun to focus on the stories of women in sports in recent years. For instance, Brown and Parker Moore (2020) considered issues of racism, classism, and sexism in baseball, interweaving historic and contemporary baseball figures Mamie "Peanut" Johnson and Mo'ne Davis with the fictional character Lizzie Bright Griffin from Schmidt's (2004) adolescent novel *Lizzie Bright and the Buckminster Boy*. Their research included an abbreviated history of women in baseball—including the Bloomer girls (1930s), All-American Girls Professional Baseball League (1940s–1950s), and the Negro Leagues (1940s–1950s)—with a focus on the trials and tribulations of Black women in baseball, including the various forms of harassment and discrimination they faced as they attempted to play a game commonly referred to as America's pastime.

Glenn and King-Watkins (2020) examined 10 middle grade and young adult novels published between 2005 and 2017 to study the experiences of female protagonists and address the question, "How are the female protagonists represented in the navigation of changing identities as they move into a male-dominated space?" (p. 309). Their findings showed that, within the 10 stories they examined, female athletes who participate in male-dominated sports often end up separating themselves from their female peers but are never fully accepted in the world of boys. The researchers added, "The institutional structures of sport reinforce traditionally masculine norms and demand conformity by female athletes even though these athletes are non-conforming in their desire to play on boys' teams" (p. 325). A novel not included within their study, *A Season of Daring Greatly* (White, 2017), offers an intriguing storyline to help students contemplate norms and representations of women in sports through young adult literature.

FOCAL YA TEXT: *A SEASON OF DARING GREATLY* BY ELLEN EMERSON WHITE

A Season of Daring Greatly is about a young woman, Jill Cafferty, and her transition from high school to professional baseball. Already a celebrity as a high school senior for her pitching acumen, particularly for her devastating breaking ball, Jill is drafted in the third round of the Major League Baseball (MLB) draft by the Pittsburgh Pirates and, therefore, becomes the first woman ever drafted by an MLB team. Supported by her mother, a college professor; her brother Theo; and a small group of close friends, Jill navigates life not only as a female professional baseball player but also as an eighteen-year-old living away from home for the first time. Supported by some teammates yet ridiculed by others, Jill relies on her intelligence, personality, and wit to learn the ropes, in some ways fitting in but in others standing apart, including having her own dressing room separate from the general locker room. Jill is harassed throughout the start of her career from all corners of the baseball universe (namely fans, agents, and players) and regularly questions her decision to pursue professional baseball instead of attending college at Stanford. Despite the media firestorm and the verbal harassment she faces in every city, Jill finds new friends in the game who support her, advocate for her, and give her the strength to overcome obstacles and face her fears of failure and being a role model for little girls everywhere.

Author Ellen Emerson White is a writer, photographer, and baseball fan who coaches baseball in East Harlem and knows what it is like to be one of the few women engaged in what is often viewed as a sport for men and boys (Kalb, 2017). *A Season of Daring Greatly* has been awarded multiple honors, including a Cooperative Children's Book Center Choices 2018 selection in the category of Fiction for Young Adults and a 2017 Blue Ribbon for Fiction from The Bulletin of the Center for Children's Books.

INCORPORATING *A SEASON OF DARING GREATLY* INTO THE SECONDARY ELA CLASSROOM

Much of *A Season of Daring Greatly* revolves around Jill's experience as the first, and only, female baseball player drafted into professional baseball, including the realities and concerns that come with feeling the weight of the world to succeed on your shoulders. With that in mind, the following activities are designed to help students respond to these four essential questions:

- What does it mean to dare greatly?
- What possibilities, pressures, pitfalls, and predicaments arise based on a woman's presence on a male-dominated sports team?
- How does an exploration of women in baseball allow for an examination of intersectionality and representation?
- What does it mean to be a trailblazer in sports, and what role do allies play in blazing the trail?

Prior to Teaching the Novel

Before beginning a whole-class reading of *A Season of Daring Greatly*, teachers can incorporate activities that help students predict and problematize the book's title, examine how women fit into what Lipsyte (2011) called "jock culture," and create identity narratives that examine the privileges and prejudices real students and fictional characters face.

Predicting Titles

A book title can tell us a great deal or leave us questioning. In the case of *A Season of Daring Greatly*, the title can do both. Before giving students a physical copy of the text, teachers can ask them what or who they believe will be the subject of the book based on the title. Once students have guessed, teachers can encourage them to break down the title by individual words, focusing on "season," "daring," and "greatly," in particular. If they know nothing about the book or the author at this point, students may not imagine baseball as a focus area, despite the word "season" having a baseball connection (e.g., the MLB season is 162 games long). Students are likely to be interested in the juxtaposition of multiple phrases: "a season of daring" and "daring greatly." We recommend asking students what a "season of daring" might entail, asking them what it means to "dare greatly," and providing examples, given that "daring" is also an adjective commonly defined as adventurous while "greatly" is an adverb usually meaning very much or a considerable amount.

When students consider a "season of daring," their responses could range from a motorcyclist jumping over a river canyon in winter to a skateboarder landing a 900 in the summer. On the other hand, students may provide examples of people, and specifically athletes, who have "dared greatly," including Jackie Robinson (baseball), Muhammad Ali (boxing), and, more recently, Ada Hegerberg (soccer). At the close of this activity, teachers may put the book's title in a different context, such as the athletes on the 2017 US women's national hockey team, who risked their careers by threatening to boycott the world championship if USA Hockey did not increase wages and support for women to levels equal to the men's national team. The team's daring was not only great for their own livelihoods but also for future athletes, thanks to the formation of a Women's High Performance Advisory Group to support women's and girls' youth hockey (Berkman, 2017).

Examining Jock Culture

A few years ago, Alan Brown, one of the authors of this book, and his former students used the lens of critical sports literacy (Brown & Rodesiler, 2016) to define the unwritten rules of high school sports (Brown et al., 2019). That project was the culmination of an exploration into what Lipsyte (2011) has labeled "jock culture," a concept succinctly described by Brown et al. (2019) as "a distortion of sports . . . overwhelmed by masculinity and power, fueled by greed and desperate competition, and pressurized by ambitious parents and coaches with a commitment to enforcing a win at all costs attitude" (p. 19). As students explored these unwritten rules through their own lived experiences and in young adult literature, four themes emerged: (1) benefits of sports in K–12 schools, (2) increased social status of student athletes, (3) greater emphasis on men's sports over women's sports, and (4) greater emphasis on athletic achievement over academic achievement.

As students prepare to read *A Season of Daring Greatly*, considering the findings of the third theme related to the emphasis on men's sports may be useful, especially as a starting point for later conversations about women who participate in male-dominated sports. Brown et al. (2019) found three categories within the theme, namely the presence of greater attention paid to men's sports, sexism in high school sports, and greater attendance for men's athletic events. Interestingly, while the second category, sexism in high school sports, is on display early in protagonist Jill Cafferty's experience, the other two categories are boosted because Jill's very presence on the baseball diamond serves to heighten the attention paid to men's sports and to increase the attendance on the days that she pitches.

Returning to the notion of jock culture (Lipsyte, 2011), a quotation from early in the novel not only sets the stage for conversations about masculinity and femininity in sports but also the role of women in sports. In preparation for a baseball game, Jill asks her coach, Mr. Portman, about how many photographers are at the game. He responds, "At least a dozen, maybe more" (White, 2017, p. 6), at which point:

> Jill checked her hair, able to feel that the chignon was still reasonably well in place. She'd never been a big fan of the perky ponytail-stuck-through-the-back-of-the-cap look, and her friend Lauren had come up with what she described as an 'if Audrey Hepburn were a *serious* jock' look, which she had been using during games since tenth grade. (p. 6, emphasis in original)

The statement about Audrey Hepburn offers potential writing and/or discussion prompts for students:

- What does it mean to be a jock?
- What is the difference between a jock and a serious jock?
- What look does a serious jock have?
- What is the difference between Audrey Hepburn's look—described as "slim, elegant, and unfailingly stylish" ("Actress," 2020)—and a serious jock look?

These questions can support an important conversation about either/or binaries, namely thinking about baseball as masculine or feminine, whereas masculinity has a connotation of physicality while femininity may be thought of according to aesthetics, which historically has also led to questions about female sexuality (Glenn & King-Watkins, 2019). In their examination of fictional female athletes who move into male-dominated spaces, Glenn and King-Watkins submitted that the masculine/feminine binary is common in sports-related young adult literature. Their findings suggested, "If the protagonists are athletes, they are also expected to be feminists, role models, or pioneers in order to resist this hegemonic masculinity; however, they cannot be feminine and must adhere to traditionally masculine expectations" (Glenn & King-Watkins, 2019, p. 295). They went on to say that female athletes must often choose one identity, athlete or female. As a result, resisting binaries is important for many reasons but perhaps most importantly because they disregard any potential for intersectional identities.

Voices from the Field
Challenging the Status Quo: Opportunities That Matter for Representation and Inclusion

Crystal L. Beach
Teacher and Academic Specialist,
Union County Schools, North Carolina

Coming back at night from a recent literacy conference, I smiled. Through that darkness, lights shone brightly on fields of play below me where I envisioned young and old alike enjoying sports on their respective fields, tracks, and courts. I reflected on the conference talk my colleagues and I gave in which we encouraged teachers to consider the value that stories of sports afford us in creating powerful and relevant connections in developing our students' overall literacy skills, and, arguably just as important, exploring our students' lived experiences (Dredger et al., 2022).

Though secondary English language arts (ELA) teachers can incorporate stories of sports to provide students with relevant learning opportunities, we must remember the dark side of sports culture, too—the fact that sexism and misogyny still play a dominating role in what and how stories are told today. Thus, being intentional about text selection is a way to challenge the status quo and push back against the oppressive narratives that are woven throughout sports culture.

Challenging the status quo is hard work, and it can often make people uncomfortable. However, we must advocate for all our students in order to create equitable learning spaces and experiences. These opportunities also allow us to hit state standards, but more important, they help us teach our students about empathy, compassion, and the realities that others face (Brown, 2021). Texts selected to challenge and rethink stereotypes, abilities, and stories of sports do not just demonstrate to female student athletes that your classroom is an inclusive learning space in which all voices are represented and valued; these stories help ALL students better understand why all voices and experiences matter (Brown & Rodesiler, 2016; Garland et al., 2021).

In addition, texts such as *A Season of Daring Greatly* by Ellen Emerson White (2017) remind us of the reality that many female student athletes experience daily. How many have been told they couldn't do something? How many have been told they wouldn't make it? How many have experienced comments about what their bodies look like instead of what their strong, athletic bodies can do physically? How many have had their sexuality brought into the discussion of their competitive and athletic endeavors? How many have had their outfits critiqued during impressive and dominating competitions? How many have been told to "suck it up" when struggling mentally or assumed that a physical violation was, sadly, normal and a part of their sport experience? Questions like these should inspire teachers to see and challenge the ways in which athletic stereotypes of female athletes have developed from years of sexist and misogynistic viewpoints that still dominate sports culture.

What does this look like in the secondary ELA classroom, anyway? As previously mentioned, it means we should look at texts that share stories of female athletes. There are lots of great young adult literature options available to pair with nonfiction texts that help create opportunities to teach, validate, and challenge (Price, 2021). For example, White's (2017) novel could be paired with news stories of women joining Major League Baseball programs (Alder & Simon, 2022) as students investigate language choices and the lived experiences of the women in comparison to the protagonist's experiences. In other words, they could consider how (literary) characterization plays out in real-life application. Another example includes examining news articles and media focusing on female athletes. Whether using "mentor texts written by athletes that have called out and disrupted confining narratives" or "calling out text that objectifies, sexualizes, or censures" (Beach & Dredger, 2021, p. 171), sharing stories of female athletes provides a variety of ways to engage student learners and challenge sexism and misogyny. The reality is that the rhetoric surrounding female athletes and their performances is out there (Beach &

Dredger, 2018, 2021), and using literature to connect to relevant, real-world experiences is what secondary ELA teachers do best. What better way than showcasing powerful sports examples from which students can learn?

The question always comes up about the place, even the value, of sports within the classroom. However, if we as teachers stay caught between the in- and out-of-school dichotomy, we will miss out on those powerful connections for our students and their learning within our classrooms. It is instead important for us to consider the ways we are engaging youth (Alvermann, 2008), which includes valuing sports culture and challenging sexism and misogyny in the process through powerful text selections. It is easy (and comfortable) to proceed with the status quo; however, our students deserve better, and they deserve classrooms that are inclusive of all voices and experiences from which they can learn. We must *dare greatly*.

References

Alder, D., & Simon, A. (2022). *These women broke barriers in baseball*. MLB. https://www.mlb.com/news/women-break-barriers-in-baseball-history

Alvermann, D. E. (2008). Why bother theorizing adolescents' online literacies for classroom practice and research? *Journal of Adolescent & Adult Literacy, 52*(1), 8–19.

Beach, C. L., & Dredger, K. (2018). Sporty girls and tomboys: Negotiating the rhetoric surrounding female athletes. In I. Renga, & C. Benedetti (Eds.), *Sports and K–12 education: Insights for teachers, coaches, and school leaders* (pp. 119–134). Rowman & Littlefield.

———. (2021). Performance, style, and substance: The female athlete. In K. Garland, K. Dredger, C. L. Beach, & C. Leogrande (Eds.), *Stories of sports: Critical literacy in media production, consumption, and dissemination* (pp. 171–190). Lexington Books.

Brown, A., & Rodesiler, L. (Eds.). (2016). *Developing contemporary literacies through sports: A guide for the English classroom*. National Council of Teachers of English.

Brown, B. (2021). *Atlas of the heart: Mapping meaningful connection and the language of human experience*. Random House.

Dredger, K., Beach, C. L., & Garland, K. (2022, March). *Athletic activism: Developing critical consumers of sports media*. Virginia State Literacy Association, Crystal City, VA.

Garland, K., Dredger, K., Beach, C. L., & Leogrande, C. (Eds.). (2021). *Stories of sports: Critical literacy in media production, consumption, and dissemination*. Lexington Books.

Price, T. (2021, August 6). *The best new YA books starring female athletes*. BookRiot. https://bookriot.com/ya-books-starring-female-athletes/

White, E. E. (2017). *A season of daring greatly*. Greenwillow Books.

Dr. Crystal L. Beach, a former athlete and coach, currently works in the Appalachian Mountains of Northeast Georgia. Serving as an academic specialist, she strives to create meaningful literacy learning opportunities for all, such as those that include sports literacy practices. Over the years, she has presented and published on a variety of areas focused on literacies, including identity, multimodalities, sports, and technologies in the classroom.

Writing Identity Narratives

Intersectionality, first coined by Crenshaw (1991), suggests that "because many people are unique, many identities are possible" (American Psychological Association, 2022), and recognizing overlapping identities is critical to understanding the complexities of privilege and prejudice (Kort, 2019). Jewell and Durand (2020) offered important insights into helping students consider who they are in the context of intersecting and overlapping identities. We suggest that teachers start by asking students to create a list of their identities, including anything that makes students who they are. Students can then create an identity chart by writing their names in the center and placing their identities all around it (see Chapter 9 for an example activity that supports students in creating an identity chart) before writing a brief narrative description of their own identities, considering what privileges or prejudices they may encounter as a result. Here is an example of one student's identity narrative.

> "I'm Tiffany. I'm 14 Years old. I live in a small house in New York State. I live with my mom and my twin sister. I'm a Black biracial cisgender female who has brown eyes and a lot of freckles. I have curly hair and have grown to love it, slowly, over time. I love to read and bake. I love to dance with my friends and I write terrible poetry that only I will ever read. All of that is who I am . . . and I'm so much more. (Jewell & Durand, 2020, p. 11)"

Once students write about their own identifiable characteristics, teachers can share with them an identity narrative for Jill Cafferty (see Figure 2.1), the protagonist of *A Season of Daring Greatly*. Students can use this information to hypothesize what they believe her experience will be like throughout the novel. In doing so, they should consider her own potential privileges and prejudices, not to mention the challenges she will face, as she transitions from being a high school student to the first female baseball player ever to be drafted by a Major League Baseball team.

I'm Jill Cafferty. I am an able-bodied, young White woman who just graduated from high school. I am a daughter living in a single-parent home since my father was a soldier killed in Afghanistan. I am a sister to Theo and a friend to Greg, Lauren, Cathy, and others. I am best known as being a female baseball player, a starting pitcher who was the first woman ever drafted in Major League Baseball. I gave up a chance to attend college at Stanford to pursue my dream of playing professional baseball, and I speak English and Spanish fluently, which helps me communicate with my baseball peers who are non-native speakers. I am heterosexual, despite assumptions otherwise due to being a female baseball player. I am a fierce competitor on and off the baseball diamond and am proud to throw like a girl.

FIGURE 2.1: An Example Identity Narrative for Jill Cafferty

Once students have made predictions, they are ready to begin their exploration of the full text and to survey the multiple ways in which Jill identifies herself and how her identity is framed by others.

As Students Read the Novel

There are countless activities that could engage students during their reading of *A Season of Daring Greatly*. This section invites students to better understand their rights when it comes to sexual harassment and gender-based violence, to consider what it means to be a trailblazer and an ally, and to investigate the representation of women in sports since Title IX, the historic law that students and educators alike can learn more about in an accessible manner thanks to Blumenthal's (2022) illustrated middle-grades book.

Identifying and Combatting Sexual Harassment

My School My Rights (American Civil Liberties Union of California, n.d.) offers resources for students, parents, and educators on a variety of topics, including student disability rights, student health rights, and harassment and bullying (see Chapter 9 for more information on bullying and hazing). One topic that is pertinent to Jill Cafferty's experience in *A Season of Daring Greatly* is sexual harassment and gender-based violence. The American Civil Liberties Union of California (n.d.) provides specific examples for students to look for, which are applicable to the book and to their own schools, as well as action steps if students experience sexual harassment. Examples include when someone does any of the following:

- follows you around, stalks you, or always wants to know where you are and who you are with;
- sends you repeated and unwanted texts, IMs, online messages, and/or phone calls including, but not limited to, sexual comments;
- pressures you to perform sexual acts or to have sex, or touches you

sexually against your will (including sexually grabbing, rubbing, touching, or pinching you);

- interferes with your birth control;
- verbally abuses you using anti-gay or sex-based insults;
- physically abuses you (e.g., hitting, punching, kicking, slapping, or choking); or
- makes repeated sexual comments about you to other classmates, including on social media (e.g., comments about your body, spreading sexual rumors, dirty jokes, or stories).

Jill Cafferty experiences both sexual harassment and gender-based violence on numerous occasions in the novel. To help students better understand how to recognize various forms of harassment for reporting purposes, teachers can ask students to track instances of sexual harassment and gender-based violence in the book using the examples listed above as guides. A sample list of this behavior from *A Season of Daring Greatly* can be found in Figure 2.2.

Victim	Harasser	Harassment / Violence
Jill Cafferty	Fans	"Go back to softball!" (p. 73).
Jill Cafferty	Teammates	"So, it didn't come as a complete shock that two of [the players] were naked, which—since they were parading around, practically *prancing*, as though they had been waiting for her to come out—was clearly intentional" (pp. 106-107, emphasis in original).
Jill Cafferty	Teammate (Owen)	"How those groin stretches feel for you, Cafferty?" (p. 155).
Jill Cafferty	Fans	"Go home, you bitch!" and "You don't belong here!" (p. 195).
Jill Cafferty	Teammate (Nelson)	"But, it was still hard to take in the fact that *one of her teammates had urinated in her dressing room*" (p. 243, emphasis in original).
Jill Cafferty	Prospective Agent (Mr. Marshak)	"'You unbelievable bitch,' he said through his teeth. 'Don't you have any idea how much work I've *already* done for you?'" (p. 294, emphasis in original).
Jill Cafferty	Fans	"As she walked towards the dugout, two frat-boy types came rushing up through the stands and threw a bunch of small white objects at her. She ducked, but also reflexively raised her glove to try and catch them.... Tampons? *Really*?" (p. 305, emphasis in original).
Jill Cafferty	Teammate (Caleb)	"'Ooh,' Caleb said, and turned to give Jill a big wink. 'You've been putting out, haven't you, you naughty girl?'" (p. 363).

FIGURE 2.2: Sexual Harassment and Gender-based Violence in *A Season of Daring Greatly*

As students consider sexual harassment and gender-based violence, they might pay particular attention to instances of harassment in the form of employment discrimination. The federal government declared, "Harassment is unwelcome conduct that is based on race, color, religion, sex (including sexual orientation, gender identity, or pregnancy), national origin, older age (beginning at age 40), disability, or genetic information (including family medical history)" (US Equal Employment Opportunity Commission, n.d.). For each instance of workplace sexual harassment and gender-based violence in the book, students can weigh whether the harassment is egregious enough to be considered unlawful. In other words, is the offensive conduct a condition of continued employment, or is it "severe or pervasive enough to create a work environment that a reasonable person would consider intimidating, hostile, or abusive" (US Equal Employment Opportunity Commission, n.d.)?

As students and teachers move from identifying to combatting sexual harassment, the National Center on Safe Supportive Learning Environments (2023) offers a useful resource package for preventing sexual harassment and sexual violence while creating a safe and supportive learning environment. Resources are also available for students who are victims of sexual harassment, including the organization Stop Sexual Assault in Schools (2015), which provides free resources and information to students, families, and educators.

Becoming an Ally

Early in the book, Jill's best friend, Lauren, makes a statement that would resonate throughout the remainder of the story: "'Fame is a heavy burden,' Lauren said" (White, 2017, p. 33). It is never easy breaking barriers, as Jill quickly learns upon getting drafted by the Pirates. A while later, as she thinks about the pressures she will face and the life changes coming her way, she once again confides in her closest friend and ally, Lauren:

> Because on top of everything else, she was going to have to move in with some strangers. Presumably, they were friendly, and nice—but, she didn't know them, and maybe they wouldn't get along, and her teammates were probably going to hate her, and—
>
> "Are you totally losing your nerve?" Lauren asked.
>
> Yes. "I wish there could have been someone else before me," she said.
>
> Lauren nodded. "Sucks to be the first."
>
> And how. It would be much better to be—the third female player. Or the fifth. "I can't be who they want me to be," Jill said. "I'm going to disappoint everyone."

> "They probably just want you to be yourself," Lauren said.
>
> No, a trailblazer was supposed to be impressive. *Special.* "I think they're expecting someone—I don't know," Jill said. "Inspirational, and enthusiastic, and—cuddly." Perky. Adorable. The girl next door.
>
> Lauren laughed. "I hate to be the one to break it to you, but I don't think 'cuddly' is ever going to happen." (p. 94, emphasis in original)

There are a number of ways to examine this passage, including making direct connections to Jill's aforementioned identity narrative, where students can compare and contrast how she views her own identity as a baseball player with the expectations of others around the sport. However, another possibility is to focus on the word "trailblazer." What does it mean to be a trailblazer in sports, and what role do allies play in blazing the trail?

Perhaps the best-known trailblazer in baseball was Jackie Robinson, the first African American to play Major League Baseball. Robinson faced backlash from fans, peers, and teammates as he broke through baseball's color barrier at the professional level, though his experience was much harsher as he was taunted and harassed everywhere he traveled, even receiving death threats, particularly when playing in the Jim Crow South. While Jackie Robinson was on his own as the first African American player in Major League Baseball, he did have allies, including his spouse Rachel Robinson, Brooklyn Dodgers president and general manager Branch Rickey, manager Leo Durocher, teammates Gil Hodges and Ed Stanky, and reporter Wendell Smith (Harner, 2022; Hill, 2022).

Gay (2016) argued that allyship can be beneficial because "it's a way for people to say and demonstrate that they care and (want to) help even if they cannot fully understand the lived experiences of marginalized people." However, Gay also noted that truly becoming an ally means making their fights your own, not merely supporting from a comfortable distance. It is important to note that Jill Cafferty's character should hardly be considered oppressed or marginalized; indeed, she has many privileges as a White woman with newfound wealth. Yet she is positioned as the first woman ever drafted into a male-dominated sport, which includes working in ballparks and clubhouses that were never intended for female players and around peers who are critical or jealous of her presence. These experiences make her vulnerable with a particularly heavy burden to carry. With this in mind, teachers can help students learn what it means to be an ally, including "the dos" and "the don'ts" found in Lamont's (n.d.) guide to allyship and have them create a daybook (Tedrow, 2022), a journal commonly used by students for open-ended writing prompts or teacher-directed guided questions, where they can record any instances of allyship toward Jill Cafferty and their impact throughout the novel. Students will likely write about her friends (Greg, Lauren), family (mom, Theo), teammates (Marcus, Andrew), and support staff (Sofia, Terrence).

Analyzing Data on Female Coaches

Representation is an important idea for students to grapple with during their reading of *A Season of Daring Greatly*. Throughout much of the novel, Jill Cafferty is viewed by the outside world as a representative or, rather, *the* representation of women in professional baseball. However, late in the story, when pressed by reporters about what her poor performance represented for women in baseball, Jill remarks, "I don't actually represent *all* women. I'm *one* athlete with, you know, a certain skill set, and whether I end up succeeding is going to be a combination of all sorts of factors, and gender really doesn't have anything to do with it" (p. 373, emphasis in original).

Expecting Jill to represent all women in the game of baseball would necessitate a level playing field, which is far from reality in a male-dominated sport. An activity that Alan has used to help students understand the relative disparities for women in men's sports is an examination of National Collegiate Athletic Association (NCAA) Division I head coaches by sex. Before digging into the data, it is useful to provide students with some background about the rationale for and impact of Title IX of the Education Amendments of 1972 (see US Department of Education, 2021). Flanagan (2017) provided useful background to consider the impact of Title IX on female coaches in particular:

> Much attention and worry has been devoted to the decline of female coaches at the collegiate level since Title IX was passed in 1972. This landmark legislation prohibited discrimination on the basis of sex in all educational programs that receive federal funds, and its passage compelled colleges to ramp up the number of athletic teams for girls to stay on par with what they offered boys. While nudging a record number of girls into athletics, Title IX also contributed to an unexpected and steady drop in the number of female collegiate coaches of women's teams, from 90 percent in 1972 to 43 percent in 2014. In response to Title IX, many colleges combined male and female athletic departments, which in turn often meant that men now oversaw women's teams; the law also meant pay parity for women's-team coaches, the now-lucrative salaries attracting male coaches to female sports. These phenomena, among others, pushed women out of college coaching.

Based on this information, students can analyze the number of men and women coaching Division I men's and women's sports teams using the National Collegiate Athletic Association (2023) demographic database (see Figure 2.3 for data on selected sports with more than 50 Division I head coaches in both the men's and women's sports plus four stand-alone sports: men's baseball and football and women's field hockey and softball). Inevitably, what students will notice is that men overwhelmingly coach men's athletic teams. With few exceptions, men are also coaching women's sports as well, particularly when equivalent categories of those sports exist for men. This analysis should lead to instant engagement among students as they discuss the factors that contribute to these inequities and potential ramifications.

Men's Sport	% of Male Head Coaches	% of Female Head Coaches	Women's Sport	% of Male Head Coaches	% of Female Head Coaches
Men's Baseball	100.0%	0.0%	—	—	—
Men's Basketball	100.0%	0.0%	Women's Basketball	34.7%	65.3%
Men's Cross Country	86.2%	13.8%	Women's Cross Country	78.9%	21.1%
—	—	—	Women's Field Hockey	16.9%	83.1%
Men's Football	100.0%	0.0%	—	—	—
Men's Golf	98.6%	1.4%	Women's Golf	38.8%	61.2%
Men's Indoor Track	90.0%	10.0%	Women's Indoor Track	81.4%	18.6%
Men's Lacrosse	100.0%	0.0%	Women's Lacrosse	12.6%	87.4%
Men's Outdoor Track	89.4%	10.6%	Women's Outdoor Track	81.1%	18.9%
Men's Soccer	100.0%	0.0%	Women's Soccer	72.1%	27.9%
—	—	—	Women's Softball	31.3%	68.7%
Men's Swimming	85.5%	14.5%	Women's Swimming	77.6%	22.4%
Men's Tennis	96.2%	3.8%	Women's Tennis	62.0%	38.0%

FIGURE 2.3: Select NCAA Division I Sport Coaches by Sex: Year 2023

Once students have analyzed and discussed this NCAA Division I coaching data, teachers can note that five sports, including Division I baseball, do not have a single female head coach on a men's team. What type of success must Jill Cafferty have in and/or out of baseball to someday become a head coach of a Division I baseball team? If students were the athletic director, would they consider hiring her? Why or why not? The conversation can also turn to football, where of the 674 college football coaches across all three NCAA divisions, every coach identified as male, and 81.8 percent identified as white and male in 2022. In that same year, only twelve football players in any division identified as female. Teachers may also want to introduce students to recent female college football players, including Toni Harris, Sarah Fuller, and Haley Van Voorhis, and ask students to consider what it would take for one of these young women to become a head football coach at any level, from middle school to the National Football League.

Culminating Tasks after Reading the Novel

Surveying the presence of women in coaching, including female coaches in men's and women's sports, presents an opportunity for students to consider the credentials, experience, and expertise someone must have to stay around a sport long enough to leave a legacy. Given the aforementioned essential questions, culminating activities could include writing a hall-of-fame speech about one's time in the sport and exploring female identities in male-dominated sporting spaces by changing advocacy to action.

Writing a Hall-of-Fame Speech

Former Green Bay Packers coach Vince Lombardi is credited with saying that perfection is not attainable, but in the process of chasing perfection you can catch excellence (Wojciechowski, 2006). Jill Cafferty feels immense pressure to be exemplary on and off the baseball diamond, whether that means being a "perfect role model" (p. 407) or pitching "six perfect innings" (p. 418) in a game early in her career. As students finish reading *A Season of Daring Greatly*, teachers may invite them to consider these questions: Is perfection attainable? Why or why not? Why does Jill Cafferty feel so much pressure to be perfect?

Phillips (2021) wrote, "Perfectionism is a trait that is encouraged and rewarded in our society, a society that values achievement and success above all else, but this pressure can be incredibly detrimental to mental health." This pressure to achieve perfection took center stage in the 2020 Tokyo Olympics when Simone Biles, arguably the greatest gymnast in history, took leave from gymnastics to focus on her mental health. Phillips shared strategies for adults to support students in overcoming the pressure to be perfect, including a willingness to

- talk about mental health
- practice self-care together

- teach kids about stress
- encourage breaks
- communicate that mistakes are expected
- avoid contributing to the pressure, and
- get help.

As students consider Jill Cafferty's career in baseball, teachers may invite them to contemplate what type of self-care, combined with baseball skill and professional knowledge, it would take for Jill Cafferty to someday be inducted into the National Baseball Hall of Fame. In terms of their playing career, the primary requirement for a hall-of-fame baseball player is at least 10 years of service in a Major League championship season (Baseball Writers' Association of America, n.d.), though students may research the cases, including statistics, of past inductees. Clearly Jill's case would be unique as only the second woman, behind Negro Leagues owner Effa Manley, and first female player to be inducted into the National Baseball Hall of Fame. Then, teachers can ask students to consider these factors and write a first-person hall-of-fame acceptance speech from the perspective of Jill Cafferty. A sample template, from Bakay's (2001) "Do-It-Yourself Hall of Fame Speech," can be found in Figure 2.4. Though written with humorous intent, this template stands to help students consider the shape a hall-of-fame speech might take.

I'd like to thank my __1__ for presenting me. That was a __2__ introduction, and a reminder to us all why they called you __3__.

It's an honor to stand here beside my fellow inductees. What great men, what __4__! In particular, it means so much to be entering the Hall with __5__ —I'll never forget __6__.

__7__, I was a __8__ fresh out of __9__, Standing at this podium today, I realize I've come a long way from __10__.

I see a lot of smiling faces out there. Former teammates, family, and the fans—especially those of you who drove all the way from __11__. I've always said __12__ fans are the best fans in the world!

(Wait for applause, start to get weepy.)

Come on, __13__ . I promised myself I wouldn't __14__.

(Long pause to regain composure. Blow nose.)

No one gets here __15___. The game of football __16___. Thank you for making all of my ___17___.

FIGURE 2.4: Nick Bakay's "Do-It-Yourself Hall of Fame Speech"

Changing Advocacy to Action

Having read *A Season of Daring Greatly*, students can examine stereotypes to consider how Jill Cafferty engaged in the processes of acculturation, commonly defined as assimilation to a different culture or social pattern, as she navigated existing gendered experiences in the male-dominated sport of baseball. Specifically, students can consider Glenn and King-Watkins's (2020) three themes about female protagonists changing identities in male-dominated sporting spaces. First, what was it like for Jill, who had previously played high school baseball, to move into the more pressurized environment of minor league baseball, and in what ways did she feel connected to or disconnected from her female peers? Second, did Jill express pride in competing at a higher level with her male counterparts, and, if so, how did she align or separate herself in a sport commonly thought of as masculine? Third, how was Jill denied access to aspects of baseball based on her gender, physical appearance, or other characteristics, and how did she react to that denial?

Having considered these questions, teachers can ask students to return to the title-prediction activity described earlier in this chapter. What do students think about the book's title after reading the text? Is it possible to "dare greatly" if you are forced to assimilate and are always viewed as different, or is enduring the acculturation process itself, in this case being the first woman drafted to play Major League Baseball, enough to be defined as "daring greatly?"

Next, teachers might consider the possibility of action and advocacy by assigning students to interview female athletes in their own school to learn more about their perspectives on access, opportunities, advancements, and equity in school or club athletics. For interviewees who are willing to share their stories, students may organize an online day of action (Advocates for Youth, n.d.) to raise awareness of issues affecting female athletes. This act includes students using their preferred social media platforms to share data, news, media, and/or personal stories about inequities in sports, thus becoming an outspoken ally for an issue affecting others in the school community.

CONCLUSION

In May 2022, Kelsie Whitmore became the first woman to start a game in the history of the Atlantic League of Professional Baseball. On that day, she started in left field and batted ninth for the Staten Island FerryHawks (Axisa, 2022). Soon thereafter, Whitmore, a two-way player, became the first woman to pitch in an Atlantic League game. On Twitter that evening, her team summarized her successful relief appearance, but instead of saying she made history, it used the hashtag "#HERstory" (Randhawa, 2022). The stories of women in sports, not only the initial trailblazers but also the players who overcome the odds and follow in their footsteps, deserve our attention. While sexism and misogyny too often dominate the headlines, and for good reason, students and teachers can use the power of reading and writing to imagine and work toward a future where women are not forced to dare greatly just to level the playing field with their male counterparts.

Options for Book Clubs

Teachers looking to facilitate book clubs in which students explore sexism and misogyny in sports culture can incorporate *A Season of Daring Greatly* alongside titles like the following:

Michigan vs. the Boys (Allen, 2019)
Michigan Manning is a hockey player without a team until she joins the boys' team in her town and experiences loneliness, abandonment, hazing, and bullying along the way. Determined and resilient, she strives to overcome episode after episode of sexism and misogyny to achieve her dream of playing hockey.

Girls Can't Hit (Easton, 2018)
Fleur Waters takes up boxing as a protest over gender restrictions at the boxing club but later continues training as an escape from her daily life, much to the dismay of her mother, boyfriend, and friends. She comes to love what training does for her physical and emotional confidence and hopes to make boxing more inclusive for women.

Throw Like a Girl (Henning, 2020)
Liv Rodinsky transfers to a public school after losing her scholarship to her private school for fighting during a softball game. One day, after seeing Liv throw a football, injured quarterback Grey persuades Liz to join the football team. While having the star quarterback in your corner is a plus, there are countless obstacles Liz must overcome in her attempt to become the school's starting quarterback.

Dangerous Play (Kress, 2021)
Zoe Alamandar is a field hockey player with dreams of a state championship until she is sexually assaulted and assembles her teammates with a new goal of saving girls from predatory boys.

Furia (Méndez, 2020)
Camila Hassan is a young woman in Argentina living a double life as an exemplary fútbol (soccer) player with dreams of joining a North American team but with parents who would not knowingly allow their daughter to participate in sports.

Options for Film Study

Teachers who want to use films to augment students' discussions about sexism and misogyny in sports culture can incorporate *A Season of Daring Greatly* alongside titles like the following:

Battle of the Sexes (Dayton & Faris, 2017)
This feature film tells the story of the world number-one tennis player and women's rights advocate Billie Jean King (Emma Stone) and her 1973 tennis match, commonly referred to as the Battle of the Sexes, with former men's champion Bobby Riggs (Steve Carell).

Power Meri (Lester, 2018)
This award-winning documentary film follows the PNG Orchids, Papua New Guinea's first national women's rugby league team, through the 2017 World Cup in Australia as they struggled against sexism and prejudice in their own country while fighting for equity in terms of funding, resources, and respect.

Girls Can't Surf (Nelius, 2020)
This documentary film offers reflections from a group of female surfers in the 1980s who fought abuse and persecution as athletes, sought gender equality in their sport, and challenged the male-dominated surfing world to turn women's surfing into the main event.

Limitless (Samartha, 2017)
This documentary film tells the stories of eight ordinary women from across India who took up running at various stages in their life and explores their experiences, both exuberant and disheartening, as they navigate a society that often looks down upon their athletic interests.

Nine for IX: Let Them Wear Towels (Sundberg & Stern, 2013)
This documentary film chronicles the history of female journalists working in men's locker rooms, including the groundbreaking story of Lisa Olson, a reporter for the *Boston Herald,* who was sexually harassed by players on the New England Patriots in 1990.

Young Adult Literature

Allen, C. S. (2019). *Michigan vs. the boys*. Kids Can Press.

Easton, T. S. (2018). *Girls can't hit*. Feiwel & Friends.

Henning, S. (2020). *Throw like a girl*. Poppy.

Kress, E. (2021). *Dangerous play*. Roaring Brook Press.

Méndez, Y. S. (2020). *Furia*. Algonquin Young Readers.

Schmidt, G. D. (2004). *Lizzie Bright and the Buckminster boy*. Clarion.

White, E. E. (2017). *A season of daring greatly*. Greenwillow.

Other Texts for Classroom Use

Advocates for Youth. (n.d.). *Youth activist toolkit*. http://www.advocatesforyouth.org/wp-content/uploads/2019/04/Youth-Activist-Toolkit.pdf

American Civil Liberties Union of Southern California. (n.d.). *Harassment & bullying*. My School My Rights. https://www.myschoolmyrights.com/harassment-and-bullying/

Bakay, N. (2001). *Do-it-yourself hall of fame speech.* ESPN Page 2. https://www.espn.com/page2/s/bakay/010803.html

Blumenthal, K. (2022). *Let me play: The story of Title IX: The law that changed the future of girls in America.* Atheneum Books for Young Readers.

Dayton, J., & Faris, V. (Directors). (2017). *Battle of the sexes* [Film]. Cloud Eight Films; Decibel Films; TSG Entertainment.

Jewell, T. (2020). *This book is anti-racist: 20 lessons on how to wake up, take action, and do the work* (A. Durand, Illus.). Frances Lincoln Children's Books.

Lamont, A. (n.d.). *Guide to allyship.* https://guidetoallyship.com/

Lester, J. (Director). (2018). *Power meri* [Film]. Media Stockade.

National Center on Safe Supportive Learning Environments. (2023). *Safe place to learn.* https://safesupportivelearning.ed.gov/safe-place-to-learn-k12

National Collegiate Athletic Association. (2023). *NCAA demographics database.* https://www.ncaa.org/sports/2018/12/13/ncaa-demographics-database.aspx?id=1729

Nelius, C. (Director). (2020). *Girls can't surf* [Film]. FINCH; Pursekey Productions; Whipped Sea.

Samartha, V. (Director). (2017). *Limitless* [Film]. Believe Films.

Stop Sexual Assault in Schools. (2023). https://stopsexualassaultinschools.org/

Sundberg, A., & Stern, R. (Directors). (2013). *Nine for IX: Let them wear towels* [Film]. ESPN Films.

US Department of Education. (2021, August). *Title IX and sex discrimination.* Office for Civil Rights. https://www2.ed.gov/about/offices/list/ocr/docs/tix_dis.html

REFERENCES

Actress Audrey Hepburn dies. (2020, January 16). History.com. https://www.history.com/this-day-in-history/actress-audrey-hepburn-dies

American Psychological Association. (2007). *Report of the APA task force on the sexualization of girls.* https://www.apa.org/pi/women/programs/girls/report?item=1

American Psychological Association. (2022, July). *Intersectionality.* https://apastyle.apa.org/style-grammar-guidelines/bias-free-language/intersectionality

Aron, N. R. (2019, March 8). What does misogyny look like? A brief history of the #MeToo moment's touchstone term. *The New York Times.* https://www.nytimes.com/2019/03/08/style/misogyny-women-history-photographs.html?

Axisa, M. (2022, May 1). *Kelsie Whitmore becomes first woman to start game in Atlantic League of Professional Baseball.* CBS Sports. https://www.cbssports.com/mlb/

news/kelsie-whitmore-becomes-first-woman-to-start-game-in-atlantic-league-of-professional-baseball/

Bailey, A. (2021, November 27). 'Disgusting and utterly unacceptable': Female athletes main target of online abuse during Tokyo Olympics. *USA Today*. https://www.usatoday.com/story/sports/olympics/2021/11/27/female-athletes-online-abuse-tokyo-olympics/8776654002/

Baseball Writers' Association of America. (n.d.). *Hall of Fame election requirements*. https://bbwaa.com/hof-elec-req/

Berkman, S. (2017, March 28). U.S. women's team strikes a deal with U.S.A. Hockey. *The New York Times*. https://www.nytimes.com/2017/03/28/sports/hockey/usa-hockey-uswnt-boycott.html

Brown, A., Dunn, W., Knapp, C. A., Okeke, S., & Shalaway, E. (2019). Writing the unwritten rules of high school sports with young adult literature. *The ALAN Review, 46*(2), 18–26.

Brown, A., & Parker Moore, D. (2020). Lizzie, Mamie, & Mo'ne: Exploring issues of racism, classism, and sexism in baseball. *Study & Scrutiny: Research on Young Adult Literature, 4*(2), 57–78.

Brown, A., & Rodesiler, L (Eds.). (2016). *Developing contemporary literacies through sports: A guide for the English classroom*. National Council of Teachers of English.

Chatterjee, R. (2018, February 21). *A new survey finds 81 percent of women have experienced sexual harassment*. NPR. https://www.npr.org/sections/thetwo-way/2018/02/21/587671849/a-new-survey-finds-eighty-percent-of-women-have-experienced-sexual-harassment

Crenshaw, K. (1991). Mapping the margins: Intersectionality, identity politics, and violence against women of color. *Stanford Law Review, 43*(6), 1241–1299.

Flanagan, L. (2017, July 28). The field where men still call the shots. *The Atlantic*. https://www.theatlantic.com/education/archive/2017/07/the-field-where-men-still-call-the-shots/535167/

Fowler, T. A. (2021). Exposures of hypermasculinity: Aesthetic portrayals of disengaged "hockey boys" in a specialized sports academy. *Sociology of Sport Journal, 38*(4), 355–366.

Gay, R. (2016, July 11). On making Black Lives Matter. *Marie Claire*. https://www.marieclaire.com/culture/a21423/roxane-gay-philando-castile-alton-sterling/

Glenn, W. J., & King-Watkins, D. (2019). Being an athlete or being a girl: Selective identities among fictional female athletes who play with the boys. *Children's Literature Association Quarterly, 44*(3), 290–309.

———. (2020). Fictional girls who play with the boys: Barriers to access in the transition to male-dominated sports teams. *Children's Literature in Education, 51*(3), 309–331.

Harner, A. (2022, March 14). *Jackie Robinson's struggle as the first Black player in MLB*. HowTheyPlay. https://howtheyplay.com/team-sports/Jackie-Robinson-and-the-struggle-of-becoming-the-first-black-player-in-Major-League-Baseball

Hill, J. B. (2022, April 15). *How sports writer Wendell Smith helped Jackie Robinson break baseball's color barrier 75 years ago*. CBS Sports. https://www.cbssports.com/mlb/news/how-sports-writer-wendell-smith-helped-jackie-robinson-break-baseballs-color-barrier-75-years-ago/

Kalb, D. (2017, May 13). *Q&A with Ellen Emerson White*. Book Q&As with Deborah Kalb. http://deborahkalbbooks.blogspot.com/2017/05/q-with-ellen-emerson-white.html

Kort, J. (2019, June 25). Understanding intersectional identities. *Psychology Today*. https://www.psychologytoday.com/us/blog/understanding-the-erotic-code/201906/understanding-intersectional-identities

Lipsyte, R. (2011, July 27). Jocks vs. pukes: Jock culture is a distortion of sports. *The Nation*. https://www.thenation.com/article/archive/jocks-vs-pukes/

Mervosh, S., & Caron, C. (2019, March 8). 8 times women in sports fought for equality. *The New York Times*. https://www.nytimes.com/2019/03/08/sports/women-sports-equality.html

Parker, K., & Funk, C. (2017, December 14). *Gender discrimination comes in many forms for today's working women*. Pew Research Center. https://www.pewresearch.org/fact-tank/2017/12/14/gender-discrimination-comes-in-many-forms-for-todays-working-women/

Phillips, M. (2021, August 20). *The pressure of perfection*. UTHealth Psychiatry Blog. https://med.uth.edu/psychiatry/2021/08/20/the-pressure-of-perfection/

Randhawa, M. (2022, May 4). *Kelsie Whitmore makes history pitching for FerryHawks*. MLB. https://www.mlb.com/news/kelsie-whitmore-first-woman-to-pitch-in-atlantic-league

Rokos, B. (2022, May 11). Ex-Riverside basketball coach convicted of lewd conduct with players; school district sued. *The Press-Enterprise*. https://www.pe.com/2022/05/11/ex-riverside-basketball-coach-convicted-of-lewd-conduct-with-players-school-district-sued/

Russell, J., & Sasani, A. (2023, January 22). Women's March holds nationwide rallies on 50th anniversary of Roe. *The New York Times*. https://www.nytimes.com/2023/01/22/us/politics/womens-march-roe-wade.html

Santhanam, L. (2017, November 21). *Poll: A third of women say they've been sexually harassed or abused at work*. PBS NewsHour. https://www.pbs.org/newshour/nation/poll-a-third-of-women-say-theyve-been-sexually-harassed-or-abused-at-work

Sidik, S. M. (2022, August 10). The effects of overturning *Roe* v. *Wade* in seven simple charts. *Nature*. https://www.nature.com/articles/d41586-022-02139-3

Srivastava, K., Chaudhury, S., Bhat, P. S., & Sahu, S. (2017). Misogyny, feminism, and sexual harassment. *Industrial Psychiatry Journal, 26*(2), 111–113.

SteelFisher, G. K., Findling, M. G., Bleich, S. N., Casey, L. S., Blendon, R. J., Benson, J. M., Sayde, J. M., & Miller, C. (2019). Gender discrimination in the United States: Experiences of women. *Health Services Research, 54*(2), 1442–1453. https://doi.org/10.1111/1475-6773.13217

Taranto, S. (2021, November 4). *Students face discipline for yelling sexually explicit chants at female goalie during high school hockey game*. CBS Sports. https://www.cbssports.com/nhl/news/students-face-discipline-for-yelling-sexually-explicit-chants-at-female-goalie-during-high-school-hockey-game/

Tedrow, M. K. (2022, August 8). *Using a daybook to promote student writing*. MiddleWeb. https://www.middleweb.com/35776/using-a-daybook-to-promote-student-writing/

Thomas, L. (2023, August 28). The kissing scandal after Spain's women's World Cup win. *The New Yorker*. https://www.newyorker.com/sports/sporting-scene/the-kissing-scandal-after-spains-womens-world-cup-win

US Equal Employment Opportunity Commission. (n.d.). *Harassment*. https://www.eeoc.gov/harassment#:~:text=Offensive%20conduct%20may%20include%2C%20but,and%20interference%20with%20work%20performance

Wasike, B. (2017). Jocks versus jockettes: An analysis of the visual portrayal of male and female cover models on sports magazines. *Journalism, 21*(10), 1432–1449. https://doi.org/10.1177/1464884917716818

Weber, J. D., & Carini, R. M. (2012). Where are the female athletes in *Sports Illustrated*? A content analysis of covers (2000–2011). *International Review for the Sociology of Sport, 48*(2), 196–203.

Williams, V. (2006, June 26). Wimbledon has sent me a message: I'm only a second class champion. *The Times*. https://www.thetimes.co.uk/article/wimbledon-has-sent-me-a-message-im-only-a-second-class-champion-f056h05hmzq

Wojciechowski, G. (2006, February 3). *Lombardi turned Packers into winners*. ESPN. https://www.espn.com/espn/columns/story?columnist=wojciechowski_gene&id=2318158

3

Protesting Systemic Racism in Schools and Society

The beatings were no comparison. The reasons for the beatings were no comparison. I wasn't going to stand there and pretend I knew what life was like for Rashad. There was no way. We lived in the same goddamn city, went to the same goddamn school, and our lives were so very goddamn different.

—*Quinn Collins,* ALL AMERICAN BOYS *(Reynolds & Kiely, 2015, p. 261)*

Though many people turn to sports to escape society's harsh realities, sports culture—like our greater society—is marred by racism. That much is evident from the following reports:

- MLB's Boston Red Sox organization acknowledged a history of racism endured by Black players and employees at Fenway Park (Bonesteel, 2020).
- Kick It Out, an organization striving to overcome discrimination in English football, noted that half of surveyed fans witnessed racist acts at professional games in 2018 ("More than 100 Hate Offences," 2022).
- Patrick Mahomes and Jalen Hurts led their teams to Super Bowl LVII in 2023, which was the first time two Black quarterbacks had started the championship game in a league where approximately 70 percent of players are people of color (Vrentas, 2023).
- Cameras caught National Association for Stock Car Auto Racing (NASCAR) driver Kyle Larson uttering a racist slur during a live-streamed virtual race (Booker, 2020).

Given the prevalence of racism in sports and in society, this chapter is designed to help students challenge racism by exploring the ways many athletes—real and fictional, historical and contemporary, amateur and professional—have spoken out against injustice, refusing to remain silent in the face of racism and bigotry.

THE SOCIAL CONCERN OF SYSTEMIC RACISM

Acts of racism like those in the aforementioned examples are undoubtedly harmful, yet systemic racism, the sort that is "manifested in all societal institutions" (Feagin, 2006, p. xiii), is especially damaging because it contributes to inequities in systems such as economics, education, health, and government. While recognizing that systemic racism affects many groups of people, this brief examination of racial disparities is limited to Black and White people, for those are the groups featured in this chapter's focal YA text, Reynolds and Kiely's (2015) *All American Boys*.

Disparities reflecting systemic racism are evident in the weekly earnings of Black and White US citizens. According to the US Bureau of Labor Statistics (2022), Black people between the ages of 25 and 54 made less money than their White counterparts during 2022's first quarter. The median pay for a Black woman at the time was $866/week; White women made $1,005/week. The median pay for a Black man during that time was $893/week; White men made $1,175/week. Such disparities are not explained away by education; Black people 25 to 34 years old had lower median earnings—$15,000 less for workers with a bachelor's degree and $8,300 less for workers with a master's degree or higher—than White people of the same age and education level in 2021 (National Center for Education Statistics, 2023).

Disparities in illness and mortality experienced by marginalized groups in the US compared to their White counterparts are well-documented (National Center for Health Statistics, 2016), and the COVID-19 pandemic has only magnified those differences. According to a report from the Centers for Disease Control and Prevention (2021), Black, non-Hispanic people were hospitalized due to COVID-19 at a rate 2.8 times higher than White, non-Hispanic people, and they died from COVID-19 complications at a rate 1.9 times higher than White, non-Hispanic people. The CDC acknowledged that inequities in social determinants of health (e.g., access to health care, socioeconomic status) contribute to such findings.

Systemic racism is also evident in how Black US citizens are governed compared to others. Mapping Police Violence (2022), a collaborative researching police violence across the nation, reported that "Black people were more likely to be killed by police, more likely to be unarmed and less likely to be threatening someone when killed." Data support this claim. Black people constituted just 12 percent of the US population in 2022, yet 26 percent of people killed by the police that year were Black; 33 percent of unarmed people killed by the police were Black; and 32 percent of nonthreatening (i.e., unarmed and not attacking) people killed by police were Black.

RACISM AND RESISTANCE IN SPORTS CULTURE

Athletes across sports culture have actively worked to turn viewers' attention from the spectacle of their athletic feats to the scourge that is systemic racism. Colin Kaepernick, formerly a quarterback in the National Football League (NFL), emerged as the modern face of protesting athletes in 2016 when, following consultation with former Green Beret and NFL player Nate Boyer (Martin, 2018), he kneeled during pre-game performances of the US national anthem in an effort to draw attention to police violence against Black people (Wyche, 2016).

Kaepernick's action inspired athletes—professionals and amateurs—across the sports landscape. In the weeks and months that followed, professional athletes such as Megan Rapinoe (2016) of the National Women's Soccer League (NWSL) and Bruce Maxwell (Bryant, 2020) of Major League Baseball (MLB) followed Kaepernick's lead by kneeling during the playing of the US national anthem, as did amateurs such as Matthew Abdullah, Michael Lynn III, Kabbash Richards, and Roje Williams, football players at Lansing (MI) Catholic High School (Couch, 2017).

Athletes protesting during the US national anthem were panned by critics within and outside sports culture. Criticism came in part due to headlines framing the actions as "anthem protests," which suggested that protestors unpatriotically disapproved of the anthem itself. Many citizens, fellow athletes (Underhill, 2016) and elected officials (Graham, 2017) included, opined that kneeling was disrespectful to the flag and to the military. For these reasons, and perhaps myriad others, not all athletes participated in on-field protests or spoke out publicly. Critics may have overlooked the fact that kneeling is a gesture of reverence as Boyer explained to Kaepernick; athletes kneel when addressed by a coach or when competitors are befallen by injury. Regardless, more citizens would be killed by police before critics would acknowledge the importance of the protestors' message.

As lives were lost and blood was shed, resistance to police violence increased in the years after. Following three high-profile cases of White police officers shooting and/or killing Black US citizens in 2020—an officer of the Louisville (KY) Metro Police Department killing Breonna Taylor in March, an officer of the Minneapolis (MN) Police Department killing George Floyd in May, and an officer of the Kenosha (WI) Police Department shooting Jacob Blake in August—the summer months saw massive protests in the nation's streets and stadiums, including boycotts and postponements from the WNBA, NBA, MLB, and MLS (Stein, 2020), among other professional organizations.

Against a backdrop of many modern athletes combatting systemic racism and fighting for social justice, this chapter supports teachers in using historical research and sports-related YA literature to help students understand the history of the activist-athlete and to learn how specific athletes are striving to build a more equitable world for all despite fervent opposition from others, including some fans and fellow athletes. Further, this chapter pushes against any insinuation that a book such as *All American Boys* (Reynolds & Kiely, 2015) should not be read by students for reasons such as indoctrination (Slocum, 2018) or divisiveness (Damon, 2022) because its very purpose is to spark conversations about equity, fairness, and justice.

FOCAL YA TEXT: *ALL AMERICAN BOYS* BY JASON REYNOLDS AND BRENDAN KIELY

All American Boys (Reynolds & Kiely, 2015) is an ideal text for exploring the intersections of racism, police violence, and athletes fighting for social justice. Further, the text offers educators an opportunity to engage students in critical dialogue with community members, researchers, activists, athletes, and police officers to learn more about policies and practices that could prevent police violence in the future.

The novel is told through multiple, alternating voices: that of Rashad Butler, a teen artist and ROTC member, and that of Quinn Collins, Rashad's classmate and a member of their school's varsity basketball team. Neither teen's life would be the same after Rashad, who is Black, is brutally assaulted by a White police officer, Paul Galluzzo, for a crime he did not commit. Rashad is hospitalized and forced to come to grips with being at the center of a growing movement within his community and in the middle of a conflict within his family. Meanwhile, Quinn, who views Galluzzo as a father figure, struggles to make sense of the assault he witnessed firsthand, refusing to believe that someone in his inner circle could enact such brutality in a prejudice-driven attack upon one of his peers.

As the narrative unfolds, the town, the school, and its basketball team show signs of division. Quinn's basketball coach, Coach Carney, insists on players leaving their concerns at the gymnasium door and prohibits them from taking action in response to the social injustice that has rocked the community, yet Quinn recognizes that to be silent is to be complicit. So, the "All-American" boy must decide whether to fall in line as directed or to join teammate English Jones and others in the growing movement and fight for what he knows is right.

As challenges to books featuring diverse characters and authors increase in America, including to the likes of *All American Boys* (Damon, 2022; Slocum,

2018), "divisive concepts" legislation is becoming more common in states across the country. Recently, the National Coalition Against Censorship (2021) and the National Council of Teachers of English, among other organizations, crafted a non-partisan coalition statement that offered five specific reasons why such policies aimed at censoring or banning books are potentially dangerous:

1. First Amendment principles forbid censorship based on ideological viewpoint.
2. The proposed bans conflict with well-established requirements that students be exposed to different interpretations of history and learn to think critically about them.
3. The language of the laws is often vague and thus would chill academic freedom.
4. [Bans] impose State indoctrination.
5. The laws may set a dangerous precedent of political manipulation of the curriculum.

Instead of being viewed as divisive, a book like *All American Boys* (Reynolds & Kiely, 2015) has greater potential if used to help students explore alternative viewpoints through constructive and collaborative conversation about important sociopolitical issues.

Upon publication in 2015, *All American Boys* received starred reviews from multiple reputable outlets, including *Booklist*, *School Library Journal*, and *Publishers Weekly*. In the years since, the novel has been honored with numerous awards. These include the Walter Dean Myers Award for Outstanding Children's Literature, the Amelia Elizabeth Walden Book Award, a Coretta Scott King Honor Award, YALSA's 2017 Top Ten Quick Picks for Reluctant Young Adult Readers, and a Junior Library Guild selection.

INCORPORATING *ALL AMERICAN BOYS* INTO THE SECONDARY ELA CLASSROOM

To frame a unit of study featuring *All American Boys*, we encourage inviting students to grapple with essential questions as they move through the novel. The following activities are intended to support students as they consider three essential questions:

- How and why have athletes throughout history fought for social justice?
- What attempts have athletes made to protest or enact change in racist social structures?
- What is the relative success of athletes' attempts of subverting systemic racism?

Prior to Teaching the Novel

One of the culminating events in *All American Boys* (Reynolds & Kiely, 2015) is the hashtag-inspired protest (#RashadIsAbsentAgainToday) that takes the form of a peaceful march for Black lives and against police brutality. Against mounting pressure from some of his family, friends, and coaches to sit out the protest, Quinn's fear grows when he sees a tank slowly moving down city streets. Quinn's growing sense of unease becomes a focal point for the reader and one that students may connect to as they examine what it means to be an All-American.

Defining an All-American

Before reading the novel, ask students to define for themselves what it means to be an All-American in different contexts. Students may begin with a discussion of qualities and characteristics that may have historically been associated with perceived American ideals, such as honesty, attractiveness, and masculinity. This conversation will undoubtedly lead to the honor of being called one of the best in America, such as in college athletics where the best players are often labeled All-Americans and the best student-athletes are called Academic All-Americans. Inviting students to consider if athletes should be considered All-Americans for other reasons, such as activism, will help prime the pump for discussions about athlete-activism.

Considering Athlete-Activism at the 1968 Summer Olympics

Sports Illustrated named five world-class athletes as their sportspersons of the year in 2020. These athletes—LeBron James, Breanna Stewart, Patrick Mahomes, Naomi Osaka, and Laurent Duvernay-Tardif—all had one thing in common: They were activist athletes ("SI's 2020 Sportsperson," 2020). These athletes took up issues that included voter suppression, racial justice, police violence, and public health. However, these were far from the first athletes whose activism has at least partially defined their legacy. Prior to teaching *All American Boys* (Reynolds & Kiely, 2015), teachers might consider introducing students to three interracial activist-athletes from the 1960s: Tommie Smith and John Carlos, who are Black and hail from the United States, and the less-heralded Peter Norman, who was White and hailed from Australia. At the height of racial tensions during the Civil Rights Movement in America, the 1968 Summer Olympics was taking place in Mexico City. According to Blakemore (2023), Smith and Carlos were discouraged by what they perceived to be a lack of action on the part of protesters of racial injustice.

Although initially planning to boycott the Olympics, Smith and Carlos eventually decided to compete in hopes of using their accomplishments to promote the need for human rights changes globally. In Mexico City, they ultimately won gold and bronze medals, respectively, in the 200-meter race with Norman winning the silver medal. After the race, Smith and Carlos stepped to the podium and each raised a fist covered by a black glove to show support for oppressed Black people around the world. Norman demonstrated his support as an ally by wearing a badge for the Olympic Project for Human Rights (Blakemore, 2023).

Smith and Carlos faced immediate backlash, including death threats, for their actions, and they were banned from competing in future Olympics. Yet they did have brief careers in professional sports and became global icons for standing up to racial injustice. Norman, in a similar way, was blackballed in his home country of Australia, which never again allowed him to compete in the Olympics despite him holding record times. Looking back, Norman once said, "I won a silver medal. . . . But really, I ended up running the fastest race of my life to become part of something that transcended the Games" (Wise, 2000).

There are myriad resources to support teaching students about these track stars from the 1968 Olympics whose activism pulled the levers of social change both nationally and internationally, including *Victory. Stand! Raising My Fist for Justice* (Smith et al., 2022), a work of graphic nonfiction for young adults, as well as documentaries such as *1968—A Mexico City Documentary* (NBC Olympics, 2018) and *The Stand: How One Gesture Shook the World* (Ratcliffe et al., 2020). Sharing these resources with students will help to provide important context for what it takes to attempt to overcome racist social structures through activism.

Examining Influence on Social Change

Learning about Smith, Carlos, and Norman's protest sets the stage for teachers to introduce an activity called the "Sports and Social Change Continuum." The purpose of this activity is for students to learn about historical and contemporary activist-athletes and the influence they had on social change regarding systemic racism. Students are challenged to identify where on a numeric continuum particular activist-athletes should be placed based on a specific moment or act of athlete activism and how students perceive the level of influence each athlete used to effect social change at that time.

With the continuum marked left to right from zero to ten, students could identify a number (e.g., 3.7, 5.2, 8.5) that corresponds with the athlete's placement and justify their decision. The continuum is meant to be a sliding scale, so as students learn more about activist-athletes' actions, they can add or adjust each placement accordingly in terms of influence on social change. Part of this negotiation is for students to consider how quickly social change can occur or how long social change takes to lead to societal transformation; after all, students have the benefit of historical memory, which can demonstrate how other experiences can positively or negatively affect the ability to create change.

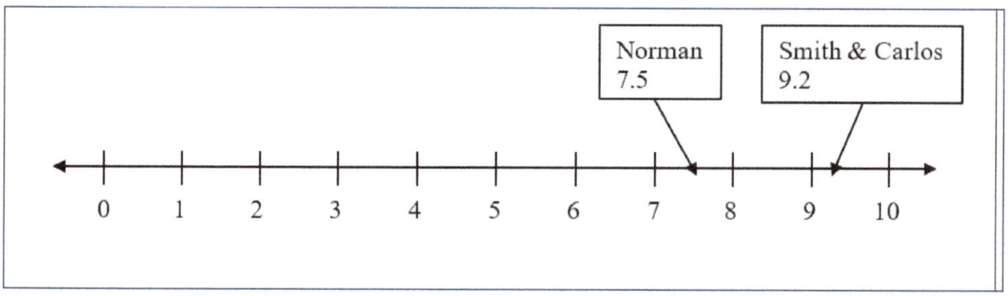

FIGURE 3.1: Example Sports and Social Change Continuum

As observed in Figure 3.1, Smith, Carlos, and Norman would be the first entry on students' "Sports and Social Change Continuum," although students should deliberate on whether they believe the three activist-athletes should be a single entry or placed on the continuum separately as they research more about the historical legacy of their collective protest. Every student in the class can create their own continuum. Some students might not value acts of protest like those carried out at the 1968 Olympics and, subsequently, may place those activist-athletes lower on their continuum. Regardless of how students perceive specific acts of protest, their rationales should be informed by textual evidence. At the end of the unit, students can average their numbers for each individual or group of activist-athletes to create a whole-class "Sports and Social Change Continuum" that represents their collective views of influence.

As Students Read the Novel

Students can consider and record how characters in *All American Boys* try to enact change in racist social structures and can determine the relative success of these attempts at change. At the same time, they can continue learning about historical and contemporary activist-athletes who have sacrificed to protest systemic racism around the world.

Exploring Multiple Perspectives

Because the story of *All American Boys* is told through two narrators, readers experience multiple perspectives of the same events, thereby allowing them to create a more complex understanding of how different characters think and feel about those events. Since this multiperspectivity reveals distinct viewpoints, it can dispel a common misunderstanding that there is one "correct" truth about personal experience and social issues (Lewis & Bruce, 2018). As a way to prepare students to add to their own "Sports and Social Change Continuum," teachers should ask students to document the characters' perspectives as they read.

One approach for documentation is a character journal in which students record central characters' thoughts, feelings, and actions related to key plot points. Teachers can identify central moments prior to teaching the novel and then assign journal entries when students are reading that section of the novel. An example is from early in the novel when Quinn is struggling to separate himself from his father's identity, which is what leads him to question what it means to be an All-American:

> No, I wasn't a stand-in for Dad. Nobody could be that. When the IED got him in Afghanistan, he became an instant saint in Springfield. I wasn't him. I'd never be him. But I was still supposed to try. That was my role: the dutiful son, the All-American boy with an All-American fifteen-foot deadeye jump shot and an All-American 3.5 GPA. (Reynolds & Kiely, 2015, p. 27)

In this case, a teacher may ask students what it means to be dutiful, defined as obediently fulfilling a duty, and under what conditions or circumstances it is okay to conscientiously question that duty. Students can then share their entries in small groups to discuss their varied opinions, which would further amplify their comprehension of Quinn's story, in this case.

Voices from the Field
Justice through Literature

Guy Hill
Teacher, Harnett County Schools, North Carolina

I began my teaching career 27 years ago in hopes of having a positive impact on young people by engaging students with literature. In short, I wanted to change the world. The writings of Ralph Waldo Emerson and Frederick Douglass, in particular, spoke to me and showed me how liberating literature can be. In my Advanced Placement and Composition class, we analyze famous and impactful speeches when we study rhetorical devices and strategies. Dr. Martin Luther King Jr.'s (2008) "I Have a Dream" speech is a perfect lesson in the power of rhetoric. In discussing the context of the speech and considering its impact today, we must talk about protesting systemic racism because that is why there was a "March on Washington," an "I Have a Dream" speech, a Civil Rights Movement, and a Martin Luther King Jr. as a national leader. Teaching the content and structure of this speech and other speeches by Dr. King and his historical predecessors and contemporaries cannot and should not be done in a vacuum without addressing the moral and societal context and implications of the author's words. We have an obligation as teachers to teach the text in its contextual entirety.

By the speech's end, I begin making connections to modern protests and discussing what systemic racism is and to what degree it still exists. When discussing King's dream at the end of his speech, we are forced to confront whether the US has achieved that dream and what evidence supports, or does not support, this conclusion. From there, I ask students to draw connections between Dr. King's, Muhammad Ali's, and Colin Kaepernick's peaceful protests through questions like the following: What was similar? What was different? What was the perception of the protests at the time they occurred, and what is the perception of the protests in hindsight? Additionally, I inform students of the disdain with which Dr. King was perceived at the time when he was protesting and how that was different from the reverent way he is commonly framed today. I also require them to analyze why this might be and what the implications of these perceptions are. We repeat this process as we read and analyze other speeches by the likes of Dr. King, Abraham Lincoln, Frederick Douglass, and John F. Kennedy.

I normally have some athletes in my English classes, AP or otherwise. They are usually aware of Colin Kaepernick's protests, and even if students are not athletically inclined, they generally have an opinion about kneeling during a performance of the national anthem before a nationally televised athletic contest. Most of the African American students I teach are sympathetic toward the concept of protesting systemic racism because they perceive racism as a problem they must confront daily. They have a vested interest in the problem of systemic racism being eradicated, and they usually want to see it happen by any peaceful means necessary.

My African American male students, in particular, frequently gravitate toward this line of thinking. They seem to be engaged by the larger moral and societal context of literature and the comparison of ideas and tactics to address society's ills. In short, they never thought to compare Dr. King to Muhammad Ali or Colin Kaepernick (e.g., Moore, n.d.), and I would assert that these connections make the writing of the people of the distant past seem more relevant to students today. Many times, in classroom discussions of these topics or through students' writing in response to prompts about systemic racism, my students confess that they had neither thought about the purpose behind the words of the aforementioned authors, nor had they thought about the context of the words, nor had they contemplated comparing the past to the present in such a manner. This process seems to give them a more comprehensive historical perspective as well as to help them see repetitive patterns in society, ideas, and the written word. I see and hear many students of different backgrounds respond in kind to this type of analysis; however, this process seems to have a profound effect on a larger percentage of African American males.

My hope is that at the very least, as their teacher, I can foster a deeper understanding of literature and specifically how people protest injustice through writing, whether it is Ralph Waldo Emerson, Frederick Douglass, Dr. Martin Luther King Jr., or their own authentic selves (e.g., through social media). I hope students can view literature as a liberating medium by which they can explore issues of inequality, injustice, and systemic racism, and my goal is to help them find their own voices by reading the voices of others. I believe this to be monumentally important in helping students understand themselves, in what they believe, and for what they are willing to fight. In schools and communities where race can still be a determining factor for opportunities, this is a valuable lesson for students to learn.

References

King, M. L. (2008). *I have a dream* [Speech transcript]. The Avalon Project. https://avalon.law.yale.edu/20th_century/mlk01.asp (Original work published 1963)

Moore, L. (n.d.). *50 voices for 50 years series: Martin Luther King Jr., and the Black athlete protest tradition*. National Civil Rights Museum. https://www.civilrightsmuseum.org/50-voices-for-50-years/posts/martin-luther-king-jr-and-the-black-athlete-protest-tradition

Guy Hill is a teacher of regular and honors ninth- and tenth-grade English as well as Advanced Placement Language and Composition at Triton High School in Harnett County. Originally from the Bronx, New York, he has a bachelor's degree in English from the University of North Carolina at Chapel Hill and a master's degree in English education from Wake Forest University. He has 27 years of teaching experience and has served as a member of the Board of Directors and President of the North Carolina English Teachers Association. He has been a recipient of the "Champion of Education" award presented by the North Carolina Department of Public Instruction, and he currently serves as an Executive Board member for North Carolina Governor Roy Cooper's DRIVE (Developing a Representative and Inclusive Vision for Education) Task Force.

Looking for Statements of Solidarity

In *All American Boys*, students will find instances of characters engaging in activism-focused activities. For example, English, who is agitated by his teammates' unwillingness to stand up to racial injustice, successfully runs a play called "Fist" three times. Before beginning the play the third time, "[English] put his fist in the air, he paused and said, 'Rashad,' and waved his fist like a flag before zigzagging in a fierce line to the hoop, banging and slipping past nearly everybody. He yelled and slapped the backboard as he went up for the layup and nailed it" (Reynolds & Kiely, 2015, p. 256). This form of protest is meant as a statement toward his teammates.

Quinn, for one, receives the message loud and clear. At that moment during English's protest, Quinn recognizes that he "couldn't just separate basketball from the rest of [his] life, just like we couldn't separate history from the present, just like we couldn't have racism in America without racists" (Reynolds & Kiely, 2015, p. 256). If the purpose of protests is to raise awareness, then English succeeded, though it will be up to students to place that protest and its influence on the "Sports and Social Change Continuum." The image of English raising his fist and calling out Rashad's name should also invite comparisons to Olympians Tommie Smith and John Carlos, figures students learned about prior to reading the novel.

Quinn also has moments of protest that support the narrative of him as an activist-athlete. Once he decides to join the protest, he makes a statement by creating and wearing a t-shirt that says, "I'M MARCHING" on the front and "ARE YOU?" on the back (Reynolds & Kiely, 2015, p. 252). His statement serves multiple purposes: (1) a chance for him to publicly display his stand against police brutality, (2) a silent demonstration of support as an ally for other activists fighting against racist social structures, and (3) a public statement to push back against authority figures (i.e., Coach Carney) who prioritize winning basketball games over supporting basic human rights.

Just like Peter Norman after the 1968 Olympics, Quinn gets scolded and harassed for wearing a statement of solidarity with protestors of systemic racism, although, as with English, it will be up to students to place his moment of protest and its influence on the "Sports and Social Change Continuum." One approach for helping students understand the social culture of protests is to look for signs, figuratively and literally, of statements of solidarity with people around particular social issues. These could come in many forms (e.g., t-shirts, bumper stickers, yard signs, billboards) and allow students to evaluate the effectiveness of messaging through written protest.

Identifying Methods for Practicing Activism

In 2020, exactly fifty years after the Syracuse 8 boycotted their own football games to demand the hiring of a Black football coach at Syracuse University ("Syracuse 8," n.d.), the National Collegiate Athletic Association (2023) finally began recognizing the important role that athletes play in social justice activism, including creating a national unity pledge and logo. As part of that recognition, they cite various ways that athletes can practice activism, such as campaigning, protesting, demonstrating, advocating, organizing, launching groups, building community, and developing communication strategies.

The NCAA's list of methods for practicing activism can provide a useful template for helping students map out the various forms of activism happening throughout the novel (e.g., graffiti, t-shirts, marching) and understand the power that athletes have in promoting social change through activism (Wulf, 2019). One way students can identify, explore, and name methods for practicing activism is to learn about the efforts of historical and contemporary athletes like those presented in Figure 3.2 and identify how the methods they used toward social justice activism helped them raise awareness or effect social change.

Historical and Contemporary Figures	Activism
Jesse Owens and Mack Robinson	Participated in the Berlin Games in the shadow of Nazi Germany in 1936
Jackie Robinson	Integrated Major League Baseball for Branch Rickey's Brooklyn Dodgers in 1947
Althea Gibson	Integrated professional tennis in 1950
Lew Alcindor (aka Kareem Abdul-Jabbar)	Boycotted the 1968 Olympics in Mexico City in support of the Olympic Project for Human Rights led by Dr. Harry Edwards
Arthur Ashe	Negotiated for an integrated tennis stadium in apartheid South Africa in 1973
Mahmoud Abdul-Rauf	Was suspended from the National Basketball Association in 1996 for refusing to stand for the national anthem in protest of social ills such as health care inequality
Toni Smith	Turned her back to the US flag during the national anthem of a Manhattanville College (NY) women's basketball game to protest the war in Iraq in 2003
Ariyana Smith	Silently protested the shooting death of unarmed teenager Michael Brown in 2014 before a Knox College (IL) women's basketball game
Minnesota Lynx Players	Wore warm-up shirts that declared "Change Starts with Us—Justice & Accountability" and "Black Lives Matter" in 2016 to protest police violence against Black civilians
Nathan Braaten and Taylor Ricci	Launched a mental health awareness initiative at Oregon State in 2018

FIGURE 3.2: Examples of Social Justice Activism by Athletes throughout History

For example, Lew Alcindor, who would later change his name to Kareem Abdul-Jabbar, was a star basketball player at UCLA who protested racial segregation by boycotting the 1968 Olympics in Mexico City (Brewer, 2018). Asking students to differentiate his form of activism from that of American athletes Tommie Smith and John Carlos, who decided to participate in the Olympics but protested by raising gloved fists on the medal podium, allows students to engage in meaningful conversation about the decision-making process that goes into activist-athletes using their influence for the sake of social justice. We recommend providing students with the youth activist toolkit (Advocates for Youth, n.d.) as they consider questions about organizing, creating a strategy, crafting a message, building and using collective power, and sustaining a movement. As students learn about new historical and contemporary athletes, they should place them along the "Sports and Social Change Continuum."

Redefining an All-American

Late in the novel, Quinn's friend Jill calms his nerves by reminding him that they are part of a movement, as she points to a quote from Desmond Tutu, an archbishop who opposed apartheid in South Africa and received the Nobel Peace Prize. Tutu's quote reads, "If you are neutral in situations of injustice, you have chosen the side of the oppressor" (Reynolds & Kiely, 2015, p. 290). At that moment, Jill turns to her friend and reminds him, "This is like a real moment in history, Quinn" (p. 291).

Soon thereafter, Quinn joins some of his basketball teammates as they become activist-athletes. While English Jones, the star basketball player at Central High School, stands up for his friend Rashad and expresses outrage from the beginning, Quinn is a more reluctant activist until he begins to think about his father, a decorated soldier who died serving his country in Afghanistan, and recognizes the importance of the protest at that moment in time: "I thought about what English had said to me . . . and it made me wonder how many times I'd remained neutral in the past too, and what that meant. What did Dad do? He ran right into the face of history. I couldn't duck now, just because I was scared" (p. 291). Quinn realizes that to protest for what you believe is right is not at all un-American. In this case, to protest against racism and bigotry, now more than ever before, is All-American, and Quinn wants to be an activist-athlete on the right side of history.

As students conclude their reading of the novel, invite them to reconsider their earlier definition of an All-American with Rashad, Quinn, and English in mind. Do they consider these characters All-American Boys? Why or why not? Then, have students imagine an award for activist-athletes similar to the honor the National High School Coaches Association (2023) provides to "Academic All Americans," whose qualifications include at least a 3.6 grade point average and high school athletic accomplishments. Invite students to consider what qualifications an Activist-Athlete All American would need to be honored in such a way and rationalize the qualifications they identify.

Culminating Tasks after Reading the Novel

Following an examination of the role of activist-athletes in social culture, teachers can ask students to write two follow-up chapters that detail how Quinn and English's basketball season finished, adding a new moment of activism that connects the two activist-athletes, before displaying their final "Sports and Social Change Continuum" via a gallery walk.

Writing Follow-Up Chapters

The work of an activist is never truly finished, particularly when the struggle is against social and political systems where racism, or other areas of concern such as sexism and homophobia, are embedded within those systems. Just as Tommie Smith and John Carlos's activism did not end after the 1968 Olympics in Mexico City, it is safe to wonder whether Quinn and Rashad will continue their activism in the future.

Suggesting these characters may have more work to do, teachers can ask students to write two follow-up chapters, encouraging them to reflect on the authors' organizational structure of dual-voice narrators. Students could write the first additional chapter from Quinn's perspective as he and English plan and implement their protest and the second chapter from Rashad's perspective as he observes their activism. For example, students could write about a moment that takes place during the first basketball game after the #RashadIsAbsentAgainToday protest or a moment later in the season during an important playoff game. Alternatively, students could write about Coach Carney attempting to punish Quinn and English for their participation in the protest, essentially for refusing to "shut up and dribble" (Sullivan, 2018), which could lead them to walk away from basketball much like WNBA star Maya Moore did in 2019 to pursue criminal justice reform (Herring & Paine, 2020). Ideally, the second chapter would end with some recognition of how Quinn and English's activism influenced them, their team, their school, and their community.

Talking the Talk and Walking the (Gallery) Walk

In her 2021 TEDx Talk, Hanna Testa spoke about the power of youth activating their voices to create action that leads to sustainable change. Based on her experience and examination of other social change movements, Testa cited three main steps to help youth get involved in activism: (1) Find your why; (2) Educate yourself; and (3) Advocate for change. As technology and social media provide young people with tools to amplify their voices louder than ever (Carnegie, 2022), providing a space for students to share what they have learned about activist-athletes and how they advocated for change seems like a logical final step.

After students have written their follow-up chapters, ask them to add English and Quinn's collaborative protest to the "Sports and Social Change Continuum" and, once again, justify their placement. Then, create a space for students to share their new chapters as part of an authors' celebration in which they share their vision for Quinn and English's activism, read a brief excerpt from their own writings, account for the placement of English and Quinn's culminating protest on the continuum, and post their final continuum for other students to see as part of a gallery walk exhibit.

During the gallery walk, students can record their classmates' ratings and then tabulate each character's average continuum number to determine a whole-class "Sports and Social Change Continuum" for *All American Boys.* Teachers might also encourage students to tabulate the collective ratings of the historical and contemporary activist-athletes to create a "Sports and Social Change Historical Legacy Continuum" to be displayed prominently in one of the school's academic buildings or athletic facilities to publicly showcase the influence of activist-athletes.

CONCLUSION

Teachers should invite students to return to the previous discussion of the 1968 Olympics in Mexico City to consider similarities and differences between English Jones and Quinn Collins's protests in *All American Boys* and Tommie Smith, John Carlos, and Peter Norman's historic protest for human rights. Connecting these real and fictional events with historical and contemporary backdrops will help students better understand what it means to speak out against injustice by refusing to remain silent in the face of racism and bigotry. These series of activities may even inspire students and athletes to consider their purpose and activate their own voices for causes that hold great meaning to them.

Options for Book Clubs

Teachers eager to employ book clubs as students explore protesting systemic racism in schools and society through *All American Boys* should also consider these titles:

Light It Up (Magoon, 2020)
This series of vignettes from multiple narrators details the aftermath of a White police officer murdering a thirteen-year-old Black girl, Shae Tatum, in the Underhill neighborhood. A follow-up to *How It Went Down*, this story explores how the repeated trauma of police brutality can devastate Black communities. This selection provides an option that is not sports-related.

I Am Alfonso Jones (Medina, Robinson, & Jennings, 2017)
In this graphic novel, Alfonso Jones is killed by an off-duty police officer while shopping for a suit. He wakes up in the afterlife on a train of ancestral victims of police shootings where he learns not only about the impact of his life and death but also about the long history of police brutality on Black lives. This selection provides an option that is not sports-related.

Anger Is a Gift (Oshiro, 2019)
Moss Jefferies's father was murdered by an Oakland police officer six years ago. Since then, Moss has suffered anxiety-induced panic attacks that are exacerbated by new regulations at West Oakland High School, where he and his friends are treated like criminals—that is, until they pull together to organize and demonstrate against a system that threatens their livelihood. This selection provides an option that is not sports-related.

Dear Martin (Stone, 2018)
Justyce McAllister is a potential Ivy League student who, along with his best friend and star basketball player Emmanuel "Manny" Rivers, attends a predominantly White private school in Atlanta. After experiencing racial profiling by a White police officer, Justyce writes a series of journal entries to Dr. Martin Luther King Jr. as he tries to reckon with his place in a corrupt system overrun by racial injustice, White privilege, and police brutality.

The Hate U Give (Thomas, 2017)
Starr Carter is a sixteen-year-old girl trying to find her identity in two worlds: a fancy, predominantly White prep school where she studies and plays basketball and the poor, predominantly Black community where she lives. Starr witnesses the death of her friend Khalil at the hands of a White police officer and experiences the traumatic aftermath as she testifies against the officer and becomes a community activist against police brutality.

Options for Film Study

Teachers looking to extend students' exploration of protesting systemic racism in schools and society might consider screening one of the following films:

Shut Up and Dribble (Chopra, 2018)
This three-part documentary series, which first aired in 2018, explores the intersections of race, social activism, and sports primarily through the lens of the National Basketball Association. Though criticized for paying limited attention to the activism of Black women, the series does provide opportunities for considering the role of athletes in the greater sociopolitical landscape.

Not Just a Game: Power, Politics & American Sports (Earp, 2010)
Starring Dave Zirin, sports editor for *The Nation*, this documentary from the Media Education Foundation challenges the notion that sports stand free of the sociopolitical issues in the world around us. Addressing the ways American sports culture has fostered racism, sexism, and more, Zirin also accounts for activist-athletes who have worked to challenge the status quo.

Salute (Norman, 2008)
This award-winning documentary focuses on the demonstration at the 1968 Olympics in Mexico City with silver medalist Peter Norman as the film's primary subject. The fallout resulting from the Australian's actions at the podium and his support of Tommie Smith and John Carlos is documented, as is a reunion between the three medal winners.

Fists of Freedom: The Story of the '68 Summer Games (Roy, 1999)
Covering events that unfolded before, during, and after Americans Tommie Smith and John Carlos raised their fists on the podium at the 1968 Summer Olympics, this award-winning documentary shines a light on the repercussions the sprinters experienced in the aftermath of their iconic protest.

Young Adult Literature

Magoon, K. (2020). *Light it up*. Square Fish.

Medina, T. (2017). *I am Alfonso Jones* (S. Robinson & J. Jennings, Illus.). Tu Books.

Oshiro, M. (2019). *Anger is a gift*. Tor Teen.

Reynolds, J., & Kiely, B. (2015). *All American boys*. Atheneum/Caitlyn Dlouhy Books.

Smith, T., Barnes, D., & Anyabwile, D. (2022). *Victory. Stand! Raising my fist for justice*. Norton Young Readers.

Stone, N. (2018). *Dear Martin*. Ember.

Thomas, A. (2017). *The hate u give*. Balzer + Bray.

Other Texts for Classroom Use

Advocates for Youth. (n.d.). *Youth activist toolkit*. http://www.advocatesforyouth.org/wp-content/uploads/2019/04/Youth-Activist-Toolkit.pdf

Chopra, G. (Director). (2018). *Shut up and dribble* [Film]. Showtime.

Earp, J. (Director). (2010). *Not just a game: Power, politics & American sports* [Film]. Media Education Foundation.

National Collegiate Athletic Association. (2023). *Student-athlete activism*. https://www.ncaa.org/sports/2021/7/23/student-athlete-activism.aspx

National High School Coaches Association. (2023). *Academic all Americans*. https://nhsca.com/academic-all-americans/

NBC Sports. (2018, October 17). *1968 - A Mexico City documentary*. [Video]. You Tube. https://www.youtube.com/watch?v=7Ss6qavj29c

Norman, M. (Director). (2008). *Salute* [Film]. Wingman Pictures.

Ratcliffe, T. (Director). (2020). *The stand: How one gesture shook the world* [Film]. Juno Films.

Roy, G. (Director). (1999). *Fists of freedom: The story of the '68 summer games* [Film]. HBO Sports; Black Canyon Productions.

REFERENCES

Blakemore, E. (2023, March 30). *How the Black Power protest at the 1968 Olympics killed careers*. History.com. https://www.history.com/news/1968-mexico-city-olympics-black-power-protest-backlash

Bonesteel, M. (2020, June 11). Red Sox acknowledge racism at Fenway Park 'is real', promise action. *The Washington Post*. https://www.washingtonpost.com/sports/2020/06/11/red-sox-acknowledge-racism-fenway-park-is-real-promise-action

Booker, B. (2020, October 20). *NASCAR reinstates racer Kyle Larson after suspending him for using n-word*. NPR. https://www.npr.org/sections/live-updates-protests-for-racial-justice/2020/10/20/925741441/nascar-reinstates-racer-kyle-larson-after-suspending-him-for-using-n-word

Brewer, J. (2018, May 28). In a time of chaos, 1968 was a breakout year for black athletes. *Chicago Tribune*. https://www.chicagotribune.com/sports/ct-spt-black-athletes-1968-story.html

Bryant, H. (2020, July 8). *The exile of Oakland A's Bruce Maxwell and the birth of MLB's Black player movement*. ESPN. https://www.espn.com/mlb/story/_/id/29414410/the-exile-oakland-bruce-maxwell-birth-mlb-black-player-movement

Carnegie, M. (2022, August 8). *Gen Z: How young people are changing activism*. BBC. https://www.bbc.com/worklife/article/20220803-gen-z-how-young-people-are-changing-activism

Centers for Disease Control and Prevention. (2021, April 23). *Risk for COVID-19 infection, hospitalization, and death by race/ethnicity*. https://stacks.cdc.gov/view/cdc/105453

Couch, G. (2017, October 6). Lansing Catholic football players kneel during anthem, start the game on the bench. *Lansing State Journal*. https://www.lansingstatejournal.com/story/sports/high-school/2017/10/06/lansing-catholic-anthem-protest-game-night/741556001/

Damon, L. (2022, January 27). "Challenged" novel on police brutality sparks discussion at Tiverton School committee meeting. *The Newport Daily News*. https://www.newportri.com/story/news/local/2022/01/27/all-american-boys-novel-jason-reynolds-and-brendan-kiely-sparks-discussion-tiverton-ri-schools/9229895002/

Feagin, J. (2006). *Systemic racism: A theory of oppression*. Routledge.

Graham, B. A. (2017, September 23). Donald Trump blasts NFL anthem protesters: "Get that son of a bitch off the field." *The Guardian*. https://www.theguardian.com/sport/2017/sep/22/donald-trump-nfl-national-anthem-protests

Herring, C., & Paine, N. (2020, June 11). *Maya Moore gave up more to fight for social justice than almost any athlete*. FiveThirtyEight. https://fivethirtyeight.com/features/maya-moore-gave-up-more-to-fight-for-social-justice-than-almost-any-athlete/

Lewis, M. A., & Bruce, E. (2018). Multiperspectivity in *How it went down:* A more just way of "seeing." *SIGNAL Journal, 43*(2), 27–31.

Mapping Police Violence. (2022). *2022 police violence report*. https://policeviolencereport.org/

Martin, M. (Host). (2018, September 9). The veteran and NFL player who advised Kaepernick to take a knee [Audio podcast episode]. In *All Things Considered*. NPR. https://www.npr.org/2018/09/09/646115651/the-veteran-and-nfl-player-who-advised-kaepernick-to-take-a-knee

More than 100 hate offences in London football stadiums. (2022, July 13). BBC. https://www.bbc.com/news/uk-england-london-62160946

National Center for Education Statistics. (2023, May). *Annual earnings by educational attainment*. https://nces.ed.gov/programs/coe/indicator/cba/annual-earnings

National Center for Health Statistics. (2016). *Health, United States, 2015: With special feature on racial and ethnic health disparities*. https://www.cdc.gov/nchs/data/hus/hus15.pdf

National Coalition Against Censorship. (2021, June 23). *Non-partisan coalition statement opposing "divisive concepts" legislation*. https://ncac.org/news/divisive-concepts-statement-2021

Rapinoe, M. (2016, October 6). *Why I am kneeling*. The Players' Tribune. https://www.theplayerstribune.com/articles/megan-rapinoe-why-i-am-kneeling

SI's 2020 sportsperson of the year: The activist athlete. (2020, December 6). *Sports Illustrated*. https://www.si.com/sportsperson/2020/12/06/sportsperson-2020-james-stewart-mahomes-osaka-duvernay-tardif

Slocum, R. (2018, August 1). The hate u give *and* all American boys *challenged by Charleston County police*. The Office for Intellectual Freedom of the American Library Association. https://www.oif.ala.org/oif/the-hate-u-give-and-all-american-boys-challenged-by-charleston-county-police/

Stein, M. (2020, September 4). Led by N.B.A., boycotts disrupt pro sports in wake of Blake shooting. *The New York Times*. https://www.nytimes.com/2020/08/26/sports/basketball/nba-boycott-bucks-magic-blake-shooting.html

Sullivan, E. (2018, February 19). *Laura Ingraham told LeBron James to shut up and dribble; he went to the hoop*. NPR. https://www.npr.org/sections/thetwo-way/2018/02/19/587097707/laura-ingraham-told-lebron-james-to-shutup-and-dribble-he-went-to-the-hoop

Syracuse 8. (n.d.). Syracuse University. https://cuse.com/sports/2020/9/16/the-syracuse-8-legacy.aspx

TEDx Talks. (2021, March 19). *Youth activism: Activating your voice* [Video]. YouTube. https://www.youtube.com/watch?v=D2xcoDM6EWw

Underhill, N. (2016, August 30). Saints' Drew Brees: I support Colin Kaepernick's stance, not his method of protest. *The Times-Picayune/The New Orleans Advocate*. https://www.nola.com/sports/saints /article_d3ff1886-d9bb-522f-87b9-f10447ebe7ff.html

US Bureau of Labor Statistics. (2022, April 15). *Usual weekly earnings of wage and salary workers: Table 3. Median usual weekly earnings of full-time wage and salary workers by age, race, Hispanic or Latino ethnicity, and sex, first quarter 2022 averages, not seasonally adjusted*. https://www.bls.gov/news.release/wkyeng.t03.htm

Vrentas, J. (2023, February 13). Black quarterbacks in the Super Bowl reflect progress and lost opportunity. *The New York Times*. https://www.nytimes.com/2023/02/12/sports/football/nfl-black-quarterbacks.html

Wise, M. (2000, September 17). Sydney 2000: The third man in Mexico City. *The New York Times*. https://www.nytimes.com/2000/09/17/sports/sydney-2000-the-third-man-in-mexico-city.html

Wulf, S. (2019, January 30). Athletes and activism: The long, defiant history of sports protests. *The Undefeated*. https://theundefeated.com/features/athletes-and-activism-the-long-defiant-history-of-sports-protests/

Wyche, S. (2016, August 27). *Colin Kaepernick explains why he sat during national anthem*. NFL. https://www.nfl.com/news/colin-kaepernick-explains-why-he-sat-during-national-anthem-0ap3000000691077

4

Challenging Homophobia in Sports and Society

"The last place to go was the rink. Caitlin, Lindsay, the team . . . and I couldn't do it."

—*Tillie Walden,* SPINNING *(2017, p. 254)*

In her graphic-novel memoir reflecting on her ice-skating career as a child and young teenager, Tillie Walden not only describes her experiences on the ice but also her personal experiences with her first girlfriend and revealing her sexual orientation to family and friends. While she is able to tell her family and school friends about her orientation, she is unable to take the same steps with her skating teammates. The reasons behind this decision are complicated, but a primary one is her perception of how "difference" was viewed within the culture of her skating team. Tillie's experience is not unique and, while many views within the sports community have slowly shifted toward more inclusive perspectives, homophobia and the rights of lesbian, gay, bisexual, transgender, queer, and nonbinary (LGBTQ+) athletes remain contemporary issues. For example, consider these stories:

- LGBTQ+ youth are significantly less likely to participate in team sports than their heterosexual, cisgender peers, 22.5 percent as compared to 49.1 percent, and they often choose to avoid sports due to fear of bullying (Goldberg et al., 2023; Ramirez, 2021).
- A 2023 World Cup qualifier between Mexico and the United States (US) was ended early by the referee due to fans' repeated use of homophobic slurs and chants aimed at US players, which was just the latest instance of such behavior by Mexican soccer fans resulting in punishments, bans, and fines (Balta, 2018; Bernal, 2021; Hernandez, 2023).
- Between 2020 and 2023, 23 US states passed laws restricting and/or banning transgender athletes' participation in school-sponsored sports at the K–12 and college levels (Movement Advancement Project, 2023).

- Clay Davies, an elite British cyclist, came out as gay after a near-death experience, despite his discomfort with doing so due to what he characterized as the "closed mindset, a not-quite-as-worldly" cycling community (Reimer, 2021).

In response to these stories, this chapter aims to support teachers using sports-related young adult literature to advance secondary students' literacy skills and knowledge as they consider how those who identify as LGBTQ+ are treated in our society.

THE SOCIAL CONCERN OF HOMOPHOBIA

In The Trevor Project's most recent National Survey on LGBTQ Youth Mental Health (2023), 41 percent of LGBTQ+ youth reported that they "seriously considered attempting suicide" in the past year, and almost 50 percent of transgender and nonbinary youth surveyed had considered suicide in the past year. This rate is about twice as high as the approximately 19 percent of all high school youth who report contemplating suicide (United Health Foundation, 2022). In The Trevor Project survey, LGBTQ+ youth that reported experiencing discrimination (60 percent of respondents), physical violence (24 percent), and/or being threatened with or subjected to conversion therapy (15 percent) were twice as likely to attempt suicide. The argument for why our society and schools should be more affirming of diverse sexual orientations should end with these statistics, particularly if we layer on reporting from The Trevor Project survey that indicates youth who see positive LGBTQ+ representations in media and popular culture, have reliable access to mental health care, and attend schools they view as LGBTQ-affirming are significantly less likely to plan or attempt suicide.

Yet in recent years, there have been renewed efforts to erase the stories of LGBTQ+ experiences from public libraries and school classrooms. For example, such stories have been removed from shelves in Texas schools due to pressures from anti-LGBTQ+ groups demanding their banishment due to their representations of characters with diverse sexual orientations, along with books that discuss other "divisive" concepts like race and gender (Hixenbaugh, 2022). Beyond the single state of Texas, PEN America tallied 1,586 decisions to *ban* a book from a library, classroom, or curriculum from July 2021 to March 2022 (Pendharkar, 2022). This number is in stark contrast to the 377 *challenges* to books recorded by the American Library Association in 2019 (2020), especially since not all challenges result in ultimate banning of the targeted text. Importantly, the two most frequently banned books in the PEN America report were memoirs by LGBTQ+ authors: *Gender Queer: A Memoir* (Kobabe, 2019) and *All Boys Aren't Blue* (Johnson, 2020). The fifth most commonly banned book was a collection of transgender biographies, *Beyond Magenta: Transgender Teens Speak Out* (Kuklin, 2015). Of all the banned selections, 33 percent included LGBTQ+ protagonists and/or topics. This movement to silence these stories contributes to the discrimination and rejection LGBTQ+ youth feel, thereby demonstrating how homophobia remains a predominant concern in US society.

HOMOPHOBIA IN SPORTS

Sports leagues, teams, and athletes have slowly shifted their views about diverse sexual orientation in positive ways in the past couple of decades. Throughout the latter half of the 1900s, the number of public LGBTQ+ athletes was few, and it only seemed "socially acceptable" for those athletes to be cisgender lesbians participating in individual sports, such as tennis star Billie Jean King and gold-winning Olympic track and field star Babe Didrikson Zaharias. As time passed and societal views became more inclusive, many retired professional athletes disclosed their orientation, ranging (to name only three) from former NFL player Dave Kopay to former MLB player John Dillinger to former NBA player John Amaechi. However, these men's stories greatly differ. Kopay played professionally in the 1960s and 1970s but remained closeted during his career. Three years after retiring, he disclosed his sexual orientation publicly in 1975 but remained ostracized by the sports world for the rest of his life (Ennis, 2016). Dillinger played for the Pittsburgh Pirates in the 1990s but did not tell his teammates he was gay because of the homophobic slurs he heard in the locker room. Yet 10 years after retiring, he was encouraged to come out by former teammates and colleagues (Buzinski, 2012). Amaechi retired from the NBA in 2003 and then disclosed his sexuality in his memoir, *Man in the Middle*, in 2007. While many initial responses were negative, he is now viewed by most as a positive role model for younger LGBTQ+ athletes, particularly athletes of color (Andrews, 2020). In the contemporary sports landscape, moreover, there are several athletes who played as openly LGBTQ+, such as NFL player Carl Nassib, US Women's National Team soccer star Megan Rapinoe, WNBA all-pro Sue Bird, NHL player Luke Prokop, and the first transgender Olympian Laurel Hubbard, a weightlifter from New Zealand. These stories reveal the overall shifting views toward acceptance of LGBTQ+ athletes in the sports world.

However, the sports world still has much room to grow in regard to the views and treatment of LGBTQ+ athletes. For example, Nassib disclosed his sexuality in June 2021 and was applauded and supported by most, including the NFL front office, and many advocates declared the NFL's embrace of Nassib coming out as a signal that sports was moving away from toxic masculinity and homophobia (Alfonseca, 2021). Yet only four months later, Nassib's head coach resigned after a long history of personal emails filled with homophobic, misogynistic, and racist statements was made public (Belson & Rosman, 2021). We should also remember that while Nassib's and Prokop's stories are positive steps forward, they remained the only two openly gay players in the four major US men's sports in 2022, probably due to the ongoing risks male athletes face for coming out (Hernandez, 2021). These risks remain present in women's sports as well, as former cricket player Alex Blackwell attested to the misconception that homophobia is a lesser issue in women's sports in her own complicated decision to disclose her sexual orientation (ABC News, 2020). Her experiences are supported by a survey of LGBTQ+ youth athletes that showed 36 percent of girls in youth sports report being targets of homophobic behavior (Denison et al., 2021).

Homophobic experiences also turn adults away from sports participation. Based on data retrieved through the National Sports and Society Survey, which interviewed 20,000 US adults aged 21 to 65, Knoester and Allison (2021) found that 40 percent of adult athletes who identify as a sexual minority report being mistreated in a sports-related setting. They also found that adults who identify as LGBTQ+ are less likely than heterosexual, cisgender adults to have played sports regularly, to have attended a sporting event, and to have even talked about sports over the previous year. These findings correlate with LGBTQ+ youth experiences as well. In The Trevor Project's 2021 National Survey on LGBTQ Youth Mental Health, 68 percent of the respondents stated that they had never participated in school or community sports due to the stress-inducing atmosphere of sports-related events. Further, 18 percent reported hearing from a sports leader or coach negative statements about people who identify as LGBTQ+, and only 16 percent reported hearing such figures express positive statements. Most telling, just 4 percent of respondents reported feeling comfortable turning to a sports leader or coach for help with issues related to mental health (Ennis, 2021). So, while overarching views might be shifting toward more inclusive perspectives, it seems the reality for LGBTQ+ athletes and non-athletes remains largely negative if not harmful.

FOCAL YA TEXT: *SPINNING* BY TILLIE WALDEN

Tillie Walden (2017) shares her experiences as a figure and synchronized ice skater, which she took up at the age of five, in her graphic-novel memoir *Spinning*. She describes the nuances between her figure skating team and her synchronized skating team, her relationships with peers and coaches, and her personal motivations to keep skating for 12 years. Tillie also explains why she stopped skating at age seventeen: a desire to pursue her interests in fine arts and the growing disconnect between her personal life and the views of the skating world. Particularly, she begins a relationship with her first girlfriend, Rae, which she keeps secret from her family, friends, and teammates because of her fears about what they might think.

When Rae's mother discovers the girls' secret relationship, she bans Tillie from seeing and even speaking with her daughter. Tillie's mother also reacts extremely negatively when she finds out about her sexual orientation. Her father and brother have problematic reactions, too, but Tillie initially still decides to tell everyone else. Unfortunately, her friends also react poorly, so she ultimately changes her mind about coming out to her skating coach and teammates. The only positive reaction she receives is from her music tutor. Tillie concludes her memoir sharing how her skating career ended and what those experiences meant for her during that time and later in life.

Spinning was extremely well received, earning starred reviews from *Kirkus Reviews*, *Booklist*, and *Publishers Weekly*. The graphic-novel memoir was selected as a New York City Public Library Notable Best Book for Teens, a 2017 Chicago Public Library Best Book, a 2017 *Booklist* Youth Editors' Choice, and a 2018 YALSA Great Graphic Novel. Most impressively, *Spinning* was named the 2018 Eisner Award for Best Reality-Based Work, which also made Tillie Walden, at age twenty-two, the youngest ever Eisner Award winner. These distinctions support making this memoir part of any secondary ELA literature curriculum.

INCORPORATING *SPINNING* INTO THE SECONDARY ELA CLASSROOM

Tillie uses ice skating to better understand herself, particularly her sexual orientation but also her family dynamics and personal friendships. With this focus in mind, we suggest framing a literature unit anchored by this memoir with these essential questions:

- If sports leagues and teams have a responsibility to include athletes of all backgrounds, what practices should they embrace to uphold that responsibility?
- In what ways do athletes express connections between their sporting and personal lives?
- How can we use personal interests to help us understand our own identities and relationships?

Prior to Teaching the Memoir

It is important to establish background knowledge about LGBTQ+ experiences in sports and society prior to teaching *Spinning.* As part of that process, we also believe that asking students to reflect on their own identities and how they are viewed by others is vital in establishing a community of learners willing to be vulnerable and to make more empathetic judgments about people whose social and cultural backgrounds may differ from their own. However, as Blackburn and Schey (2018) reminded us, it is improbable that any space can be completely free of homophobic or transphobic thoughts and actions, so we recognize that these prereading activities can only support building safer spaces for LGBTQ+ youth and discussions about their experiences in sport and society. If concerned about how to respond to anti-LGBTQ+ language and/or views, we encourage teachers to review the Human Rights Campaign Foundation's Welcoming Schools (2023) resource for teachers.

Exploring LGBTQ+ Experiences in Sports and Society

Many heterosexual, cisgender youth might not recognize the concerns related to LGBTQ+ experiences in sports because they are part of the sexual majority, and their experiences are normalized. As well, those in the sexual majority are less likely to recognize mistreatment toward LGBTQ+ athletes (Knoester & Allison, 2021). Therefore, an important first step prior to reading and discussing *Spinning* would be to share examples of LGBTQ+ athletes' experiences, both positive and negative, with students. Teachers could have students explore the statistics reported in The Trevor Project's annual surveys, view excerpts of *Changing the Game* (see "Options for Film Study"), a documentary about transgender high school athletes, and read news reports about recent laws restricting K–12 transgender athletes' participation in interscholastic sports (Movement Advancement Project, 2023). For more positive examples, teachers could share stories about the 2020 Tokyo Olympic Games, which included the most openly LGBTQ+ athletes ever to participate in a single Olympic Games (Leicester,

2021), and the National Federation of State High School Associations' Executive Order on Preventing and Combatting Discrimination on the Basis of Gender Identity or Sexual Orientation (Green, 2021). Another important aspect of these stories to discuss is how an athlete being open about their sexual orientation and gender identity positively affects their mental health; seventeen-year-old English footballer Jake Daniels cited this as a primary reason for coming out as gay (Sky Sports, 2022).

Voices from the Field
Creating Change Starts with the Story: Just Listen

Rick Joseph
Language Arts and Social Studies Teacher,
Birmingham Public Schools, Michigan

"We're creating an environment where it's not sinister. I think the fact that we're having this conversation means we're getting close."

—Billy Bean, former MLB player who came out as gay in retirement

For people who are LGBTQ+, the opportunity to share the story of the realization of their identity and orientation can be both liberating and lifesaving. As sports are a microcosm of our larger society, the importance of honoring the stories and voices of athletes and all people who are LGBTQ+ cannot be overstated.

Stories present mirrors that reflect our own lives, windows into the lives of others, and sliding glass doors that enable us to emulate the lived experiences of characters we value (Bishop, 1990). Providing students with books that represent people who are LGBTQ+ fosters an environment of inclusion that uplifts everyone. The challenge for educators is frequently found in how to provide access to students in a range of ways.

One of the least obtrusive ways to promote the consumption of literature that features characters who are LGBTQ+ is to have a classroom library book bin marked "LGBTQ+." While all the bins in my classroom library are labeled by a variety of familiar genres, from realistic fiction to fantasy, I introduce this particular bin to my students at the beginning of every school year by explaining that the books contain at least one character who is LGBTQ+. The American Library Association (2021) cautions educators about labeling books in this way, but I justify the bin's existence by briefly mentioning the history of marginalization and violence that people who are LGBTQ+ have faced and continue to face. I am also quick to address any misuse of the bin and am ready to remind students that disrespect for any of the titles in the bin in any context will not be tolerated. Titles range from picture books to YA fiction that I have purchased or borrowed from both the school and public library. The availability of books deliberately identified as LGBTQ+ themed can be lifesaving for students who feel isolation and alienation as they seek to understand who they are.

I begin every school year reading a picture book with an LGBTQ+ character to my fifth-grade students. I ask them to consider themes in the book and how a younger reader, who may pick up this book on their own, might interpret the themes. Most recently, I have selected *I Am Jazz* by Jessica Herthel and Jazz Jennings (2014). The effectiveness of using a picture book is its simplicity and accessibility. The emphasis on asking students to consider how a younger reader would interpret the text disarms students and provides a purpose for reading a story that is seemingly too juvenile. Students create their own meaning through an inquiry-based approach. Upon completion of the read-aloud, I prefer to have students follow a think-write-pair-share approach, which helps them process the themes of the book. It is quite possible to simply read a book aloud and ask students to think without discussion. The decision regarding how extensively I want to analyze the story depends on my instructional goals and the level of sensitivity of both my students and the particular topic of the book.

My social-action book club unit provides students with an opportunity to select, read, and discuss books around a justice-based theme. For example, one group of students decided they wanted to read a book that explored life for people who are LGBTQ+, given the higher-than-average levels of suicide that affect this group. They considered a number of possible titles that ranged from *Aristotle and Dante Discover the Secrets of the Universe* by Benjamin Alire Sáenz (2012) to *Melissa* (previously published as *George*) by Alex Gino (2022). They also examined *Felix Ever After* by Kacen Callender (2020) and *All Boys Aren't Blue* by George M. Johnson (2020) before selecting *Rick by* Alex Gino (2020). The chance to select the book from a number of options provided students with the voice and choice necessary to maintain high levels of motivation to read. The students then chose from a range of end-of-book projects to present to their classmates the key components of the book that impacted them the most.

I am mindful of the considerable support I receive from my building principal and the overwhelming majority of parents as I offer titles that feature characters who are LGBTQ+. Every educator must gauge the potential impact of the books they select and consider how best to proceed. Stories that feature people who are marginalized change the culture of a classroom and both the school and larger community. Indeed, to some, they may provide a lifeline.

References

American Association of School Librarians. (2021). *Position statement on labeling practices.* https://www.ala.org/aasl/sites/ala.org.aasl/files/content/advocacy/statements/docs/AASL_Labeling_Practices_Position_Statement_2021a.pdf

Bishop, R. S. (1990). Mirrors, windows, and sliding glass doors. *Perspectives: Choosing and Using Books for the Classroom, 6*(3), ix–xi.

Callender, K. (2020). *Felix ever after.* Balzer + Bray.

Gino, A. (2020). *Rick.* Scholastic Press.

———. (2022). *Melissa.* Scholastic Press.

Herthel, J., & Jennings, J. (2014). *I am Jazz.* Dial Books.

Johnson, G. M. (2020). *All boys aren't blue: A memoir-manifesto.* Farrar, Straus and Giroux.

Sáenz, B. A. (2012). *Aristotle and Dante discover the secrets of the universe.* Simon & Schuster Books for Young Readers.

Rick Joseph is a National Board-Certified Teacher and has taught fifth and sixth grade at Covington School in suburban Detroit since 2003. He previously served as a bilingual educator (Spanish) and trainer for nine years in the Chicago Public Schools. Rick has a bachelor's degree in English from the University of Michigan and a master's degree in elementary education from the University of Illinois—Chicago. He is pursuing a doctorate in literacy from Walden University. He has served on NCTE's LGBTQ Advisory Committee. Rick is the 2016 Michigan Teacher of the Year.

Writing Reflective Journeys

Writing a memoir can be a considerably vulnerable process. The author is usually sharing inner thoughts about moments of their life that few people, if anyone, have previously known. *Spinning* is one of those vulnerable memoirs because Tillie is sharing intimate thoughts and feelings about past teammates, former coaches, and, in particular, her family's reactions to her coming out. One way to prepare secondary students who may not have read such personal stories previously is to ask them to embrace a vulnerable position in terms of their own lives.

As one way to meet this goal, we suggest engaging students in a reflective journey through writing. The task asks students to reflect on a particular aspect of their identity, perhaps something that others do not know about them or might find surprising, or something for which they have faced discrimination or negative bias from others. Students then draft a reflective essay, approximately two to three pages, explaining their identity marker, why it is an important aspect of themselves, and reactions others have toward that aspect of their identity or, if it is still secret, the reactions they imagine others would have if they disclosed it. Teachers should explain to students that these are personal essays and will only be read by others, including the teacher, if the students give permission. (The aim is to provide an outlet for students to write about themselves in a safe space and not as an evaluative or assessment task.) Students will use these essays during the following discussion-based activity in preparation for reading *Spinning*. In the spirit of teachers being vulnerable when asking students to be vulnerable, we encourage teachers to share their own essay as a model for students to follow.

Facilitating an Anonymous Share

As a next step, we suggest engaging the classroom community in an anonymous share, a discussion-based strategy in which community members can share aspects of their identity in a safer space. First, ask students to consider what they wrote about in their reflective journey essays, particularly related to their personal identities and how others have perceived their identities either explicitly or implicitly. Second, distribute index cards to everyone in the classroom—students and teachers—and ask individuals to respond to the following prompt on the card: "Describe a time in which you were treated differently due to some aspect of your identity or heard someone say something that kept you silent about some aspect of your identity." Remind students that they could write about any primary or secondary identity markers that they included in their reflective journey essays. The index-card statements should be written in first person or "I-statements." Whenever using this strategy with students, Mark Lewis, one of the authors of this book, has also participated as a way to demonstrate his willingness to be a vulnerable community member, and we recommend teachers who use this strategy to participate as well. Third, collect all the index cards, shuffle them, and redistribute one to every classroom member. Fourth, ask everyone to read what is written on their card verbatim, so they would use the first-person language, thereby metaphorically owning the statement as well. Finally, open the floor for discussion on how the students felt during the activity, what they heard that affected them, and what they learned about their classroom community. This discussion step could first be completed with a partner or small group to build a sense of comfort and safety.

When concluding this activity, it is important to collect the index cards immediately after the discussion. This eliminates any possibility of the cards being distributed or shared outside of the classroom and helps to maintain as much anonymity as possible. Also, we encourage teachers to remind students about the personal nature of the activity and the need to respect the privacy of everyone in the classroom.

Identifying Artistic Features in Graphic Novels

While graphic novels are growing in popularity, teachers should not assume that all students are knowledgeable about the medium and its unique structures and features. Therefore, as a way to provide some background knowledge, it is important to provide students with terminology about the structural and artistic features included in this medium and some practice identifying those structures and features. To meet this goal, Mark usually provides a list of terminology with definitions that he and his students have accumulated over time (see Figure 4.1) for students to read and discuss, answering any questions they might have about the nuances between the terms. He then gives small groups sample pages borrowed from graphic novels that use different features from the aforementioned list and asks students to annotate the images by identifying those features and explaining the effect each feature has on how they read and view what appears on the page. When engaging students with this activity, Mark provides each group with different pages, each with its own unique features, to create a more dynamic discussion. He usually uses pages from *Saturn Apartments* (Iwaoka, 2010) and the graphic adaptation of *The Metamorphosis* (Kafka, 2003) because the artists provide high-quality examples of various artistic features. Groups then present their analyses during a whole-class discussion to ensure that all students have a deep understanding of the different features. Teachers might also post these annotated images in the classroom for students to refer to as they read *Spinning*.

Artistic Features within Graphic Novels

Accent: to stress/single out as important. As applied to art, it is the emphasis given to certain elements in a composition that allows them to attract more attention.

Aerial Perspective: refers to creating a sense of depth in painting by imitating the way the atmosphere makes distant objects appear less distinct than they would be if nearby.

Chiaroscuro: a technique employed in the visual arts to represent light and shadow as they define three-dimensional objects.

Close-Up: close-range presentation of a character or a thing within the narrative, often to create intimacy or emphasize importance.

Focal Point: a specific area, element, or principle that dominates a work of art; the area in a work that the reader's eye is most compelled to view.

Frame: something made to enclose a picture, a mirror, or a separate scene.

Gutter: space included in between panels.

Hierarchical Scale: presenting the "most important" person/object/scene of a particular artistic composition as larger than the rest of the elements of the composition in order to emphasize the significance or power of the enlarged person/object/scene.

Horizon Line: a level line where land or water ends and the sky begins. Vanishing points (where two parallel lines appear to converge) are typically located on this line. A horizon line is used to attain the perspective of depth.

Illustrated Emotion: clearly indicates a character's unspoken emotions or the tone of a given situation/frame.

Juxtaposition: the act of placing or positioning items in the image area or frame side by side or next to one another to illustrate some comparison.

Layout: the configuration of the entire page, including all elements of the frame, panels, and gutters.

Linear Perspective: a system for creating the illusion of depth on a two-dimensional surface. The system is based on implied lines that intersect at a vanishing point on the horizon. Linear perspective determines the relative size of objects from the foreground of an image to the background.

Narrative Bubble: indicates omniscient third-person perspective or may be words spoken by individuals not shown in/not involved in a given frame.

Negative Space: the unoccupied or empty space left after the positive shapes have been laid down by the artist; however, because these areas have boundaries, they also function as shapes in the total design.

Panel: cell or box that contains a single image and text.

Point of View: the position from which something is seen or considered; for instance, head-on, from overhead, from ground level, etc.

Scream Bubble: indicates that the character is screaming or shouting their dialogue, generally made with sharp angles.

Shading: showing change from light to dark or dark to light in a picture by darkening areas that would be shadowed and leaving other areas light. Shading is often used to produce illusions of dimension and depth.

Speech Bubble: indicates the characters' spoken words.

Thought Bubble: indicates a character's unspoken thoughts and is typically drawn distinctly different from a speech bubble.

Vanishing Point: the point on the horizon in the distance where two lines seem to converge and visibility ends.

FIGURE 4.1: Artistic Features and Definitions

As Students Read the Memoir

Beyond traditional literature-reading activities, such as maintaining reading logs, engaging in book club discussions, and creating plot charts, we suggest engaging students with specific tasks related to the subject matter of *Spinning* and the essential questions framing a unit of study anchored by Walden's (2017) graphic memoir.

Modeling Reading about LGBTQ+ Characters

Since it is possible that many students have never chosen to read a story about/ with LGBTQ+ characters and related social concerns, an important first step is to model ways to interpret representations of those characters and concerns. Borrowing from Burke and Greenfield (2016), one approach would pair a children's literature selection with *Spinning*, as children's books tend to be more concrete and explicit due to their intended audience of younger children. Burke and Greenfield use *And Tango Makes Three* (Richardson et al., 2005), which tells the story of two male penguins who want to raise a baby. First, students would individually read the opening 25 pages of *Spinning* and record any insights they have about Tillie, her thoughts, her interactions with her teammates, and any illustrated facial expressions. Second, teachers would explain that the students will conduct a practice analysis of a children's book addressing similar themes as *Spinning*. While reading *And Tango Makes Three* aloud, students could consider the following questions:

- How are the characters' identity markers, such as gender and sexual orientation, represented?
- How does the story disrupt or reinforce common perspectives about LGBTQ+ individuals?
- What is the theme of the story related to LGBTQ+ experiences?
- What words, phrases, and/or images support your answers?

After the conclusion of the read-aloud and using a think-pair-share discussion format, teachers should provide students time to individually record their responses, then pair with a partner to discuss their responses, and close by sharing their partner responses with the entire class. Teachers can record key ideas during the whole-class discussion.

Finally, students can reread the first 25 pages of *Spinning* while considering the same questions posed during the practice analysis of *And Tango Makes Three*. After rereading, students should have time to reflect on their initial responses and add to those responses based on the inquiry questions. Students then return to their partner and discuss their responses before participating in a whole-class discussion about what the opening pages of *Spinning* might reveal about Tillie's identity markers and representations of LGBTQ+ youth and their experiences.

Responding with Image and Metaphor Sketch Journals

As part of supporting students to grapple with the second essential question—"In what ways do athletes express connections between their sporting and personal lives?"—and preparing them for the culminating tasks, they could keep sketch journals as a form of reading response. As they read, students would be asked to identify salient images that represent metaphors for how Tillie is feeling about her identities, her position on the ice-skating teams, her family and friend relationships, and any other themes students identify as important to her story.

FIGURE 4.2: Image and Metaphor Sketch Journal Example

The journals could be organized in a top-to-bottom page format (see Figure 4.2). The top half of the page would be reserved for students' own sketches of images or a summary of a collection of images they chose from the book. The bottom half would be reserved for students to draft a paragraph in which they explain why they chose the image; present their metaphorical analysis of what they believe Tillie was trying to represent about her life experiences, particularly related to her sexual orientation; and include corresponding page numbers from the memoir for future reference. This paragraph should also identify any artistic features employed in the image and how those contribute to the students' analyses.

We suggest that students identify two to four images for each chapter, whether small images, such as a single face, or large images, such as an entire team skating. If all students have their own copies of *Spinning,* then these journal entries would work well as homework assignments to extend the in-class reading and discussion. As always, it would be important for teachers to model a sample journal entry, which students could tape inside the cover of their journals for reference. This teacher model might also include a reminder definition of how a metaphor can function in narrative texts, as well as identification of any artistic elements that enhance the interpretation of the image. We also suggest teachers share new entries to their own journal sporadically as students progress through the book. At the end of each chapter, students can gather in small groups to share their sketches and analyses. They can record any feedback from their peers in their journal entries, including alternative interpretations of their selected images. These journals would be useful for students' interpretations of Tillie's experiences as they read, and they can be used to support their "personal passion graphic memoir" projects, which are described in the following section.

Culminating Tasks after Reading the Memoir

To address all three essential questions, we suggest closing the literature unit with the following culminating activities, which are meant for students to answer the questions in personal and authentic ways.

Writing Advocacy Statements

In self-selected teams, ask students to identify a local youth, interscholastic, or professional sports league that interests them and/or in which they participate. Based on the resources they explored during the literature unit, students craft an advocacy statement for that league related to LGBTQ+ athletes. The statement should consist of an opening defense for the need of such a statement and a bulleted list of suggested advocacy practices for coaches, parents, and athletes that are more inclusive for LGBTQ+ athletes. Students could research professional leagues' practices to be used as examples, such as the NFL's "Football Is Gay" advertising campaign (Yurcaba, 2021), MLB's participation in "Spirit Day" (Landry, 2020), or English Premier League's "Rainbow Laces" program (Premier League, 2021). It would also be important to address any issues that have arisen as leagues carried out these practices as a way to demonstrate that this type of advocacy work can be damaging if not executed properly. For example, the Texas Rangers did not actually mention the LGBTQ+ community in their tweet about the 2021 Spirit Day, which angered many of their fans (Grant, 2021). With the aim of taking social action, these statements can be shared with students' chosen local leagues with the hope that they opt to engage in such advocacy practices.

Creating Personal Passion Graphic Memoirs

In *Spinning,* Tillie uses a particular ice-skating move to title each of her chapters, draws herself attempting that move, and provides a definition of that move (for example, Chapters 1 through 3 open with a waltz jump, scratch spin, and flip jump on pages 7, 29, and 73, respectively). Further, the story she shares in each chapter metaphorically links to that ice-skating move. So, as a culminating activity, teachers could ask students to create their own mini-graphic memoir based upon a personal passion and their own identities. The students should identify a particular activity in which they enjoy participating, such as developing a set of sports-related skills, learning to play an instrument, performing on stage, creating fine arts, or engaging in a hobby. They then need to identify a set of six to eight particular skills that they need in order to be successful with that activity, and they need to draft definitions for each skill. The definitions should use language non-experts would understand. For each skill and definition, the students then depict themselves engaged in that skill, similar to how Tillie draws herself attempting each ice-skating move on the first page of each chapter. The students add the name of the skill and definition to their depictions. Finally, the students add a brief paragraph explaining how each skill metaphorically connects to some aspect of their identity. We recommend that teachers create their own model for students to refer to in addition to Tillie's examples. Providing this model further demonstrates teachers' willingness to be vulnerable by sharing their own passion and how it connects to some aspect of their identity.

CONCLUSION

Reading Tillie Walden's (2017) *Spinning* and taking up these literacy-based activities will provide students with multiple opportunities to consider the unit's essential questions as well as their own perspectives about LGBTQ+ youth and their rights for participating in sports. The hope is that after experiencing this curriculum secondary students will have more multifaceted and socially just views about diverse sexual orientations.

Options for Book Clubs

Teachers looking to facilitate book clubs in which students explore the experiences of LGBTQ+ youth can incorporate *Spinning* alongside titles like the following:

The Passing Playbook (Fitzsimons, 2021)
Every soccer team needs a great left foot, and Spencer Harris has been graced with that gift. Spencer desperately wants to play for his school's soccer team, but his parents are more hesitant because they want to protect him from what might happen if his teammates discover his secret—Spencer is a transgender boy. He decides to join the team anyway, which takes his life down an unexpected path.

The Other Boy (Hennessey, 2019)
Shane Woods is a transgender boy; it is a fact that he has so far kept hidden from everyone at his new school, including his best friend on the baseball team, his other teammates, and a romantic interest. Yet, that secret is in jeopardy because a bully from a rival team is trying to out him by sharing pictures of him presenting as a girl when he was in elementary school.

Openly Straight (Konigsberg, 2013)
Rafe Goldberg is openly gay but often dreams about being more than simply "the gay guy." So, when he transfers to an all-boys boarding school, he decides to hide his orientation and become a "jock," just like all the other boys. His plan is disrupted when he falls in love with one of his new classmates.

True Letters from a Fictional Life (Logan, 2016)
James Liddel is known as the fun-loving star athlete in his Vermont town who is also the boyfriend of a popular girl, Theresa. Privately, he writes letters about his real feelings, including his disinterest in Theresa and his true romantic interest in a local boy. He never intends to send these letters, but someone else does, and he must make a decision about what to tell everyone.

Honor Girl: A Graphic Memoir (Thrash, 2017)
Maggie Thrash spent almost every summer during her childhood and early teens attending Camp Bellflower for Girls. She focuses her memoir on the summer when she was fifteen, becoming better at rifling and experiencing a crush on a female counselor. Yet she struggles with what to do about the crush because the camp imposes oppressive views about homosexuality.

Options for Film Study

Teachers looking to incorporate film study to support students' exploration of the experiences of LGBTQ+ youth can consider the following options:

Changing the Game (Barnett, 2019)
This documentary tells the stories of three transgender high school athletes as they compete and advocate for their rights to participate. They share their stories in vulnerable ways that provide insight into what it means to be transgender and an athlete.

1:54 (England, 2016)
Tim (Antoine Olivier Pilon) is a victim of bullying. He is also a runner and competes on his high school track team along with his primary bullying nemesis, Jeff (Lou-Pascal Tremblay). As Tim slowly works to replace Jeff's position as the top runner on the team, Jeff increases his bullying behavior, which leads to tragic ends.

Alone in the Game (Metzger & Rohrbaugh, 2018)
This documentary shares the recurring obstacles LGBTQ+ athletes face at the highest levels of sport, including major US professional leagues, the NCAA, and the Olympics. It shows how the business of sports works to exclude and silence LGBTQ+ athletes in favor of keeping viewers watching and spending money.

Game Face (Thomas, 2015)
The stories of Fallon Fox, MMA's first transgender fighter, and Terrence Clemons, a gay college basketball player, are compared. The documentary follows their coming-out experiences and the obstacles they continually face throughout their careers.

Young Adult Literature

Fitzsimons, I. (2021). *The passing playbook.* Dial Books.

Hennessey, M. G. (2019). *The other boy.* HarperCollins.

Iwaoka, H. (2010). *Saturn apartments.* VIZ Media.

Johnson, G. M. (2020). *All boys aren't blue: A memoir-manifesto.* Farrar, Straus and Giroux.

Kafka, F. (2003). *The metamorphosis* (P. Kuper, Illus.). Three Rivers Press. (Original work published 1915).

Konigsberg, B. (2013). *Openly straight.* Scholastic.

Kuklin, S. (2015). *Beyond magenta: Transgender teens speak out.* Candlewick.

Logan, K. (2016). *True letters from a fictional life.* HarperTeen.

Thrash, M. (2017). *Honor girl: A graphic memoir.* Candlewick.

Walden, T. (2017). *Spinning.* First Second.

Other Texts for Classroom Use

Amaechi, J. (2007). *Man in the middle.* ESPN.

Barnett, M. (Director). (2019). *Changing the game* [Film]. SuperFilms!

England, Y. (Director). (2016). *1:54* [Film]. Cinémaginaire Inc.

Kobabe, M. (2019). *Gender queer: A memoir.* Oni Press.

Metzger, N., & Rohrbaugh, M. (Directors). (2018). *Alone in the game* [Film]. DLM Entertainment Group.

Richardson, J., & Parnell, P. (2005). *And Tango makes three* (H. Cole, Illus.). Simon & Schuster Books for Young Readers.

Thomas, M. (Director). (2015). *Game face* [Film]. Passion River Films.

REFERENCES

ABC News. (2020, December 2). *Alex Blackwell says homophobia remains a serious problem in women's sports despite "misconceptions."* https://www.abc.net.au/news/2020-12-03/alex-blackwell-homophobia-womens-sport-gay-lesbian/12946396?utm_campaign=abc_news_web&utm_content=link&utm_medium=content_shared&utm_source=abc_news_web

Alfonseca, K. (2021, June 26). *Carl Nassib's coming out signals shift from toxic masculinity, homophobia in sports, advocates say*. ABC News. https://abcnews.go.com/Sports/carl-nassibs-coming-signal-shift-toxic-masculinity-homophobia/story?id=78432672

American Library Association. (2020). Issues and trends. *The State of America's Libraries 2020.* https://www.ala.org/news/state-americas-libraries-report-2020/issues-trends

Andrews, K. (2020, September 17). John Amaechi: How the first NBA player to come out is now teaching us all about white privilege. *The Guardian.* https://www.theguardian.com/society/2020/sep/17/john-amaechi-first-nba-player-to-come-out-now-teaching-us-all-about-white-privilege

Balta, V. (2018, June 18). "Homophobic and not very clever": Why puto chants haunt Mexican football. *The Guardian.* https://www.theguardian.com/football/2018/jun/18/puto-chants-mexico-football-world-cup

Belson, K., & Rosman, K. (2021, October 11). Raiders coach resigns after homophobic and misogynistic emails. *The New York Times.* https://www.nytimes.com/2021/10/11/sports/football/what-did-jon-gruden-say.html

Bernal, R. (2021, November 1). Fans banned from two World Cup qualifying games in Mexico due to anti-gay chants. *The Hill.* https://thehill.com/latino/579412-fans-banned-from-two-world-cup-qualifying-games-in-mexico-due-to-anti-gay-chants/

Blackburn, M. V., & Schey, R. (2018). Shared vulnerability, collaborative composition, and the interrogation and reification of oppressive values in a high school LGBTQ-themed literature course. *Journal of Literacy Research, 50*(3), 335-358.

Burke, B. R., & Greenfield, K. (2016). Challenging heteronormativity: Raising LGBTQ awareness in a high school English language arts classroom. *English Journal, 105*(6), 46–51.

Buzinski, J. (2012, October 24). *John Dillinger, on living life in baseball's closet.* SB Nation. https://www.sbnation.com/2012/10/24/3545938/john-dillinger-interview-outsports

Denison, E., Jeanes, R., Faulkner, N., & O'Brien, K. S. (2021). The relationship between "coming out" as lesbian, gay, or bisexual and experiences of homophobic behaviour in youth team sports. *Sexuality Research and Social Policy, 18*(3), 765–73.

Ennis, D. (2016, January 11). The surprisingly long history of gays in pro football. *The Advocate.* https://www.advocate.com/sports/2016/1/10/surprisingly-long-history-gays-pro-football

———. (2021, September 15). Why are LGBTQ youth avoiding sports in school? Fear of discrimination, research shows. *Forbes.* https://www.forbes.com/sites/dawnstaceyennis/2021/09/15/why-are-lgbtq-youth-avoiding-sports-in-school-fear-of-discrimination-research-shows/?sh=61b267cb4195

Goldberg S. K., Lewis T., Kahn E., & Watson R. J. (2023). *2023 LGBTQ+ youth report.* Human Rights Campaign Foundation. https://hrc.im/youthreport2023

Grant, E. (2021, October 22). Rangers omit LGBTQ acknowledgement during MLB-wide Spirit Day initiative, frustrating advocates. *The Dallas Morning News.* https://www.dallasnews.com/sports/rangers/2021/10/22/rangers-omit-lgbtq-acknowledgment-during-mlb-wide-spirit-day-initiative-frustrating-advocates/

Green, L. (2021, March 9). *High school sports participation rights of LGBTQ students.* National Federation of State High School Associations. https://www.nfhs.org/articles/high-school-sports-participation-rights-of-lgbtq-students/

Hernandez, C. (2023, June 16). *Referee ends USMNT rout over Mexico early amid anti-gay chants.* ESPN. https://www.espn.com/soccer/story/_/id/37861934/usmnt-rout-mexico-ends-early-referee-discretion

Hernandez, J. (2021, July 21). *Why there are few openly gay athletes in men's professional sports.* NPR. https://www.npr.org/2021/07/21/1018404859/openly-gay-athletes-in-mens-pro-sports-few

Hixenbaugh, M. (2022, February 1). *Banned: Books on race and sexuality are disappearing from Texas schools in record numbers.* NBC News. https://www.nbcnews.com/news/us-news/texas-books-race-sexuality-schools-rcna13886

Human Rights Campaign Foundation Welcoming Schools. (2023). *What do you say to "that's so gay" & other anti-LGBTQ comments?* https://hrc-prod-requests.s3-us-west-2.amazonaws.com/welcoming-schools/documents/NEA_HRCF_Stop_Anti_Gay_and_LGBTQ_Comments.pdf?mtime=20200713131629&focal=none

Knoester, C., & Allison, R. (2021). Sexuality, sports-related mistreatment, and U.S. adults' sports involvement. *Leisure Sciences: An Interdisciplinary Journal.* Advance online publication. https://doi.org/10.1080/01490400.2021.1895009

Landry, K. (2020, October 15). *MLB spreads message of love on Spirit Day*. MLB. https://www.mlb.com/news/billy-bean-mlb-celebrate-spirit-day

Leicester, J. (2021, July 27). *"About time": LGBTQ Olympic athletes unleash a rainbow wave*. AP News. https://apnews.com/article/2020-tokyo-olympics-sports-lifestyle-nhl-ap-top-news-4c4d04b03dc0f3a070e287be092c50d4

Movement Advancement Project. (2023). *Bans on transgender youth participation in sports*. https://www.lgbtmap.org/equality-maps/youth/sports_participation_bans

Pendharkar, E. (2022, April 7). How prevalent are book bans this year? New data show impact. *EducationWeek*. https://www.edweek.org/teaching-learning/how-prevalent-are-book-bans-this-year-new-data-show-impact/2022/04

Premier League. (2021). *Rainbow laces*. https://www.premierleague.com/RainbowLaces

Ramirez, M. (2021, September 16). LGBTQ youths are less likely to play sports because of bullying—and advocates fear they're missing out. *USA Today*. https://www.usatoday.com/story/news/2021/09/16/lgbtq-youth-mostly-avoid-sports-citing-bullying-and-discrimination/8347727002/

Reimer, A. (2021, August 25). *Elite cyclist comes out, calls out his sport for homophobia*. Outsports. https://www.outsports.com/homophobia/2021/8/25/22641481/clay-davies-british-cycling-gay-homophobia

Sky Sports. (2022, May 17). *Jake Daniels: Blackpool forward becomes UK's first active male professional footballer to come out publicly as gay*. https://www.skysports.com/football/news/11095/12614531/jake-daniels-blackpool-forward-becomes-uks-first-active-male-professional-footballer-to-come-out-publicly-as-gay

The Trevor Project. (2021). *National survey on LGBTQ youth mental health 2021*. https://www.thetrevorproject.org/survey-2021/

———. (2023). *2023 U.S. national survey on the mental health of LGBTQ young people*. https://www.thetrevorproject.org/survey-2023/

United Health Foundation. (2022). *Teen suicide in United States*. https://www.americashealthrankings.org/explore/health-of-women-and-children/measure/teen_suicide/state/ALL

Yurcaba, J. (2021, June 29). *NFL proudly declares "football is gay" in new video*. NBC News. https://www.nbcnews.com/nbc-out/out-news/nfl-proudly-declares-football-gay-new-video-rcna1300

5

Upending Ableist Perspectives in the Arena and in Life

I'm doing this for Rosa. And yeah, at first I just wanted her to experience a run—to cross a finish line and hear people cheering for her—because that's something she wanted. But you know what? Her biggest wish isn't to cross a finish line or have people cheer for her. It's to have people see *her* instead of her condition. That's all anybody with a disability wants.

—*Jessica Carlisle,* The Running Dream *(Van Draanen, 2011, pp. 306–7, emphasis in original)*

Some athletes are not only used to having people cheer for them as they perform but also actually crave the adoration and use it as motivation. Other athletes, however, do not need such external motivation because the internal drive to achieve a personal athletic goal—running faster, jumping higher, enduring long distances—sustains them. This latter group of athletes often uses sports to show others they are more than what is on the surface and to help them build an inner strength to achieve. For example, the following stories highlight how athletes with physical and/or mental disabilities have met their personal goals:

- Jacky Hunt-Broersma, an amputee ultra-runner who set the record for running the most marathons in consecutive days at 104 marathons in 104 days, shared how irritated she became when people told her there were things she could not do, so she used running to show them otherwise (Lewis, 2022).
- Mallory Weggemann, who won two gold medals and a silver at the 2020 Summer Paralympic Games, discussed how she uses her story as a swimmer to show others that a disability should not be viewed as someone's sole identity marker (Renuart, 2021).

- Zion Clark, a wrestler and mixed martial arts fighter born without both legs, described how he approached physical challenges and bureaucratic obstacles to continue engaging in the sports he loves (Hockensmith, 2022).
- Chris Nikic, the first person with Down syndrome to complete an Ironman Triathlon, talked about how striving to achieve as an athlete helped him succeed with other goals in his life (Holohan, 2021).

As Jessica Carlisle from *The Running Dream* (Van Draanen, 2011) explains in this chapter's epigraph, people with disabilities want to be understood as complex individuals who hold multiple identities beyond their particular physical or mental characteristics. Students without direct experiences knowing someone with disabilities may not have nuanced understandings about or may hold damaging misconceptions related to disability and ableism. Reading stories that provide positive representations of people with disabilities can work to upend preconceived conceptions and ableist perspectives, as well as educate readers about related issues of access and trauma that often affect both people with disabilities and their family and friends.

THE SOCIAL CONCERN OF ABLEISM AND DISABILITY

In 1973, Section 504 of the Rehabilitation Act was passed by the US Congress; this was the first time that people with disabilities were recognized and designated as a class of people who could not be banned from receiving federal funds based on their disability alone (Mayerson, 1992). Prior to this law, people with disabilities were routinely denied access to basic rights, as activist Judith Heumann outlines in her memoir *Being Huemann: An Unrepentant Memoir of a Disability Rights Activist* (2020). In 1949, Heumann contracted polio as a child and lost her ability to walk. She first experienced discrimination when she was denied enrollment in kindergarten because the principal designated her and her wheelchair as a "fire hazard." Later, she was also denied a teaching license because, again, the New York Board of Education deemed her a fire hazard who could not escort her students to safety. After winning that lawsuit and receiving her teaching license, Heumann, along with many others, went on to advocate for civil rights for people with disabilities. Their activism led to the passing of Section 504 and, eventually, the passing of the Americans with Disabilities Act (ADA) in 1990, which extended equal rights for people with disabilities across "public accommodations, employment, transportation, state and local government services, and telecommunications" (ADA National Network, 2022). However, change for the lives of people with disabilities in terms of access and civil rights continues to be slow.

The history of civil rights for people with disabilities from a schooling perspective, as outlined by the US Department of Education (2022), is a revealing example of the slow progress of positive change. Again, federal action for people with disabilities first took place in the 1970s with the passage of the Education for All Handicapped Children Act (EHA), which extended Section 504 to children and youth aged 3 to 18 as well as their families. The EHA has undergone several reauthorizations since, with each iteration showing how views on disability shifted in society. The 1986 EHA reauthorization extended services to families and their children from birth to age three. The 1990 reauthorization changed the name to the Individuals with Disabilities Education Act (IDEA) and extended students' individualized education programs to include post-secondary life, and IDEA added traumatic brain injury and autism as conditions eligible for services. Then, the 1997 IDEA reauthorization established that students with disabilities should have access to the same curriculum as all learners. We could continue reviewing this history of incremental changes through several reauthorizations and legal cases, establishing and extending civil rights related to educational services for people with disabilities over the course of the next 25 years up to today. Most important, it would be clear from such a review that change has been slow, despite all of these improvements in services, as the National Center for Education Statistics (2022) recently reported that 13 percent of students with disabilities aged 14 to 21 dropped out of school in 2019–2020, which is significantly higher than the overall 5.3 percent dropout rate of all high school students in 2020. Our society still has work to do in providing equitable access for people with disabilities.

Voices from the Field
Starting with Language: Teaching about Disabilities in the ELA Classroom

Rachel Roloff
English Teacher and Department Chair,
Washington Middle School, Olympia, Washington

Media sometimes show people with disabilities as "pitiable, helpless, or evil with the plot leaving them cured or dead at the end. Or they become unlikely heroes whose disability somehow 'saves the day'" (Dunn, 2022), yet these inaccurate labels are harmful when seen or taught in the classroom. The words we use and the words we find in books matter. The goal for teachers should be to read novels, short stories, and other texts that do not portray negative stereotypes of people with disabilities and, if they do depict such stereotypes, to teach students how to ask critical questions that "invite [them] to recognize and challenge those stereotypes" (Dunn, 2010, p. 17).

Challenging stereotypes means first explaining why stereotypes are harmful. In the classroom, this allows me to return to concerning language, as needed, throughout the year—whether in relation to a story we read or comments from students. For instance, if a student makes a comment about a character with a physical disability that shows a bias or reinforces a stereotype (e.g., helplessness), I will ask: *What's the definition of the bias or stereotype? Where does the portrayal of people with that physical disability come from (e.g., movies, television)? What evidence do we have to suggest this bias or stereotype may or may not be true? What language can we use to create a more accurate depiction of the person with the disability?* By discussing language at the beginning, I allow students a chance to see that their words do matter.

Recently, I taught a lesson on point of view using a chapter of Jason Reynolds's (2016) novel *As Brave as You*. Reynolds's book is about Genie, a twelve-year-old boy, who visits his grandparents' house for the summer with his brother Ernie. Genie has no idea what to expect while visiting his grandparents, and he is surprised to find out his Grandpop has glaucoma. Reynolds's story depicts the physical disability of blindness authentically, and the empathy that students feel usually keeps them interested throughout the book. During class discussions, we talked about how the story might change if written from the point of view of a character other than Genie. When we discussed how the novel would be different if written from Grandpop's perspective, I asked the question, "How does Grandpop see himself?" Some of my middle school students laughed, saying he's blind so he can't see himself, which prompted a conversation about identity and perception.

The National Center on Disability and Journalism [NCDJ] (2021) has a "Disability Language Style Guide" that urges people to "refer to a disability only when it's relevant to the story being told." In this instance, Grandpop being blind is relevant to the story, but context matters. NCDJ's recommendation is that

> "Blind" may be used for people who have complete or almost complete loss of sight. Other terms are acceptable for those with some vision loss. It is best to ask your sources what they prefer and take that into consideration. Similarly, ask whether the person prefers identity-first or people-first language. Many prefer "blind" or "blind person," while others prefer "a person with blindness."

Other commonly used terms include "limited vision," "low vision," "partially sighted," and "visually impaired," though some object to the latter because it incorporates deficit language. Providing this information to students can create a space for conversation about ableist perspectives.

With every unit I teach, I always focus on language. Whether it is the language I use while teaching or the language I hope my students will use, this is the area in which I am most cognizant. When teaching social justice topics, specifically about characters with physical disabilities, I try to use language that is not othering to ensure that what I say does not uphold society's ableist perspective, which NCDJ (2021) describes as "['Ableism'] . . . discrimination and social prejudice against people with disabilities. Ableism comes in all forms, from overt prejudice to more subtle microaggressions."

Self-reflection and checking for stereotypes are essential for teachers and students. I discuss with students the importance of language—both what I say and what they say; what a word means (denotation) and what feelings it invokes (connotation). I often worry that some students might shut down or not engage in class discussion or small-group work due to the fear they will say something wrong. To cultivate a safe environment, I explain to students that they may not always know the correct words to say right away but that attempting to learn new words and phrases to meet the moment or being open to correction if something comes out wrong is the best way to engage one another in a respectful manner. Books can be a helpful tool in teaching this lesson, particularly when students have a chance to examine diverse points of view and language use around a topic as important as discerning ableist perspectives.

References

Dunn, P. (2010). Re-seeing (dis)ability: Ten suggestions. *English Journal, 100(2)*, 14–26.

———. (2022, June 8). Quashing disability myths through the lived experience of authors: Three new middle grade books. *National Council of Teachers of English*. https://ncte.org/blog/2022/06/quashing-disability-myths-through-the-lived-experience-of-authors-three-new-middle-grade-books/

National Center on Disability and Journalism. (2021, August). *Disability language style guide*. https://ncdj.org/style-guide/

Reynolds, J. (2016). *As brave as you*. Atheneum/Caitlyn Dlouhy Books.

Rachel Roloff has been teaching seventh- and eighth-grade English at Washington Middle School in Olympia, Washington, for the past six years. She graduated from Washington State University with a BA in English with certification in secondary teaching. She has presented at the National Council of Teachers of English Convention twice and is coauthor of "Learning to Live Authentically: Studying Transgender Young through Being Emily,*" a chapter in* Queer Adolescent Literature as a Complement to the English Language Arts Curriculum *edited by Paula Greathouse and Henry "Cody" Miller, and author of "Learning How to Speak for Social Justice" in* English Journal's *From Campus to Classroom column.*

ABLEISM AND DISABILITY IN SPORTS

The history of access for people with disabilities to sports activities and competitions has followed a similar trajectory as access in society and school. For example, today's Paralympic Games have become a shining example of inclusion as these events hold international competitions in the same manner and in the same location as the Olympic Games every four years. At the 2022 Winter Paralympic Games in Beijing, for instance, over 500 athletes representing 45 countries competed in 78 events (International Paralympic Committee, 2022). This success, however, took decades to achieve. The first reported sport clubs for people with disabilities were those for the deaf in 1880s Germany. It was not until 1944 when Dr. Ludwig Guttmann opened a clinic for servicemen with spinal issues after World War II, at which he used sport as part of his rehabilitation program, that sports for people with disabilities started becoming more mainstream. Dr. Guttmann also hosted the first competitions for wheelchair athletes on the same day as the opening of the 1948 Summer Olympic Games in London. From there, the first official Summer Paralympic Games were held in Rome in 1960 and have been held every four years since. The Winter Paralympic

Games were added in 1976, and every Summer and Winter Paralympic Games since 1988 have been held in the same city as the corresponding Olympic Games (International Paralympic Committee, 2022). Again, this history represents a slow but rather successful progress toward building access for athletes with disabilities on an international scale.

However, this success is tempered by the media coverage of athletes with disabilities. A rather problematic example is how stereotypical descriptions of athletes with disabilities still prevail in sports media. Silva and Howe (2012) identified this type of representation as following a "supercrip" narrative in which athletes have somehow "overcome" or have fought against their impairments to achieve "unlikely" success (p. 178). They argued that this narrative, rather than expressing celebratory and value-based views, actually undermines athletes with disabilities by characterizing their achievements as beyond social expectations and only on the individual and personal responsibility level, thereby ignoring other social and institutional factors that both propel and impede athletes' relative success. While Pearson and Misener (2019) saw a positive shift toward representing Paralympians as athletes first, they also found that media coverage often used the verb "participate" as opposed to "compete" when describing Paralympians playing in the Games and often used the term "cyborg," in reference to their adaptive technologies, to describe Paralympians' athletic abilities. This "cyborg" characterization problematically highlights the technology used to enhance athletes' success in their sport over their own athletic abilities, which they have spent years honing in preparation to compete at the international level. Similarly, Darlene Hunter, a member of the US Women's Basketball team that won a bronze medal at the 2020 Summer Paralympic Games, referred to media portrayals that focus on athletes' disabilities rather than their athletic performances as "inspiration porn" (Knapp, 2021). Hunter argued such media coverage objectifies athletes with disabilities for the entertainment of the viewing public, which detracts from other messages, particularly those that inspire youth with disabilities to also achieve in the athletic arena. Viewed uncritically, such portrayals can propagate stereotypical and limited perspectives about all people with disabilities—perspectives this unit of study aims to disrupt.

FOCAL YA TEXT: *THE RUNNING DREAM* BY WENDELIN VAN DRAANEN

Jessica Carlisle is a runner, but readers do not meet her crossing the finish line of a 400-meter track race or enduring a road marathon at the beginning of *The*

Running Dream (Van Draanen, 2011); they meet her in a hospital bed trying not to look at the "monstrosity" of her "red and bulging" stump that now ends her right leg just below the knee (p. 4). After a successful high school track meet in which she bested her rival and set a personal record in the 400-meter, her team's bus is hit by a truck, flipping the bus, killing one of her teammates, and crushing her lower right leg. More than Jessica's leg is crushed, however, as she wonders if she will ever be able to run again. And if she cannot run, then she also wonders if she can ever find a purpose for her life again. Van Draanen's story weaves together Jessica's physical recovery with her mental recovery as part of learning how to walk and, eventually, how to run again. Jessica is lucky to have strong support from those around her. Her parents and sister push her to get out of bed and back to school. Kyrokowski, her track and field coach, who everyone on the team calls Coach Kyro, shows her how she can learn to run with a prosthetic. Her teammates, particularly Fiona, her best friend, encourage her by organizing fundraisers to purchase the prosthetic running leg. Gavin Vance, a possible romantic interest, also promotes her story through the local media. Along the way, Jessica establishes an unexpected new friendship with Rosa, a girl in her math class. As Jessica learns about Rosa and how she has endured cerebral palsy, she discovers both a personal connection with Rosa and a renewed purpose to her running—not only to run for herself but also for Rosa.

The Running Dream has received numerous positive reviews and honors. Van Draanen's novel was listed on YALSA's 2012 Best Fiction for Young Adults. It was named the 2013 Golden Sower Award winner, an award selected by children and young adults across Nebraska. Most impressively, the novel also earned the American Library Association's Schneider Family Book Award for 2013, which identifies stories that positively express disability experiences for children and youth.

INCORPORATING *THE RUNNING DREAM* INTO THE SECONDARY ELA CLASSROOM

While the primary aim of this literature study is to explore issues related to ableism, disability, and sports, Van Draanen's (2011) story also provides opportunities to think about how someone handles traumatic life events. With these two aims in mind, the outlined instructional tasks are meant to support students' exploration of the following essential questions:

- What is disability?

- How does access impede and/or encourage participation in sports and other extracurricular activities?
- How might obstacles complicate reaching personal goals?

These essential questions are phrased carefully due to particular stigmas attached to words often used to describe people with disabilities and their experiences. For instance, Simi Linton (2010) argued that the notion of "overcoming" was not developed by people with disabilities; rather, it has been used and propagated as a form of wish fulfillment by those outside the disability community. Dunn (2010) elaborated on this concern in terms of teaching about ableism and disability through literature in the secondary ELA classroom. She cautioned teachers about the content of questions posed to youth about fictional characters with disabilities, including any questions that imply stereotypical assumptions about the effects of a disability on a person's life, such as the supposed desire people have to overcome disability as something that can be eventually set aside and that a disability is automatically limiting. Stratman (2015) argued that youth readers should focus on two broad inquiries when considering characters with disabilities. First, readers should identify exactly what the characters are attempting to "overcome" and then, determine the factors that are motivating their attempts. We encourage teachers to keep these ideas about "overcoming" and related descriptors in mind as they engage youth with the following tasks aimed at exploring Jessica's and Rosa's experiences in *The Running Dream.*

Prior to Teaching the Novel

An important first step to any literature study is to determine background knowledge students will need to engage with the story and to consider responses to the framing essential questions. For *The Running Dream,* readers would need opportunities to explore terminology related to ableism and disability, the use of prosthetics, and the effects of traumatic events. These prereading instructional tasks aim to provide opportunities for examining these topics.

Establishing Vocabulary Groundwork

While many students might be familiar with the general term *disability,* they might not have as much background regarding the nuances of the term nor related legal issues. We suggest teaching terminology related to disability in context, as opposed to through isolated memorization instruction that focuses solely on learning definitions. For example, students could be asked to follow a "vocabulary note-taking" process (Zygouris-Coe, 2015, p. 151). This process begins by providing a list of important terminology and a content-specific text. For *The Running Dream*, the supplemental text should focus on disability and access. Documents from the World Health Organization, ADA National Network, and the Council for Exceptional Children are viable because they use a variety of relevant vocabulary. Then, with a reading partner, students would 1) identify the definition of each vocabulary word found in the text and note the corresponding page number and/or paragraph, 2) note how the text provides evidence for and expands upon the definition, 3) make connections between the word and their own prior knowledge, and 4) craft a summary about what they learned about disability and access using the assigned terminology. The fourth step should be completed after the first three steps have been accomplished for all assigned vocabulary since students should attempt to use all the terminology in their summaries. As students read *The Running Dream*, they could note when they come across the terminology in the novel and add to their definitional understandings. Figure 5.1 provides a starter list of important vocabulary words and a possible format students could use for the note-taking strategy.

Vocabulary Term	**Definition Found in Text (with page/ paragraph number)**	**Textual Evidence and Expansion for Definition**	**Connections to Your Prior Knowledge**	**Connections Found in *The Running Dream***
Disability	*Individual with a "physical or mental impairment that substantially limits one or more major life activities" (p. 3)*	*Definition expanded in multiple bullets that add details. They refer to where in the ADA Act I can find the definition.*	*I knew that a disability meant someone had something different about them.*	*Jessica losing her leg limits her ability to run track.*
Accommodation				
Discrimination				
Impairment				
Transitory				
Liability				
Summary of what you learned using all terms:				

Source: ADA National Network. (2021). *What Does it mean to be "Regarded as Having an Impairment" under the Americans with Disabilities Amendments Act (ADAAA)?* https://adata.org /sites/adata.org/files/files/Regarded%20 as%20Having%20Impairment_FINAL.pdf

FIGURE 5.1: Vocabulary Note-Taking Strategy Example

Providing Background on Prosthetics and Running

Another unique aspect to Jessica's story in *The Running Dream* is her use of two different prosthetics—one for walking and another for running—to support her mobility after she lost her leg in the accident. Van Draanen describes multiple medical procedures through conversations between Jessica and her surgeon, Dr. Wells, and prosthetist, Hank Kruber (or, as Jessica teasingly calls him, Hankenstein). Teachers could ask students to complete an additional "vocabulary note-taking" chart with a reading on prosthetics. However, we would also advise teachers to use videos of people using prosthetics to support them walking and running in order to assist students in visualizing the scenes in which Jessica learns how to use both types of prosthetics. We suggest using resources from the Mission Gait Foundation (2021), which includes several instructional videos ranging from preparing one's leg for a prosthesis to practicing using the prosthesis to completing sports-related agility drills. Students could take vocabulary-focused notes while viewing the videos for homework or as an in-class activity. If completing both vocabulary-based activities during class time, then we recommend setting up stations, perhaps two reading-based and two video-based, in which groups can rotate through the stations and build a robust vocabulary on disability and access in preparation for reading the novel.

One important note for teachers to consider as they prepare students to read *The Running Dream* is that Van Draanen uses Oscar Pistorius as the primary example of a successful track athlete using a prosthesis to motivate Jessica to return to running. In this scene (all of Chapter 6 in Part III, pp. 141–45), Fiona, who is clearly keeping a mysterious secret, takes Jessica to Coach Kyro's classroom during a lunch period and surprises her with videos of Pistorius, along with two other runners, successfully using prostheses. One of the other runners is identified as "Amy," whom we would guess is Amy Palmiero-Winters, an award-winning marathoner (Stanfield, 2010) who gained fame around the time Van Draanen was most likely writing her novel. The videos inspire Jessica to return to running and the track team, a dream that she had convinced herself was beyond possibility, and they spur Fiona's and Coach Kyro's involvement in raising funds for her running prosthesis. Consequently, it is a pivotal scene in the novel. However, since Van Draanen's novel was published, Pistorius has become a very problematic role model for all athletes due to being accused and ultimately convicted of murdering his girlfriend. Therefore, we recommend teachers prepare for this scene by discussing Pistorius and his entire history—from child athlete prodigy to Paralympian gold medalist to disability activist to convicted murderer (Ott, 2021). There are numerous videos of Palmiero-Winters, Hunt-Broersma, and others that could be used to present students with alternative role models.

Understanding Trauma

Finally, since Jessica experiences her own traumatic event and endures survivor's guilt over her deceased teammate, we suggest that teachers activate students' prior knowledge about these issues before beginning the novel. First, teachers should educate themselves about grief and trauma. Places to begin include studies on teaching about grief through literature, such as Dunn and Johnson's (2022) exploration of English teachers handling emotions related to loss while teaching literature, and Witte and Dail's (2021) recommendations for pairing loss narratives and young adult literature. Mark Lewis, one of the authors of this book, has also used "affective response journals" to help students write about the emotions they feel while reading stories about grief and loss (Lewis, 2018). For instance, teachers could begin with a children's picture book about grief, such as *Ida, Always* (Levis & Santoso, 2016), which tells the story of two polar bears, Ida and Gus, who have lived in New York City's Central Park Zoo for most of their lives. Ida gets sick, and she and Gus must grapple with her terminal diagnosis. At key moments in the story related to Ida's illness, students would compose journal entries addressing prompts like the following: *How are both bears grieving in response to Ida's illness? What do you think or feel about how grief and loss is presented in the story? How might you grapple with grief and loss in your own life?* This process will help prepare them to discuss Jessica's own grief about her accident and her teammate's death. We discuss teaching about death and dying in more detail in Chapter 8.

Jessica is also almost seduced by pain medicine addiction (pp. 54–56), so teachers will need to be prepared to discuss this aspect of the story as well. We examine the social concern of drug abuse and sports in depth in Chapter 11, including asking a counselor to visit the classroom to talk about the issue with students. We suggest teachers plan a similar discussion with a counselor and their students to discuss addiction related to pain medication, as well as handling grief and loss, as another way to support students to engage productively with Jessica's experiences in *The Running Dream.*

As Students Read the Novel

Van Draanen relies on many literary and poetic devices to tell Jessica's story, particularly how Jessica thinks about the new challenges her accident creates in her life. For example, both Rosa and Jessica use the idea of a "finish line" metaphorically to describe setting and achieving personal goals, as well as to understand how one's life progresses. Another important literary aspect of *The Running Dream* involves internal and external conflicts because Jessica and Rosa confront problems and obstacles brought on by outside forces and internal struggles that get in the way of achieving their goals. Therefore, we suggest asking readers to tackle the following during-reading instructional tasks to encourage them to build their understanding and use of these literary devices.

Analyzing Literary and Poetic Devices

During an early conversation in Jessica and Rosa's growing friendship, Rosa asks Jessica why she loves running and racing and about the differences between the two. In this conversation, Rosa reveals that she has clearly already thought about the meaning of crossing the finish line:

> I look at her. "You're very philosophical about the finish line." She gives a thoughtful nod. "It's symbolic." I nod too, because I'm sure I know what she means, but then she adds, "Because it's also the starting line." For some reason this thought startles me. (p. 214)

Jessica thinks further about what this symbolism means, including why starting a race is so different from finishing a race despite, as Rosa philosophizes, the actual lines the runner crosses are the same. This finish-line metaphor holds significant weight in the story in two ways. First, in a very concrete way, the finish line represents success as Jessica prepares to run for Rosa and help her feel what it is like to cross the finish line of a race. Second, in a more abstract way, the finish line represents Jessica achieving full recovery from her accident, both mentally and physically, and embracing all of the changes that have resulted from that accident. This latter, more metaphorical meaning, is solidified in the novel's conclusion that ends with Jessica realizing she is now facing a "new starting line" for the rest of her life (p. 332).

Van Draanen's metaphorical use of the "finish/starting line," along with several other running-based symbols and images, to thread the overarching themes of her novel provides an opportunity for students to identify and use the literary and poetic devices of metaphor, imagery, and symbolism. One way to examine such devices is to ask students to move through an inquiry project conducting an artifactual analysis (Pahl & Rowsell, 2010) of symbols and images employed in the novel. Mark and his colleague Emily Bruce (Lewis & Bruce, 2018) have suggested using this type of analysis with Kekla Magoon's *How It Went Down* (2014) by assigning different symbols and images, or "literary artifacts," to students prior to reading the novel and then asking them to keep a running record of when the symbols and images are discussed by different characters. Their records can then be used to conduct an artifactual analysis in which the students write about how symbols and images can hold disparate metaphorical meanings for individual characters based on their particular social and cultural backgrounds. For *The Running Dream*, a necessary first step would be for teachers to build students' knowledge about the devices of metaphor, imagery, and symbolism. This step can be accomplished by providing definitions and examples and then asking students to identify the devices in short poems or film excerpts. Then we suggest asking students to follow a similar path of artifactual analysis that Mark and Emily outlined, but focusing on symbols and images related to running and racing, such as the finish line, Rigor Mortis Bend, hurdles, and starting blocks. Figure 5.2 provides an example artifactual analysis record using Rigor Mortis Bend.

Artifact: Rigor Mortis Bend		
Part, Chapter, and Page Numbers	**Characters**	**Artifactual Analysis**
Part I Chapter 7 pp. 16–17	Jessica	Jessica explains how her team uses "rigor mortis," which refers to how a body stiffens after death, to describe the final turn before the finish line in a track race. She then compares that experience in a track race to using crutches to get from her hospital bed to the bathroom. She feels like her entire life is "living on Rigor Mortis Bend."
Part IV Chapter 4 p. 222	Jessica and Gavin	Gavin asks Jessica if she is going to stand at "Rigor Mortis Bend" to cheer on Fiona in her race. Jessica warns Gavin that he is starting to sound like he is on the team. So, for Jessica, using this term is a way to show someone is a member of the track team.

FIGURE 5.2: Artifactual Analysis Example for *The Running Dream*

As the students read the novel, it is important to provide opportunities for students with the same assigned symbols and metaphors to discuss and compare notes in a small-group setting. They can add notes to their records from their classmates' thoughts and opinions. We also suggest providing discussion opportunities for students examining different symbols and images to help them recognize and articulate connections across the running-related metaphors. The students' running records of symbols and images can then be used for students to write summaries of characters, employing their assigned symbols and images to build metaphorical understandings of the characters' lives, situations, and relationships. These summaries should focus on the essential questions related to disability, access, and obstacles.

Through this analysis, students should recognize that symbols and images can hold unique meanings for different people. Their analyses can then be used as resources for the culminating task of writing an extended metaphor poem, as described in the "Culminating Tasks" section.

Exploring Conflict

Jessica and Rosa grapple with several internal and external conflicts throughout *The Running Dream*, so it would be a useful story to support students' exploration of this plot element, a common English language arts content standard. After reviewing the five primary types of conflict—character versus self, character, society, nature, or technology—with several literary examples, teachers could ask students to take consistent notes on when Jessica and/or Rosa face a conflict, how/if that conflict becomes more complicated, and how she or they resolve the conflict. If using a class set of novels, this task can be completed using sticky notes, perhaps a different color for each unique conflict, which students can use to mark specific pages as they read. If students are sharing copies of the novel, then they can still use sticky notes but need to organize them in personal notebooks or journals. At various moments as the students progress through the novel, they can pause reading to discuss their conflict notes with small groups, adding sticky notes based upon those conversations. Teachers can then ask the small groups to sort their identified conflicts into different types. After sorting, the groups can compose a collaborative reading response outlining all the conflicts Jessica or Rosa endure throughout the story.

Culminating Tasks after Reading the Novel

After reading about Jessica and Rosa, students can reflect on what they learned about ableism, disability, and sports through the following summative assessments. These performance tasks will also provide students with opportunities to consider issues related to access and overcoming obstacles presented in the framing essential questions.

Crafting Extended Metaphor Poems

Now that students have conducted their artifactual analyses on their assigned symbols and images, as well as discussed their possible metaphorical meanings, they can use their work to craft their own extended metaphor poems. With the recognition that writing poetry can be daunting for secondary students, teachers should provide many supports for the writing process. The first support the students have is their artifactual analyses. The second support could be a lesson moving students through a scaffolded writing process using an unrelated topic to help them craft an extended metaphor poem. Mark has followed a protocol (adapted from Dr. Clarissa Thompson) using emotions as the topic for the students' poems.

First, each student receives a random emotion written on a notecard and an organizer listing several categories (see Figure 5.3). The emotion words (such as joy, dread, love, serenity, etc.) are placed face down on students' desks, one word per student, with the direction that they should keep their assigned emotion secret from their classmates. The students are then given individual think time to determine images and/or symbols for as many categories as they can. In the organizer handout, Mark provides some examples using an emotion that was not assigned to any student and explains how some images might be more personal and some might be more universal. Second, students move into small groups of three or four, and each member reads their list of images and symbols without revealing their actual emotion, and the other group members try to guess the emotion. After the guessing rounds are completed, Mark has a whole-class discussion on why and how students were able to guess correctly (or closely enough), focusing on how certain symbols and images represent particular emotions (e.g., the color yellow often signifies cowardice) and that these images can be used as metaphors to express an emotion without actually stating it. Third, Mark reads Theodore Roethke's poem "Dolor" (1943) aloud without identifying the emotion named in the title, and he asks the small groups to identify items that match the categories on the organizer and then guess the emotion Roethke was attempting to metaphorically describe. Finally, students draft their own poems using "Dolor" as a mentor text, their assigned emotion as the poem title, and their list of images and symbols to create their lines of poetry. Their small-group members are also there to help, revise, and edit each other's poems. After revising the poems for homework, teachers can facilitate an author's celebration the next day for students to read their poems.

Category	Directions: In each row, list images that match the category and your assigned emotion. Remember not to use the actual word for the emotion in your lists.
Place	(Mark's personal example for a place of "happiness"—As a kid, camping with friends in the Appalachian Mountains. Mark's universal example for a place of "happiness"—home)
Color	
Food	
Clothing	
Animal	
Smell	
Mineral	
Sound	
Flower	

FIGURE 5.3: Writing Organizer for Extended Metaphor Emotion Poems

At this point, with more experience working with metaphors and writing poetry, students can return to the artifactual records and analyses and use those documents to craft an extended metaphor related to disability and access. We suggest asking them to use a sport or hobby they engage in and reflect on what it might be like for someone with a disability to also engage in that sport or hobby. They can consider all the challenges involved, ways to embrace those challenges, and possible ways a disability might actually be an advantage in their chosen sport or hobby, using Jessica and Rosa as role models. The students might also brainstorm images and symbols using the same category-based organizer they used to write their extended metaphor emotion poems. As well, time could be provided for students to research how people with disabilities have been successful playing their chosen sport or engaging in their chosen hobby. We suggest providing time for students to move through the entire writing process, and we recommend that teachers write their own poems as models for students to use. Finally, students can share and discuss their poems, particularly how researching and writing them might have expanded their answers to the essential questions framing the entire literature study on *The Running Dream.*

Constructing a Life Road Map

When Jessica sets the goal to complete the River Run with Rosa, she faces several obstacles to her success. Namely, she must become more proficient at running with a prosthetic, build her strength and stamina as both part of her recovery and pushing the added weight of Rosa and her wheelchair, and create a plan for the challenges of the race route. She quickly learns, however, that she cannot achieve her goal independently, so she accepts help from many others during her preparation for the race and throughout the race itself. For instance, Coach Kyro creates a training regimen for her to follow, her father constructs a more aerodynamically efficient wheelchair for Rosa, her new boyfriend, Gavin, agrees to be her running partner, and Fiona organizes logistics such as designing team shirts and organizing cheer squads during the actual race. Whenever an obstacle arises, Jessica or one of her support team members determines a way to negotiate it so she can successfully finish the River Run and help Rosa cross the finish line.

Using this aspect of the story, teachers can ask students to create their own Life Road Map that identifies a single personal goal and organizes all the logistics and steps necessary to meet their identified goal. Following Jessica's experience, students might include smaller goals or "milestones" as part of the process of achieving their ultimate goals. Therefore, some aspects of the maps that students might include are setting milestones, identifying possible complications or obstacles, determining possible solutions for those complications or plans for enduring those obstacles, and considering divergent paths or routes for meeting their personal goals. To create the final project, students could choose to use a digital platform that lends itself to creating maps and/or paths, such as Prezi or a Miro board. Students could also create wall murals of their Life Road Maps using butcher paper and art materials; these murals could resemble a board game or a tourist map. For either digital or print options, and to create an interdisciplinary experience for students, partnering with an art teacher or community artist will support students in learning about and employing artistic elements in their projects.

CONCLUSION

People with disabilities should have the same access to education and other social goods, including the ability to enjoy and play sports, as anyone else. Reading stories such as *The Running Dream* and discussing everything that Jessica and Rosa must endure is one way to build empathy for people with disabilities. Ideally, youth will construct multifaceted perspectives about what it means to provide support and advocate for people with disabilities, thereby also creating a more just and inclusive society.

Options for Book Clubs

Teachers looking to facilitate book clubs in which students explore ableism and disability can incorporate *The Running Dream* alongside titles like the following:

Pinned (Flake, 2012)
Told through multiple narrators, *Pinned* shares the stories of Autumn Knight and Adonis Miller. Autumn is a star wrestler, confident that she can beat anyone on the mat. Succeeding in school is a different matter, as her learning disability often gets in the way. Adonis Miller has no problem succeeding in school and loves to read, navigating the school hallways in his wheelchair with confidence. Their lives become intertwined as they discover they can help each other.

Braced (Gerber, 2018)
Rachel Brooks looks forward to her senior year in high school, particularly as a starter on the soccer team and with the burgeoning possibility of a romantic relationship. However, those hopes are seemingly dashed when her doctor informs her that her scoliosis has worsened, which means wearing a restrictive back brace. Rachel must now consider what her condition means for how she lives her life and how she views herself.

Not If I See You First (Lindstrom, 2015)
Parker Grant does not want to be treated any differently since losing her vision, expecting anyone who wants to be her friend to follow "The Rules" she has outlined. She thinks she has a foolproof plan for her life moving forward, including an opportunity to run for

the school track team, but her life gets complicated when a former boyfriend returns unexpectedly and the circumstances of her father's death are questioned.

A Time to Dance (Venkatraman, 2015)
Dancing is central to Veda's life. She loves how she feels when completing the highly intricate *Bharatanatyam*, an ancient Indian dance, and hearing the audience applaud her achievements. When an accident damages her leg beyond repair, she must decide if she wants to, or even can, learn how to dance with a prosthetic. This novel-in-verse reveals the beauty and athleticism of dance, as well as Veda's determination to keep dancing.

Options for Film Study

Teachers who want to use films to augment students' discussions about ableism and disability can incorporate *The Running Dream* alongside titles like the following:

Walk. Ride. Rodeo. (Allyn, 2019)
This biopic shares the story of Amberley Snyder (Spencer Locke), who achieved huge success on the rodeo circuit as a barrel racer. Unfortunately, she becomes paralyzed from the waist down after crashing her truck. The film shows her initial frustration and depression due to the accident and her fear of not being able to ride a horse again, much less compete. Yet with encouragement from friends and fans, along with her own determination, she learns how to ride with a specially designed saddle and continues her rodeo racing success.

Crip Camp: A Disability Revolution (Newnham & LeBrecht, 2020)
This documentary tells the story of Camp Jened, which was one of the first summer camps specifically designed to provide access to people with disabilities. Camp Jened was open in the 1950s through the 1970s, and the film documents many of its campers, including Judith Heumann, who became activists in the disability rights movement in the US.

The Peanut Butter Falcon (Nilson & Schwartz, 2019)
Part comedy, part drama, this film features Zak (Zack Gottsagen), who has been placed in a state-run assisted living home because he has Down syndrome and no caregivers. Zak is far from happy at the home and wants to be a professional wrestler so badly that he runs away to try to join the school of his favorite wrestler, Salt Water Redneck. Along the way, he forms a friendship with another social outcast, Tyler (Shia LaBeouf), who decides to help Zak complete his journey to join the wrestling school and become a professional wrestler.

The Terry Fox Story (Thomas, 1983)
Terry Fox has the potential to be a star runner for Canada before he loses a leg to cancer. He decides to use his disability to raise cancer research awareness and organizes the Marathon of Hope, which will follow his attempt to run across Canada. The film documents his life from before his diagnosis through his attempt to finish his cross-country run.

Young Adult Literature

Flake, S. G. (2012). *Pinned*. Scholastic.

Gerber, A. (2018). *Braced*. Scholastic.

Lindstrom, E. (2015). *Not if I see you first*. Poppy.

Magoon, K. (2014). *How it went down*. Henry Holt & Co.

Van Draanen, W. (2011). *The running dream*. Knopf Books for Young Readers.

Venkatraman, P. (2015). *A time to dance*. Nancy Paulsen Books.

Other Texts for Classroom Use

Allyn, C. (Director). (2019). *Walk. Ride. Rodeo.* [Film]. Poke Prod.

Heumann, J., & Joiner, K. (2020). *Being Heumann: An unrepentant memoir of a disability rights activist*. Beacon Press.

Levis, C. (2016). *Ida, always* (C. Santoso, Illus.). Atheneum Books for Young Readers.

Newnham, N., & LeBrecht, J. (Directors). (2020). *Crip camp: A disability revolution* [Film]. Higher Ground Productions; Rusted Spoke Productions; Little Punk; Just Films; Ford Foundation.

Nilson, T., & Schwartz, M. (Directors). (2019). *The Peanut Butter Falcon* [Film]. Armory Films; Lucky Treehouse; Bona Fide Productions; Endeavor.

Roethke, T. (1943). Dolor. *Poetry: A Magazine of Verse, 63*(11), 69-70. https://www.poetryfoundation.org/poetrymagazine/browse?contentId=23707

Thomas, R. L. (Director). (1983). *The Terry Fox story* [Film]. HBO Premiere Films.

REFERENCES

ADA National Network. (2022). *What is the Americans with Disabilities Act (ADA)?* https://adata.org/learn-about-ada

Dunn, M. B., & Johnson, R. A. (2020). Loss in the English classroom: A study of English teachers' emotion management during literature instruction. *Journal of Language and Literacy Education, 16*(2), 1–21.

Dunn, P. A. (2010). Re-seeing (dis)ability: Ten suggestions. *English Journal, 100*(2), 14–26.

Hockensmith, R. (2022, December 16). *Inside Zion Clark's MMA debut and the battle over who gets to fight*. ESPN. https://www.espn.com/mma/story/_/id/35260940/zion-clark-mma-fight

Holohan, M. (2021, October 26). *Chris Nikic, first Ironman finisher with Down syndrome, shares philosophy of 1% better.* TODAY. https://www.today.com/health/chris-nikic-1st-person-down-syndrome-finish-ironman-releases-book-t235948

International Paralympic Committee. (2022). *Paralympic Games.* https://www.paralympic.org/

Knapp, G. (2021, September 5). "Inspiration porn": Paralympians know it when they see it. *The New York Times.* https://www.nytimes.com/2021/09/05/sports/olympics/inspiration-porn-paralympians-know-it-when-they-see-it.html

Lewis, M. A. (2018). Disruption of adolescent-adult and death-life binaries: The experiences of Elizabeth Hall in *Elsewhere.* In M. Falter & S. Bickmore (Eds.), *Moving beyond personal loss to societal grieving: Discussing death's social impact through literature in the secondary ELA classroom* (pp. 3–12). Rowman & Littlefield.

Lewis, M. A., & Bruce, E. (2018). Multiperspectivity in *How it went down:* A more just way of "seeing." *SIGNAL Journal, 43*(2), 27–31.

Lewis, N. (2022, May 5). *How amputee Jacky Hunt-Broersma ran 104 marathons in 104 days: "Just focus on the next step."* ESPN. https://www.espn.com/espn/story/_/id/33859427/how-amputee-jacky-hunt-broersma-ran-104-marathons-104-days-just-focus-next-step

Linton, S. (2010). Reassigning meaning. In L. J. Davis (Ed.), *The disability studies reader* (3rd ed., pp. 223–236). Routledge.

Mayerson, A. (1992). *The history of the Americans with Disabilities Act: A movement perspective.* Disability Rights Education & Defense Fund. https://dredf.org/about-us/publications/the-history-of-the-ada/

Mission Gait Foundation. (2021). *Instructional videos.* https://www.missiongait.org/instructional-videos

National Center for Education Statistics. (2022). *Report on the condition of education 2022.* https://nces.ed.gov/pubs2022/2022144.pdf

Ott, T. (2021, March 3). *Oscar Pistorius: The rise and fall of the Olympian turned killer.* Biography. https://www.biography.com/news/oscar-pistorius-rise-fall-olympics-murder-girlfriend

Pahl, K., & Rowsell, J. (2010). *Artifactual literacies: Every object tells a story.* Teachers College Press.

Pearson, E., & Misener, L. (2019). Canadian media representations of para-athletes at the 2016 Paralympic Games. *Olympika: The International Journal of Olympic Studies, 28,* 1–28.

Renuart, A. (2021, November 28). *Mallory Weggemann: "Swimming saved my life," says five-time Paralympic medalist.* CNN. https://www.cnn.com/2021/11/28/sport/mallory-weggemann-swimming-paralympics-spt-intl/index.html

Silva, C. F., & Howe, P. D. (2012). The (in)validity of *supercrip* representation of Paralympian athletes. *Journal of Sport and Social Issues, 36*(2), 174–194.

Stanfield, M. (2010, August 8). Amy Palmiero-Winters: Running for her life. *The O&P EDGE.* https://www.oandp.com/articles/2010-08_08.asp

Stratman, J. (2015). "Overcoming": Analyzing motivations in *Shark girl* and *The running dream. English Journal, 104*(4). 103–105.

US Department of Education. (2022). *A history of the Individuals with Disabilities Education Act.* https://sites.ed.gov/idea/IDEA-History#2000s-10s

Witte, S., & Dail, J. S. (2021). "The grief that fills one's heart": Pairing loss narratives and graphic young adult literature. In N. Sieben & S. A. Shelton (Eds.), *Humanizing grief in higher education: Narratives of allyship and hope* (pp. 38–48). Routledge.

Zygouris-Coe, V. I. (2015). *Teaching discipline-specific literacies in grades 6–12: Preparing students for college, career and workforce demands.* Routledge.

6

Confronting the Dangers of Contact Sports Head-On

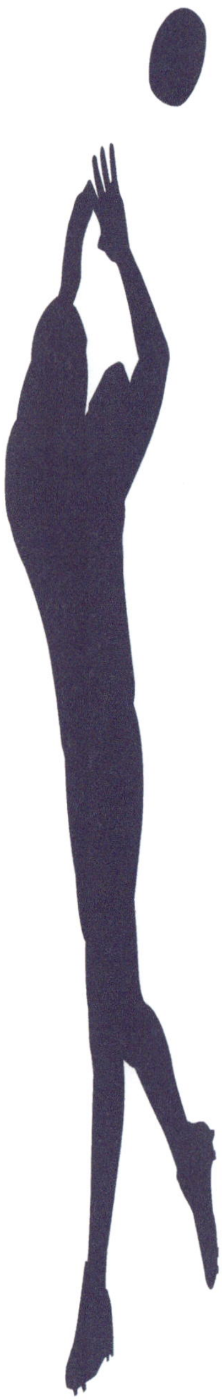

"Sometimes helmets hit helmets. Get used to it. It's a violent game, dude. Or did they forget to tell you that?"

—*Arlo Brodie,* HIT COUNT *(Lynch, 2015, p. 238)*

A child's participation in sports is generally accepted as beneficial to their physical and mental well-being. However, the dangers of suffering brain injuries when playing contact sports have prompted coaches and administrators to reconsider the protocols, practice habits, equipment, and facilities used to protect participants in youth and interscholastic sports, as evinced by stories like the following:

- Alpine School District (UT) collaborated with Intermountain Healthcare to establish academic benchmarks for students recovering from concussions (Vejar, 2021).
- Ramapo High School's (NJ) football team cut to-the-ground tackling out of its practices to reduce concussions—and the team proceeded to win a state title (Stubbs, 2019).
- A Pop Warner football team in Jupiter, FL, became the state's first to use protective caps over their helmets during practice to guard against brain trauma (Dunnan, 2021).
- Striving to reduce concussions and other injuries, Clark County School District (NV) converted 29 high school football fields from natural grass to turf (Yamashita, 2021).

Schools and youth-sports organizations have taken such measures because they recognize the tension between the benefits of athletic competition and the risk of brain trauma accompanying sports such as football, hockey, and soccer. Many students who take on roles as athletes and/or fans understand that tension well; they desperately want to play or watch sports where collisions are routine, yet they feel unsettled about the long-term effects of brain trauma. That tension creates valuable opportunities for literacy teaching and learning, particularly when explored through celebrated young adult literature and other relevant texts.

THE SOCIAL CONCERN OF TRAUMATIC BRAIN INJURIES

The Centers for Disease Control and Prevention (2015) recognize a traumatic brain injury (TBI) as a disruption of the brain's typical function, resulting from a blow to or penetration of the head. TBIs are a public health concern around the globe. In fact, Dewan et al. (2018) estimated that 64 to 74 million individuals worldwide suffer a TBI each year. These injuries vary in intensity and are categorized upon occurrence as mild, moderate, or severe. Concussions, which moved into the public eye following research investigating connections between brain trauma and participation in contact sports, are categorized as "mild" TBIs. Still, "[a]n injury of any severity to the developing brain can disrupt a child's developmental trajectory" (Centers for Disease Control and Prevention, 2018, p. 4).

TBI is a medical issue, but it is not free from the sociopolitical realm. Factors such as race and socioeconomic status, geographic location, and gender norms play a role in the outcomes people experience across the spectrum of TBIs. For instance, Haines et al. (2019) reported disparities in treatment of TBI patients based on race and socioeconomic status. According to Haines et al., uninsured patients with minority status and more severe TBIs see the greatest disproportion of outcomes, including mortality. Such findings align with data Daugherty et al. (2019) presented, indicating that some racial and ethnic groups (e.g., American Indians/Alaska Natives) have higher rates of TBI-related deaths and hospitalizations than others.

Gender norms, including those that have men believing they are somehow flawed if they show any signs of weakness, factor into how people deal with TBIs. Wallace et al. (2017) found that male high school athletes were 4-to-11 times more likely than their female counterparts to refrain from reporting a sport-related concussion for reasons focused on others' perceptions, such as not wanting to seem "weak" to teammates and coaches. (See Chapter 10 for methods and materials that support critically examining traditional masculinity ideology via YAL and related texts.) The stigma associated with disclosing a TBI is a barrier preventing some athletes from seeking a proper medical diagnosis and treatment. That fact is troubling, especially considering the number of sport-related concussions experienced by children each year in the US.

TRAUMATIC BRAIN INJURIES IN SPORTS

Bryan et al. (2016) estimated that 1.1 to 1.9 million sport- and recreation-related concussions occur annually in US residents aged 18 and under. Such concussions are often sustained through participation in contact sports. From 2001 to 2018, the highest rates of emergency department visits for children with sport- and recreation-related TBIs were associated with playing football, basketball, and soccer (Waltzman et al., 2020). Regarding the incidence and outcomes of sport-related concussions, researchers have noted sex-based differences. For example, conducting a meta-analysis of published research, McGroarty et al. (2020) found that female athletes may be more susceptible to concussions and have more prolonged symptoms after sustaining one.

Attention paid to the significance of sport-related concussions began rising in the 2000s. Omalu et al. (2005) presented the first study to link American football and chronic traumatic encephalopathy (CTE), a progressive degenerative brain disease found in people who have suffered a severe blow or repeated blows to the head. Symptoms found in individuals diagnosed with the disease include behavioral changes (e.g., impulsivity); mood disturbances (e.g., depression); and cognitive changes (e.g., memory loss) (Stern et al., 2013). Given CTE's severity, research examining connections between the disease and football has grown. For instance, Mez et al. (2019) discovered a strong relationship between the duration of football played and CTE neuropathology, with odds of disease doubling every 2.6 years of play. Findings like these may contribute to the decline of US high school athletes playing football annually, an ongoing pattern since the 2013–2014 season (National Federation of State High School Associations, 2022).

Researchers continue investigating sport-related concussions, with some suggesting measures to reduce exposure to head impacts and concussions in interscholastic and youth sports. For instance, flag football might be offered instead of tackle football, for Sarmiento et al. (2021) found that male tackle-football players aged 6–14 sustained nearly 20 times more head impacts per game than flag-football competitors. In hockey, rules could be implemented to restrict body checking, considering Ingram et al. (2019) found evidence supporting a relationship between body-checking policies and decreased incidence of concussions among male youth ice hockey players. Likewise, reducing the amount and duration of full-contact activities is an option, given that Pfaller et al. (2019) found a 57 percent decrease in the rate of sport-related concussions sustained during high school football practice following the launch of a policy limiting full-contact activities. Such measures can reduce exposure to head impacts and concussions, yet they cannot eliminate them outright. That begs the question: What is an acceptable level of risk for brain injury when a child's health and well-being are at stake? That is a sociopolitical dilemma worth pondering in the ELA classroom.

FOCAL YA TEXT: *HIT COUNT* BY CHRIS LYNCH

Hit Count (Lynch, 2015) follows narrator Arlo Brodie, a burgeoning linebacker with a penchant for making big hits, as he advances through high school from his freshman year to his senior year. Earning praise for his aggressive play from his father and his coaches, Arlo is pursuing dreams of gridiron glory—dreams his older brother Lloyd abandoned. But not everyone in Arlo's orbit is enamored with football and the violent collisions he creates with his no-nonsense approach to the game. His mother has developed "The File," a compilation of newspaper and magazine clippings about sport-related brain trauma, and Sandy, his girlfriend, cannot bear to watch him compete, yet Arlo plays on.

As the story progresses, so does Arlo's game. Displaying a tireless work ethic, he hits the weights, hardening himself for the rigors of his sport. Arlo's efforts pay off, for he earns a spot on the varsity football team as a sophomore, is dubbed "Starlo" for his exceptional play, and is named co-captain as a junior. In time, though, the kind of bone-jarring tackles that thrust Arlo into the spotlight are the same ones that increasingly raise concern among those around him, including his coach. Nevertheless, enraptured by the rush of the action and the spectators' adulation, Arlo is convinced he can play through the pain. As Arlo's coach begins tracking the number of head impacts the linebacker suffers, readers are left to wonder: What becomes of a displaced football player who has built his identity around gridiron success?

Chris Lynch, a Printz Honor Award-winning author, has earned numerous accolades for his work. In 2015, *Hit Count* was recognized as a Junior Library Guild selection in the "Sports High" category, which includes celebrated works of sports-related fiction and nonfiction. Additionally, the novel was included among the 2015 Top Ten Sports Books for Youth by *Booklist*. *Hit Count* was also one of just thirty titles selected by teen reviewers for the International Literacy Association's Young Adults' Choices 2017 Reading List, a distinction indicative of the book's appeal to teen readers. Such acclaim supports making room for *Hit Count* in the secondary ELA classroom.

INCORPORATING *HIT COUNT* INTO THE SECONDARY ELA CLASSROOM

Much of *Hit Count* revolves around the tension between Arlo's passion for the game of football and the danger the sport poses to his health and well-being. With that in mind, the following activities are designed to aid students as they explore four overarching essential questions:

- How do we reconcile our passion for contact sports with the threats they pose to the health and well-being of the athletes who play them?
- What becomes of an individual who can no longer fulfill the identity they have built for themselves?
- To what lengths should adults go to ensure a child's health and well-being?
- To what degree are health risks acceptable in interscholastic and youth sports?

Prior to Teaching the Novel

Smagorinsky (2008) advised that effective introductory activities position students to draw from their own knowledge and experiences while engaging with ideas central to the literature at hand. Facilitating student engagement in scenarios that simulate situations or decision-making relevant to the literature is one viable approach. When it comes to preparing students to discuss issues raised in *Hit Count* specifically, a value-trading scenario is apt. Likewise, inviting students to write about personal experiences relevant to what characters go through in the novel is also appropriate, as is building background knowledge.

Value Trading

Years ago, while teaching English in southeast Michigan, Luke Rodesiler, one of the authors of this book, facilitated a value-trading activity he picked up from Wilhelm (2002). As students prepared to read Washington Irving's Faustian tale "The Devil and Tom Walker," he presented a scenario that had them think about what they value and what they would sacrifice to acquire what they covet most. Luke distributed cards representing different things people value, such as health, wealth, and political power (see Figure 6.1). Then, students were charged with moving around the room and trading cards with their peers to secure those they value most. For instance, a student who really valued their familial relationships but did not have the "Family" card in the hand they were dealt was willing to trade a combination of the "Political Power" and "Fame" cards to secure it. Once the trading ceased, Luke invited students to reflect on their choices. What did they covet and why? What were they willing to sacrifice and why? The activity prepared students to read Irving's story, which prompts readers to consider what they cherish, what they sacrifice, and the consequences of their choices.

That same activity can help students begin thinking about the trade-offs one makes when playing football and, as Arlo intends, trying to carve out a career in the sport. In *Hit Count*, Arlo is lauded for his violent play, but it comes with costs, including his health and, at times, his relationship with Sandy. Still, he dreams of

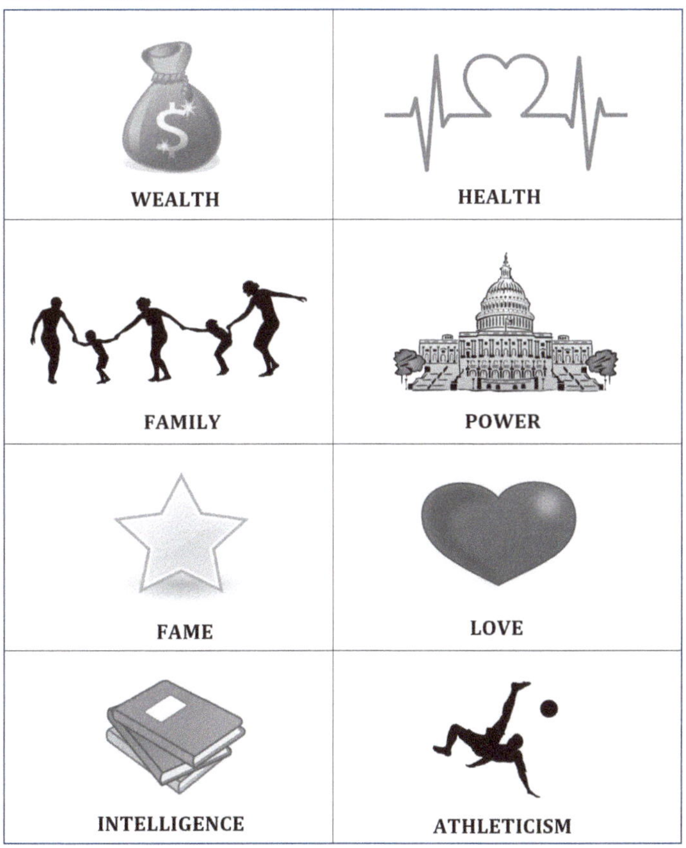

FIGURE 6.1: Example Value-Trading Cards

playing professional football and garnering the fame and fortune that come with a career in the nation's most popular sports league. Some people even parlay athletic success into political power (e.g., bodybuilder Arnold Schwarzenegger, pro wrestler Jesse "The Body" Ventura, boxer Manny Pacquiao, football player Anthony Gonzalez). But is enduring brain trauma worth the potential for wealth, fame, and political influence that could be had? Facilitating a value-trading activity using cards like those in Figure 6.1 sets students up to weigh what is most important to them and the sacrifices they would make to get it.

Writing about Personal Experiences

Alternatively, teachers might invite students to draw from personal experiences as they reflect in writing on issues relevant to *Hit Count* specifically and to the essential questions more broadly. For example, a writing prompt like the following aligns with the second essential question presented in this chapter:

> Have you ever built an identity or reputation for yourself that you had to abandon, whether by force or by choice? For example, maybe you grew out of a behavior you were known for at an earlier time in your life, or perhaps you no longer felt the desire to participate in an activity in which you were known to excel. Regardless, write about a personal experience in which you came to identify with or be known for something you left behind. As you develop your response, be sure to address the following:
>
> - What was it that you identified with or had come to be known for?
> - Why did you leave that identity or reputation behind?
> - What, if anything, made it difficult to leave that identity/reputation behind?
>
> Please be prepared to share your writing with your peers.

When students respond to this prompt and report on it, they get to mull over their own and others' experiences with a personal challenge Arlo endures in the novel: accepting the fact that the identity he built for himself is not sustainable.

Building Background Knowledge about Concussions

Prior knowledge is recognized as a key factor in reading comprehension (Daniels & Zemelman, 2014). With that in mind and considering the central role concussions play in *Hit Count*, it may be helpful for students to build knowledge about sport-related TBIs before reading Lynch's novel. For instance, it cannot be assumed that all students know exactly what a concussion is or how they occur, and many students may be unfamiliar with specific terms that arise in the story, such as "subconcussive hits" or "traumatic encephalopathy." Therefore, students may benefit from exploring resources such as those provided by the Concussion Legacy Foundation (CLF), which was founded by Drs. Chris Nowinski and Robert Cantu. The CLF (n.d.) has published web pages dedicated to concussions, subconcussive impacts, and CTE. Students could even complete the free one-hour "Concussion for Students" online course offered by the National Federation of State High School Associations (n.d.). The course helps students learn about concussions, including how to identify their signs and symptoms, what to do in response to a concussion, and how to prevent them. Students can then draw upon what they learn while reading *Hit Count*.

Relevant video resources are also available. For instance, "What Happens When You Have a Concussion?" is an animation from TED-Ed (2017) that was created by Clifford Robbins of Boston University's CTE Center. By watching the video, students can learn about the prevalence of sport-related concussions and what causes them, the damage done by subconcussive hits, and more. Teachers might play the brief video twice, inviting students to take notes while watching the second time. In discussion, teachers can invite students to share what struck them most, what questions they have, and what the science behind concussions means for the future of football, hockey, and other contact sports. With knowledge constructed by watching and discussing the video, students will be better prepared to make sense of the concerns Arlo's mother raises about football and the threats to Arlo's health and well-being that come with playing the game he loves.

In the event that students are unfamiliar with football and the violence inherent in the game—or even if they are familiar with it—teachers might share Josh Begley's (2018) *Concussion Protocol*, a short film documenting each concussion reported in the 2017–2018 NFL season. The short film is a compilation of in-game collisions that resulted in traumatic brain injuries, and each one is played in reverse and presented in slow motion. With that unique presentation of routine plays, Begley disrupts the commonplace and invites viewers to question what they actually see when they watch a football game. Insights gleaned from the short film may help students appreciate the reality of the on-field violence Lynch describes in *Hit Count*.

Voices from the Field
Toughen Up, Buttercup

Mitchell Nobis
Virtual Learning Mentor Teacher,
Birmingham Public Schools, Michigan

The purpose of an education is not merely to prepare students for what's next. Students already live in the real world, so teachers need to invite them to grapple with current problems facing them now, too. For better or for worse, in the United States, sports and academics are both school pursuits, and the dangers of sports are risks our students have to face.

Incoming middle and high school students are told to "get involved" and "join a team." What if playing that game leads to brain damage? For generations, we ignored the risks and played them off as rites of passage. We said, "I got my bell rung, too" and "Get back in there." Learning toughness definitely has merit. I'm glad I did, but we don't need to damage our kids' brains for them to get those messages. There are many ways to be tough.

How can an English teacher help students engage in critical thinking about problems like concussions? I answer that the same way I answer most questions about teaching English: We balance what we know from theory and practice, and we jump in and get messy. We know good pedagogy invites student choice and reading a wide range of texts. We want students to reflect, discuss, debate, and write. We help them learn *how to think*. How, then, might we help students think about the dangers and benefits of sports?

I've taught AP English Language and college-prep writing classes, and I use essays as grist for thinking and as writing models that might accompany the novels mentioned elsewhere in this book. We think best when doing our own writing, so I invite students to engage with various texts before writing their own essays about sports and head trauma or other problems. Since many students are already aware of football's concussion controversy, we start with a news report about a high school football player who died from a head injury (Mohney & Shapiro, 2015) before we do a group reading and discussion of Charles Pierce's (2015) "The Death of Evan Murray," a piece that takes the football controversy a step further into an ethics debate on whether we should even have high school football.

My goal is to get students to individualize their focus, though, so over the ensuing few days, I give students a list of sports essays, invite them to read a few, then discuss with partners before writing their own essays on contemporary problems related to sports. Of course, many students stick with head trauma, but this format allows students to have choice and to go in related directions if desired. There are many excellent essays that work for the readings, and here are some of the older pieces with enduring popularity that can add topics beyond football or head injury:

- "Have Sports Teams Brought Down America's Schools?" (Kolbert, 2013)
- "College Athletes of the World, Unite" (Abdul-Jabbar, 2014)
- "Man and Superman" (Gladwell, 2013)
- "When Basketball Became the Crying Game" (Shirley, 2007)
- "American Meritocracy Is Killing Youth Sports" (Thompson, 2018)

Go find your own or check out some sports-related essays highlighted on The Electric Typewriter (n.d.) and Sport Literate (n.d.).

If we allow students space to get in the pit and tussle with controversy, they'll learn and maybe even change their own thinking. Changing one's mind seems to be ridiculed in today's media, but isn't changing one's mind based on new information one of the main goals of learning in the first place?

It is.

It is also tough to do. It can be harder than getting back up after a rough fall. The elders often say kids today are soft, but the kids are not just repeating what they've been told. We have seen how it can scare the old guard and lead to backlash when the younger generation parts ways with tradition. Our students break new ground and get yelled at for it. But learning means not just doing what has been done before. Learning how to think and how to navigate a landscape of words requires teachers and students to be tough. Addressing this in our classrooms expands our definition of toughness beyond the playing field. This must be a goal of education, so let's rub some dirt on our brains and get back in there.

References

Abdul-Jabbar, K. (2014, November 12). College athletes of the world, unite. *Jacobin*. https://www.jacobinmag.com/2014/11/college-athletes-of-the-world-unite

Gladwell, M. (2013, September 2). How bad is doping, really? *The New Yorker*. https://www.newyorker.com/magazine/2013/09/09/man-and-superman

Kolbert, E. (2013, September 5). Have sports teams brought down America's schools? *The New Yorker*. https://www.newyorker.com/news/daily-comment/have-sports-teams-brought-down-americas-schools

Mohney, G., & Shapiro, E. (2015, October 6). *Seattle high school football player was brought to hospital with head injury before he died.* ABC News. https://abcnews.go.com/Health/seattle-high-school-football-player-brought-hospital-head/story?id=34290085

Pierce, C. P. (2015, September 30). *The death of Evan Murray*. Grantland. http://grantland.com/the-triangle/the-death-of-evan-murray

Shirley, P. (2007, March 30). *Journal 43: When basketball became the crying game*. ESPN. https://www.espn.com/nba/columns/story?columnist=shirley_paul&page=Journal-43

Sport Literate. (n.d.). *Best American essays*. https://sportliterate.org/about-us/best-american-essays

The Electric Typewriter. (n.d.). *50 great sports articles—examples of excellent sports writing*. https://tetw.org/Sport

Thompson, D. (2018, November 6). American meritocracy is killing youth sports. *The Atlantic*. https://www.theatlantic.com/ideas/archive/2018/11/income-inequality-explains-decline-youth-sports/574975

Mitchell Nobis is a writer and the virtual learning mentor teacher for high schools in Birmingham (MI) Public Schools. He is a past president of the Michigan Council of Teachers of English and serves as a co-director of Red Cedar Writing Project and the Teachers as Poets facilitator for the National Writing Project. He was lucky enough to be an assistant coach on a state championship high school basketball team a long time ago.

As Students Read the Novel

While reading *Hit Count*, there are various activities students can take up to extend their thinking as it relates to the essential questions. These include tracking the head impacts Arlo endures over the course of the novel, considering how characters guard Arlo's health and well-being, if at all, and making connections between Lynch's story and those of real athletes whose careers were derailed by concussions.

Tracking Arlo's Hit Count

Multiple conflicts in *Hit Count* are fueled by Arlo's aggressive play and the blows to the head he endures as a result; these include conflicts with his girlfriend Sandy, with his mother, and with his friend Dinos. By the time Arlo's a junior, Coach Fisk has even begun tallying a hit count to track the head impacts the star linebacker sustains. As students read, they can maintain their own hit count for Arlo. That is, they can track each head impact he suffers and note the ways they affect him, if at all. If tasked with framing their notes as medical reports, then students can draw from insights they gleaned while building knowledge about concussions prior to starting the novel. For example, an entry might take the shape of Figure 6.2, addressing the reason for medical assessment, symptoms, additional notes, and recommendation. When tracking head impacts, students ought to note the blows Arlo takes on the football field from freshman year on, but they should also register hits he sustains off the field as well, such as "the conk [Arlo] had given [his] own head" (Lynch, 2015, p. 138) when he broke up a fight between Lloyd and their father.

Medical Report	
Patient's Name	Arlo Brodie
Grade Level	10
Reason for Medical Assessment	The patient endured multiple high-impact collisions during practice, including an illegal head slap (pp. 141–143).
Symptoms	Symptoms include nose bleeding, headache, and ears ringing "like a great big church bell" (p. 143).
Additional Notes	The patient reported not being removed from practice despite remaining on the ground for "several seconds" (p. 143).
Recommendation	Refrain from physical contact to avoid additional blows to the head. Seek immediate medical care if symptoms worsen. Return in seven days for re-evaluation.

FIGURE 6.2: Example Medical Report

Whether students use the format of a medical report or something different, tracking Arlo's hit count stands to help them see the totality of the brain injuries he is accumulating as well as the effects he is suffering. Plus, the documentation can aid students as they discuss the story and contemplate prompts like the following:

- What effects are head impacts having on Arlo? How, if at all, do they match up with what you know about the symptoms of concussions and subconcussive hits?

- What is it about playing football that keeps Arlo hanging on despite the numerous head impacts you've documented and the effects they've had on him (and others)?
- Throughout the story, Arlo resists efforts people make to steer him away from football. Considering the effects of various head impacts you've noted, do you side with Arlo or with those who've tried to protect him? Why?
- Some people may defend football by arguing that we assume risks daily and that brain trauma can be sustained outside the arena as well. How, if at all, could that argument be supported by events you have documented? On which side of that argument do you fall?

Such questions invite students to weigh how true-to-life they find the novel, to contemplate how people reconcile passion for contact sports with the dangers inherent in them, and to ponder their own thinking about the threat football poses to the athletes competing.

Ranking Characters as Arlo's Protectors

Considering characters in relation to one another based on relevant criteria is one way to invite discussion among students around a common work of literature (Milner et al., 2017). Teachers can facilitate such work as students read *Hit Count* and, in the process, help them think about the lengths to which adults should go to ensure a child's health and well-being. For example, teachers might provide a prompt like the following as Arlo's junior year winds down:

> Some characters are more protective of Arlo's health and well-being than others. To help us figure out which characters are more or less protective, let's do some ranking.
>
> - First, take time to independently rank the following characters—Arlo, Arlo's mother, Arlo's father, Lloyd, Sandy, Dinos, and Coach Fisk—from 1–7 (i.e., from most to least protective of Arlo's health and well-being). As you analyze each character, find evidence from the text to support their ranking.
> - Then, when prompted, compare your rankings with a small group of peers. Using evidence from the text to guide your thinking, hash out any differences and establish a final set of rankings for your group. Please be prepared to share your final rankings with the class and cite the text for support as warranted.

After groups report, teachers can facilitate discussion using questions like these:

- What more, if anything, could some of these characters do to protect Arlo?
- What responsibility, if any, does Arlo bear for the brain trauma he is experiencing?
- What role does the culture around football play in Arlo's refusal to accept others' advice?
- To what lengths should adults in a teen's life go to ensure their health and well-being?
- What's an acceptable level of risk to accept when a child's health is at stake?

While plainly relevant to the novel, such questions also position students to deliberate these issues in life beyond the world Lynch created in *Hit Count*.

Considering Arlo's Story in Light of Real Athletes' Experiences

Hit Count is fiction, yet concussions forcing an individual to abandon their identity as an athlete is quite real. It is not uncommon for athletes across sports to retire after suffering brain injuries. For example, NASCAR driver Kurt Busch retired while still recovering from a concussion (Williams, 2023); Australian surfer Owen Wright, an Olympic medalist, retired from competitive surfing due to a history of concussions (Australian Associated Press, 2023); and the NFL's Jordan Reed retired in 2021 with concussion-related issues lingering (Keim, 2021). However, some athletes retire before concussions force their hand. For instance, the NFL's Chris Borland chose to retire in 2015, taking a proactive measure for his health's sake after playing just one season of professional football (Fainaru-Wada & Fainaru, 2015). Exploring real athletes' experiences and the decisions they made—by force or by choice—can extend students' thinking about the dangers of collision sports and the challenge of identity loss.

Concussions End an NHL Dream (CBC News, 2019) is one text documenting how concussions disrupted an athlete's career. In the ten-minute video, Connor Crisp, who retired at age twenty-four, describes his passion for hockey, especially the physicality and the cheers, and how losing his identity as a player deflated his ego. In that way, the short offers a powerful complement to *Hit Count*. When showing the video, teachers might invite students to consider prompts like these:

- What parallels are evident in the ways Connor Crisp and *Hit Count*'s Arlo Brodie describe the feelings they get from playing their respective sports? How might those feelings inform decisions they make about giving up their sport?
- Chelsea Burt explains a pressure that discourages players like Crisp from reporting injuries. What is that pressure, and why might that deter players like Crisp from reporting concussions? How does Arlo put similar pressure on himself?
- At one point, Crisp declares, "There's a lot I'd trade in to, you know, just feel normal." What is Arlo sacrificing for the game he loves and the benefits that accompany it? Might he regret those trades someday? Why or why not?
- Dr. Bennet Omalu asks, "Why are we placing sports above the humanity of mankind?" How might you respond to Dr. Omalu? Why embrace sports rather than protect the health that allows for experiencing humanity in full?

Bridging the real world and the fictional, such questions support students in exploring issues common to both texts. Figure 6.3 highlights other resources that can aid students in exploring the lives of athletes whose careers were derailed by concussions.

Title	Author	Date	URL
"The Right Decision"	Husain Abdullah	April 18, 2016	https://www.theplayerstribune.com/articles/husain-abdullah-chiefs-retirement-concussions
"13 Concussions"	Casey Cochran	July 6, 2016	https://www.theplayerstribune.com/articles/casey-cochran-uconn-football-concussions
"Soccer's Unspoken Problem"	Alecko Eskandarian	November 18, 2016	https://www.theplayerstribune.com/articles/alecko-eskandarian-soccer-concussions
"The Darkness"	Adam Estoclet	March 3, 2016	https://www.theplayerstribune.com/articles/adam-estoclet-hockey-concussion
"We Need to Talk About Concussions, Right Now"	Gabriel Landeskog	August 3, 2016	https://www.theplayerstribune.com/articles/we-need-to-talk-about-concussions-right-now
"Hell and Back"	Marc Savard	May 17, 2017	https://www.theplayerstribune.com/articles/marc-savard-bruins-hell-and-back

FIGURE 6.3: Other Resources Documenting Real Athletes' Experiences with Concussions

Culminating Tasks after Reading the Novel

Given the aforementioned essential questions and activities, multiple culminating tasks for students are viable, including engaging in a final discussion and writing argumentation essays.

Discussing Big Ideas via the Fishbowl Protocol

If teachers want to focus on speaking and listening, two of the English language arts that seem to be overlooked at times, while still engaging students in one last exploration of the essential questions guiding the unit and other big ideas relevant to *Hit Count*, they might do so by engaging students in a discussion via the fishbowl protocol. In terms of physical structure, a fishbowl features desks organized to form two concentric circles. Discussion takes place among students seated in the inner circle. Students in the outer circle listen to and make note of the ideas shared. When so moved, they can join the discussion by tapping the desk of someone seated in the inner circle to signal that person's dismissal and then taking their seat (Smagorinsky, 2008).

When it comes to the discussion's content, we encourage teachers to have students bring their own thoughtful, big-idea questions for the class to contemplate. Of course, it never hurts for teachers to prepare thought-provoking questions they can pitch if they want to make sure specific issues get due consideration, if discussion falls flat, or if students arrive unprepared. Teachers might consider posing questions like the following:

- Considering *Hit Count* and other texts we've studied in recent weeks, what danger, if any, is there in tying your identity to athletic success?
- Who or what is most to blame for the brain trauma Arlo suffered in *Hit Count*?
- Dr. Chris Nowinski, CEO of the Concussion Legacy Foundation, stated, "A football player's odds of developing CTE may be most determined by their parents" (Holohan, 2021). Did Arlo's parents do enough to protect his health and well-being in *Hit Count*?
- Should schools and youth organizations continue sponsoring tackle-football programs, or are the established risks of youth sustaining brain trauma simply unacceptable?

Such prompts are the sort that invite rich discussion, and they align with the essential questions established previously.

Finally, if using the culminating fishbowl discussion as a high-stakes summative assessment, we suggest incorporating the protocol at other points in the unit of study so that students have a feel for the expectations and the structure of the discussion as well as opportunities to develop as speakers and listeners.

Writing Argumentation Essays

If teachers are looking to sharpen students' writing skills as they wrestle with issues raised in *Hit Count*, they might invite students to write argumentation essays. Argument is everywhere in today's world, so it is reasonable that teachers would position students to craft formal arguments incorporating the literature they read. The four questions included as suggestions for facilitating discussion in the preceding subsection can also be used as prompts to facilitate the writing of argumentation essays. Whether or not students get the opportunity to discuss those questions with their peers, they can extend their thinking through writing as they develop original essays.

When helping students develop arguments around topics raised in *Hit Count*, teachers might present an essay like "Exactly How Dangerous Is Football?" (Chen, 2020) or "Youth Tackle Football Will Be Considered Unthinkable 50 Years from Now" (Nowinski, 2019) as a mentor text. With Nowinski's (2019) essay, for example, the topic is plainly relevant, and studying the writer's moves—including how he establishes ethos, uses statistics to support his argument, and closes the piece by posing questions—can help students consider the writerly moves available to them.

CONCLUSION

Teachers who invite students to critically examine the danger of contact sports can anticipate resistance. Researchers have established connections between football and CTE, yet the game remains arguably the nation's most popular sport. The significance of the issue and the relevance to students' lives, whether they are fans or competitors, make the struggle worthwhile. Studying *Hit Count* and related texts presents an extended opportunity for students to reconsider the violence inherent in contact sports and weigh, perhaps for the first time, just how much risk is too much risk when a child's health hangs in the balance.

Options for Book Clubs

Teachers looking to facilitate book clubs in which students explore the danger of contact sports through literature can incorporate *Hit Count* alongside titles like the following:

Game Changer (Greenwald, 2018)
In this multigenre novel, the family of thirteen-year-old Teddy tries to understand how he ended up in critical condition with possible intracranial bleeding, raising questions about the violent culture that permeates the game of football.

Cracking the Bell (Herbach, 2019)
Isaiah has benefited immensely from playing football—it brings structure to his life and offers a path to a college education—but he's compelled to reconsider everything when he sustains a concussion on the field.

Gut Check (Kester, 2019)
Wyatt's not much of an athlete, but he longs to connect with his brother, the star quarterback, before he departs their dreary town. A big win in a high-profile game would do a lot for the community, so will Wyatt reveal his brother's concussion or stay quiet?

Second Impact (Klass & Klass, 2013)
In this multigenre novel, Jerry, the star quarterback, and Carla, a reporter for the school paper, begin blogging about the football season. But when Carla seeks to pursue the issue of sports-related concussions, she meets resistance from players and adults alike.

Before the Ever After (Woodson, 2020)
In this verse novel, twelve-year-old ZJ, the son of a retired professional football player, clings to memories of better times as he tries to make sense of the changes he sees in his father, who suffered numerous concussions during his days on the gridiron.

Options for Film Study

Teachers looking to incorporate film study to help students weigh the danger of contact sports can consider the following options:

Head Games (James, 2012)
In this award-winning documentary film, director Steve James explores the dangers of collision sports from youth leagues to the pros, offering viewers a sense for the scope of the issue, which is not limited strictly to tackle football.

League of Denial: The NFL's Concussion Crisis (Kirk, 2013)
This award-winning documentary explores the connection between playing football and suffering brain injuries, as well as the National Football League's (NFL) efforts to suppress research that stands to undermine the money-making juggernaut but protect public health.

Concussion (Landesman, 2015)
This feature film recreates forensic pathologist Dr. Bennet Omalu's (Will Smith) fight against the NFL as it tries to silence him and quash his research on chronic traumatic encephalopathy (CTE), a neurodegenerative disease he found in deceased football players.

Concussions and Female Athletes (Tucker Center, 2022)
This documentary from the Tucker Center for Research on Girls & Women in Sport at the University of Minnesota incorporates insights from scholars and renowned medical professionals to address the impact concussions have on female athletes.

The Crash Reel (Walker, 2013)
This award-winning documentary film focuses on the rivalry between world-class competitive snowboarders Kevin Pearce and Shaun White, the traumatic brain injury Pearce suffered while training in 2009, and his long road to recovery.

Young Adult Literature

Greenwald, T. (2018). *Game changer*. Amulet Books.

Herbach, G. (2019). *Cracking the bell*. Katherine Tegen Books.

Kester, E. (2019). *Gut check*. Farrar, Straus and Giroux.

Klass, D., & Klass, P. (2013). *Second impact*. Frances Foster Books.

Lynch, C. (2015). *Hit count*. Algonquin Young Readers.

Woodson, J. (2020). *Before the ever after*. Nancy Paulsen Books.

Other Texts for Classroom Use

Begley, J. (2018, February 1). *Concussion protocol* [Video]. Field of Vision. https://fieldofvision.org/concussion-protocol

CBC News. (2019, January 28). *Concussions end an NHL dream* [Video]. YouTube. https://www.youtube.com/watch?v=RPH99ZgcA88

Chen, I. (2020, February 1). Exactly how dangerous is football? *The New Yorker*. https://www.newyorker.com/culture/annals-of-inquiry/exactly-how-dangerous-is-football

Concussion Legacy Foundation. (n.d.). *Subconcussive impacts*. https://concussionfoundation.org/cte-resources/subconcussive-impacts

———. (n.d.). *What is a concussion?* https://concussionfoundation.org/concussion-resources/what-is-concussion

———. (n.d.). *What is CTE?* https://concussionfoundation.org/CTE-resources/what-is-CTE

James, S. (Director). (2012). *Head games* [Film]. Head Games the Film.

Kirk, M. (Director). (2013). *League of denial: The NFL's concussion crisis* [Film]. Public Broadcasting Service.

Landesman, P. (Director). (2015). *Concussion* [Film]. Columbia Pictures.

National Federation of State High School Associations. (n.d.). *Concussion for students*. https://nfhslearn.com/courses/concussion-for-students

Nowinski, C. (2019, April 3). *Youth tackle football will be considered unthinkable 50 years from now*. Vox. https://www.vox.com/2019/3/27/18174368/football-concussion-brain-injury-cte-youth-football

TED-Ed. (2017, July 27). *What happens when you have a concussion?* [Video]. YouTube. https://www.youtube.com/watch?v=xvjK-4NXRsM

Tucker Center. (2022, April 21). *Concussions and female athletes* [Video]. YouTube. https://www.youtube.com/watch?v=uEz9zB1JM08

Walker, L. (Director). (2013). *The crash reel* [Film]. Impact Partners; Tree Tree Tree.

REFERENCES

Australian Associated Press. (2023, March 21). Owen Wright to retire from competitive surfing due to history of concussions. *The Guardian*. https://www.theguardian.com/sport/2023/mar/22/owen-wright-to-retire-from-competitive-surfing-due-to-history-of-concussions

Bryan, M. A., Rowhani-Rahbar, A., Comstock, R. D., & Rivara, F. (2016). Sports- and recreation-related concussions in US youth. *Pediatrics*, *138*(1).

Centers for Disease Control and Prevention. (2015). *Report to Congress: Traumatic brain injury in the United States: Epidemiology and rehabilitation*. https://www.cdc.gov/traumaticbraininjury/pdf/TBI_Report_to_Congress_Epi_and_Rehab-a.pdf

———. (2018). *Report to Congress: The management of traumatic brain injury in children*. https://www.cdc.gov/traumaticbraininjury/pdf/reportstocongress/managementoftbiinchildren/TBI-ReporttoCongress-508.pdf

Daniels, H., & Zemelman, S. (2014). *Subjects matter: Exceeding standards through powerful content-area reading* (2nd ed.). Heinemann.

Daugherty, J., Waltzman, D., Sarmiento, K., & Xu, L. (2019, November 22). Traumatic brain injury-related deaths by race/ethnicity, sex, intent, and mechanism of injury—United States, 2000–2017. *Morbidity and Mortality Weekly Report*, *68*(46), 1050–1056.

Dewan, M. C., Rattani, A., Gupta, S., Baticulon, R. E., Hung, Y-C., Punchak, M., Agrawal, A., Adeleye, A. O., Shrime, M. G., Rubiano, A. M., Rosenfeld, J. V., & Park, K. B. (2018). Estimating the global incidence of traumatic brain injury. *Journal of Neurosurgery*, *130*(4), 1080–1097.

Dunnan, T. (2021, April 13). *Jupiter Mustangs first Pop Warner team in state to use safety helmet caps*. WPTV. https://www.wptv.com/sports/football/jupiter-mustangs-first-pop-warner-team-in-state-to-use-safety-helmet-caps

Fainaru-Wada, M., & Fainaru, S. (2015, March 16). *SF's Borland quits over safety issues*. ESPN. https://www.espn.com/espn/otl/story/_/id/12496480/san-francisco-49ers-linebacker-chris-borland-retires-head-injury-concerns

Haines, K. L., Nguyen, B. P., Vatsaas, C., Alger, A., Brooks, K., & Agarwal, S. K. (2019). Socioeconomic status affects outcomes after severity-stratified traumatic brain injury. *Journal of Surgical Research*, *235*, 131–140.

Holohan, M. (2021, August 17). *Brett Favre urges no tackle football for children under 14.* Today. https://www.today.com/parents/brett-favre-psa-urges-no-tackle-football-kids-under-14-t228384

Ingram, B. M., Kay, M. C., Vander Vegt, C. B., & Register-Mihalik, J. K. (2019). The effect of body checking policy changes on concussion incidence in Canadian male youth ice hockey players: A critically appraised topic. *Journal of Sport Rehabilitation, 28*(7), 774–777.

Keim, J. (2021, April 20). *Jordan Reed retiring from NFL due to issues from concussions.* ESPN. https://www.espn.com/nfl/story/_/id/31295380/source-jordan-reed-retiring-nfl-7-seasons

McGroarty, N. K., Brown, S. M., & Mulcahey, M. K. (2020). Sport-related concussion in female athletes: A systematic review. *Orthopaedic Journal of Sports Medicine, 8*(7), 1–12.

Mez, J., Daneshvar, D. H., Abdolmohammadi, B., Chua, A. S., Alosco, M. L., Kiernan, P. T., Evers, L., Marshall, L., Martin, B. M., Palmisano, J. N., Nowinski, C. J., Mahar, I., Cherry, J. D., Alvarez, V. E., Dwyer, B., Huber, B. R., Stein, T. D., Goldstein, L. E., Katz, D. I., … McKee, A. C. (2019). Duration of American football play and chronic traumatic encephalopathy. *Annals of Neurology, 87*(1), 116–131.

Milner, J. O., Milner, L. M., & Mitchell, J. F. (2017). *Bridging English* (6th ed.). Pearson.

National Federation of State High School Associations. (2022, September 16). *High school participation survey archive.* https://www.nfhs.org/sports-resource-content/high-school-participation-survey-archive

Omalu, B. I., DeKosky, S. T., Minster, R. L., Kamboh, M. I., Hamilton, R. L., & Wecht, C. H. (2005). Chronic traumatic encephalopathy in a National Football League player. *Neurosurgery, 57*(1), 128–134.

Pfaller, A. Y., Brooks, M. A., Hetzel, S., & McGuine, T. A. (2019). Effect of a new rule limiting full contact practice on the incidence of sport-related concussion in high school football players. *The American Journal of Sports Medicine, 47*(10), 2294–2299.

Sarmiento, K., Waltzman, D., Devine, O., Zhang, X., DePadilla, L., Kresnow, M-J., Borradaile, K., Hurwitz, A., Jones, D., Goyal, R., & Breiding, M. J. (2021). Differences in head impact exposures between youth tackle and flag football games and practices: Potential implications for prevention strategies. *The American Journal of Sports Medicine, 49*(8), 2218–26.

Smagorinsky, P. (2008). *Teaching English by design: How to create and carry out instructional units.* Heinemann.

Stern, R. A., Daneshvar, D. H., Baugh, C. M., Seichepine, D. R., Montenigro, P. H., Riley, D. O., Fritts, N. G., Stamm, J. M., Robbins, C. A., McHale, L., Simkin, I., Stein, T. D., Alvarez, V. E., Goldstein, L. E., Budson, A. E., Kowall, N. W., Nowinski, C. J., Cantu, R. C., & McKee, A. C. (2013). Clinical presentation of chronic traumatic encephalopathy. *Neurology, 81*(13), 1122–1129.

Stubbs, R. (2019, August 27). This high school football team never tackled in practice last year. Then it won a state title. *The Washington Post.* https://www.washingtonpost.com/sports/2019/08/27/this-high-school-football-team-never-tackled-practice-last-year-then-it-won-state-title

Vejar, A. (2021, July 17). A Utah school district is reassessing how it cares for athletes after concussions. *The Salt Lake Tribune*. https://www.sltrib.com/sports/2021/07/17/utah-school-district-is

Wallace, J., Covassin, T., & Beidler, E. (2017). Sex differences in high school athletes' knowledge of sport-related concussion symptoms and reporting behaviors. *Journal of Athletic Training*, *52*(7), 682–688.

Waltzman, D., Womack, L. S., Thomas, K. E., & Sarmiento, K. (2020, July 10). Trends in emergency department visits for contact sports-related brain injuries among children—United States, 2001–2018. *Morbidity and Mortality Weekly Report*, *69*(27), 870–874.

Wilhelm, J. D. (2002). *Action strategies for deepening comprehension*. Scholastic.

Williams, D. (2023, August 26). *Concussion, health issues force Kurt Busch into early retirement from NASCAR Cup*. Autoweek. https://www.autoweek.com/racing/nascar/a44917883/concussion-health-issues-force-kurt-busch-into-early-nascar-cup-retirement

Yamashita, N. (2021, August 4). New turf in time for football. *The Progress*. https://mvprogress.com/2021/08/04/new-turf-in-time-for-football

7

Interrogating the Intersections of Sports and Sexual Violence

I'm near hysteria, I can feel it. I'm going to scream and scream and scream, to make up for the screaming I didn't do last night. I am going to pull my skin off and grind it into the floor and then I'm going to cry until I've got nothing left.

—*Hermione Winters,* Exit, Pursued by a Bear *(Johnston, 2016, p. 53)*

Incidents of sexual violence in sports culture are well documented in our society. Fans of collegiate and professional sports too often hear about stories involving sexual misconduct and sports figures:

- The Northwestern University football program was accused of hazing that involved coercing players to engage in sexual acts (Markus et al., 2023).
- An independent investigation found systemic sexual abuse in the National Women's Soccer League, leading to five of the ten head coaches in the league either being fired or stepping down (Draper, 2022).
- Deshaun Watson, NFL quarterback, was sued by over two dozen massage therapists for sexual assault and harassment (Coleman, 2021).
- Kyle Beach, former NHL player, sued the Chicago Blackhawks for ignoring his complaints that he was being sexually assaulted by a member of the coaching staff (Diaz, 2021).

Unfortunately, there are numerous stories beyond just these four about sports organizations and high-profile athletes and many more incidents involving lesser-known athletes at the high school level. Sexual misconduct, assault, and harassment are major social concerns in our society, and those concerns have been heightened by the #MeToo movement. Therefore, in this chapter, we focus on implementing a literature study on a highly recommended young adult novel in which sexual violence and related societal concerns are central to the story.

THE SOCIAL CONCERN OF SEXUAL VIOLENCE

According to the Rape, Abuse & Incest National Network [RAINN], a person in the United States is sexually assaulted every 68 seconds (2023). Further, despite the fact that more than 700,000 people in the US have self-reported to have been sexually assaulted, it is estimated that less than 40 percent of assaults are reported to the police, so the number of sexual assault cases grossly underrepresents the number of actual incidents in our society (Morgan & Oudekerk, 2019). Statistics from RAINN also show that approximately 7 out of 10 victims of sexual assaults are aged 12 to 34 years old. Within this age bracket, 8 out of 10 juvenile victims are girls, 9 out of 10 adult victims are women, and college women aged 18 to 24 are three times more likely to experience sexual violence than non-students. Further, 17 percent of US girls and women have been victims of an attempted or completed rape and, although at a lower rate, 3 percent of US boys and men have also been victims of an attempted or completed rape. Male college students aged 18 to 24 are five times more likely to have been assaulted than non-students in the same age group. It should also be noted that 21 percent of transgender, genderqueer, and non-conforming college students have been sexually assaulted. As well, in Suarez and Gadalla's (2010) meta-analysis of 37 studies, 25 articles, and 12 dissertations that reported measurements of participants' rape myth acceptance (RMA)—false beliefs used mainly to shift the blame of rape from perpetrators to victims—they found that men followed RMA viewpoints at a significantly higher rate than women and that RMA was strongly linked with these men's hostile behaviors toward and attitudes about women.

Overall, approximately 13 percent of all college students have reported experiencing unwanted, nonconsensual, or violent sexual contact (Cantor et al., 2020). Yet this percentage was based on the answers from only 33 colleges and universities that participated in the Association of American Universities survey. As well, there is a history of campuses concealing and underreporting sexual assault incidents (Yung, 2015) and poorly handling cases, which results in fewer reports (DeMatteo et al., 2015). Additionally, we know that sexual violence is underreported by victims in general (Morgan & Oudekerk, 2019), so all these numbers may be representative of a much larger problem on college campuses.

ROLES OF SPORTS AND ATHLETES IN SEXUAL ASSAULT

Recently, sexual assault has been directly tied to athletics, particularly with the notoriety of cases involving the Northwestern University's football program, the University of Michigan's athletic program, USA Gymnastics, the Baylor University football program, and the Penn State University football program. Many studies in the last three decades have found a higher incidence of sexual violence by college athletes than the general college student population (see McCray, 2019, for a complete review of the literature). For example, Crosset et al. (1995) found that athletes were involved in 19 percent of sexual assault cases while only making up 3 percent of the overall student population. In another study twenty years later, Young et al. (2017) surveyed 379 male college students about their attitudes toward "women, rape myth acceptance, and sexual coercion" (p. 798). They found that 46 percent of participants reported engaging in some form of sexual coercion. Fifty-four percent of athletes surveyed, including students on formal athletic teams and students engaged in club sports, and 38 percent of non-athletes surveyed made up the 46 percent of all participants.

Similarly, a *USA Today* investigation requested sexual misconduct reports from colleges and universities for the previous five years and found that college athletes were overrepresented in cases related to sexual misconduct. Of the thirty-five campuses that responded to the request, athletes comprised approximately 3 percent of the overall student population but comprised 9 percent of the students involved in sexual misconduct. Further, football players made up 6 percent of the students implicated with sexual misconduct while only making up 1 percent of the overall student population (Jacoby, 2019). Beaver (2019) identified several institutional factors that explain why athletes are more disposed to engaging in sexual assault and violence, including the importance of college athletics to campus life, increased abuse of alcohol and other drugs by college students, and the culture of entitlement extended to college athletes.

These numbers and factors indicate that behavior related to sexual violence is more prevalent within university athletic circles, hence the importance of examining this issue with K–12 students, particularly middle and high school athletes who may become part of college-level athletic programs. Within schools, discussions related to sexual assault prevention must start with adults. Over the years, school employees whose positions involve greater individual exposure to K–12 students (e.g., athletic coaches) have been more likely to engage in sexual misconduct (Grant et al., 2017) and therefore are often the focus of sexual assault and harassment policies and regulations involving school athletic programs (Green, 2018; Pennepacker, 2019). Still, it remains to be seen exactly what percentage of sexual assault attackers and victims—including more than 15,000 cases reported in elementary and secondary schools in 2015–2016 alone (Balingit, 2020)—come from the ranks of middle and high school athletes, making it more important than ever for school employees, including academic teachers and athletic coaches in particular, to make sure they are part of the solution for preventing sexual aggression in and around K–12 athletics (Lyndon et al., 2011).

FOCAL YA TEXT: *EXIT, PURSUED BY A BEAR* BY E. K. JOHNSTON

Johnston sensitively tackles the issue of sexual assault in the world of sports. The story begins with Hermione Winters, senior captain of the high school cheerleading squad, riding a bus with her teammates to attend the annual summer cheerleading camp at Lake Manitouwabing. The squad engages in the usual banter between the girl and boy team members and Hermione and Polly, her co-captain and best friend, rally the girls to prepare for the "best cheer year ever" (p. 3). As the bus arrives at the camp, Hermione reflects on how excited she is for this last camp, both as a senior and captain, while listening to her tough but respected Coach Caledon give her usual speech about social rules and safety. The team spends the beginning of camp training for the final cheer competition with Hermione and Polly pushing their teammates, particularly Leo, who clearly has romantic feelings for Hermione, toward a perfect routine.

The Friday afternoon and evening before the final week of camp is reserved for swimming in the lake and partying at the camp social, described by Hermione as "the last time we have for fun and laughing for the next six days, though, because starting at seven a.m. on Sunday morning, the real work starts" (p. 45). Her summer, however, ends that evening with her being drugged and raped by a male cheerleader during the social. She wakes the next morning in the hospital without any memory of what happened but immediately feels her trauma as explained in the quotation that opens this chapter. Besides her parents, Polly, many of her teammates, and Coach Caledon are her strongest supporters as she endures her senior year through the ensuing trauma. Johnston does well to engage the reader, both in terms of building empathy for Hermione—and, thereby, for others suffering similar trauma—and creating suspense for whether or not Hermione's attacker would be discovered.

Johnston's novel earned starred reviews from *Kirkus Reviews*, *School Library Journal*, *Quill & Quire*, *Publishers Weekly*, and *School Library Connection*. It was honored as a *Booklist* Best Book of 2016 and among YALSA's 2017 Top Ten Quick Picks for Reluctant Young Adult Readers. It was also included on the 2017 Amelia Bloomer Book List, which identifies high-quality children's and young adult literature that addresses feminist-related concerns. Most notably, *Exit,*

Pursued by a Bear was distinguished by the Canadian Children's Book Centre with the 2017 Amy Mathers Teen Book Award for Canadian authors of young adult literature.

INCORPORATING *EXIT, PURSUED BY A BEAR* INTO THE SECONDARY ELA CLASSROOM

Several scholars and teachers have lauded the utility of young adult literature as a platform for talking about sexual misconduct, assault, and violence with youth. For example, Malo-Juvera (2014) found that reading and discussing the novel *Speak* (see "Options for Book Clubs") with eighth-grade English language arts students significantly lowered the students' RMA (rape myth acceptance). Cleveland and Durand (2014) claimed that teaching young adult literature with scenes of sexual violence can provide space for students to join national discussions on the #MeToo movement, and Charles (2019), in her essay on the impact of young adult literature with sexual assault content, explained how reading such novels helped her grapple with her own experiences with being abused as a young child. Finally, Colantonio-Yurko et al. (2018) reminded teachers that discussing sexual assault through literature can further students' understanding of historical events, such as reading the novel *Copper Sun* (Draper, 2006) in conjunction with a history unit on colonial America as a way to examine the common practice of White owners raping enslaved people. We aim to contribute to this scholarship by promoting the teaching of sports-related young adult literature, incorporating sports culture to broaden the conversation on this important social concern.

To frame a unit of study featuring *Exit, Pursued by a Bear,* we suggest using essential questions for students to grapple with as they move through preparing, reading, and reacting to the novel. The following activities are intended to support students as they consider three essential questions:

- How are sports and athletes characterized in relation to sexual violence?
- How, if at all, does sports culture contribute to sexual violence and rape culture?
- How are sexual violence and rape culture perpetuated and/or disrupted in popular media?

Prior to Teaching the Novel

The foci of these prereading activities include addressing the terminology students will be asked to use when discussing the story as well as issues related to sexual violence and common practices related to victim blaming and rape myths. The activities are meant both to prepare students to grapple with the nuance involved in discussing sexual violence and to help them reflect on their own perspectives about the issue.

Teaching Terminology

An important first step to teaching Johnston's novel, or any young adult literature that includes scenes of sexual violence, is to have students define terminology associated with the issue and understand when to use specific words and concepts to describe disparate situations. Terminology we suggest includes victim, survivor, sexual assault, sexual battery, rape, rape culture, date rape, acquaintance rape, alcohol/drug-facilitated rape, commercial sexual exploitation, sexual harassment, incest, and stalking. RAINN (2023) and Stop Sexual Assault in Schools (SSAIS, 2023) are both reputable organizations that have definitions and resources that explain the nuance of this terminology, as well as when to use which concepts—such as using victim versus survivor—based on specific situations. We also suggest consulting your state's laws on sexual violence because different states have unique statutes using different terminology. We think it is important that students have this type of local knowledge about the legalities of the issue. For *Exit, Pursued by a Bear,* alcohol/drug-facilitated rape, victim, survivor, sexual harassment, and stalking are directly related to the story, so focusing on those words and concepts would be vital. Colantonio-Yurko et al. (2018) recommended that teachers use specific vocabulary strategies, rather than simply reviewing the terminology, so that students take the time to explore the words and concepts to deepen their understanding. One way to accomplish this goal is to have students read media stories about sexual violence and to make note of how different terminology is employed by professional journalists (Cleveland & Durand, 2014; Jackett, 2007). Other effective vocabulary strategies include concept maps and word boxes that ask students to record original definitions, determine relationships between different words, and identify examples and non-examples.

Discussing Victim Blaming and Rape Myths

Another step to take prior to beginning the novel is to discuss how victim blaming and rape myths contribute to rape culture in our society (Cleveland & Durand, 2014). As Colantonio-Yurko et al. (2018) reminded, "we must address and analyze the societal structures and systems that allow these myths and sayings to permeate society" (p. 5). As well, discussions around rape culture can help students reconsider their preconceived assumptions related to rape myths, which is particularly important for boys, who tend to have higher rates of RMA beliefs and attitudes (Malo-Juvera, 2014). One way to identify these assumptions is to complete an attitudinal survey, such as the Illinois Rape Myth Acceptance Scale (McMahon & Farmer, 2011; Thelan & Meadows, 2021), in which students indicate their level of agreement with statements related to victim blaming and rape myths. The results could be collected anonymously and reported out to small groups for discussion, followed by a whole-class conversation in which each small group shares what they discussed. We suggest anonymity at this stage to encourage honest answers and reflection when completing the survey. Then, it will be up to students to self-identify which statements they agreed or disagreed with during the small-group discussion and/or the whole-class conversation. The end goal would be to identify the statements on the survey that reflect more healthy viewpoints on sexual violence and victims of assault.

As Students Read the Novel

In general, we recommend that during-reading discussion activities begin in reading groups with membership determined by the teacher. Then, teachers can close discussions by bringing everyone together to share what they discussed and collect common perspectives about and reactions to Johnston's novel. Having difficult conversations in their reading groups first affords space for students to formulate and practice their responses before the whole-class discussion (Jackett, 2007). Additionally, Malo-Juvera (2014) recommended establishing a discussion protocol that included specific prompts for the reading groups to discuss in order to establish the focus of each small-group discussion. A possible protocol might include routines such as an initial share in which everyone voices a reaction to or opinion about what they have read since the last meeting, guidelines for how to "take" and "give" the floor, and procedures for who takes on the roles of leading the discussion, recording notes, and reporting out to the whole class. We also suggest the following prompts related to *Exit, Pursued by a Bear:*

- What personality traits help Hermione move from being a victim to being a survivor?
- What role does cheerleading play in the characters' lives as they grapple with trauma?
- What views of rape culture are presented in the story?

These groups could also follow the practices related to literature circles (Daniels, 2002), such as assigning roles to individual members to facilitate the discussion.

Reviewing Statistics on Sexual Violence

Once students begin reading *Exit, Pursued by a Bear,* we suggest sharing statistics on sexual violence in society and sports like those we presented previously. Again, RAINN and SSAIS keep updated statistics on their websites, and the US Department of Justice's Bureau of Justice Statistics also publishes regular reports on criminal victimization (see Morgan & Oudekerk, 2019, for a recent report). To address sports' and athletes' roles in the issue of sexual violence, viewing *The Hunting Ground* documentary (see "Options for Film Study") should help students see how athletes accused of perpetrating sexual violence have received preferential treatment from authorities. Sharing the statistics that point to the overrepresentation of athletes in cases of sexual violence on college campuses will also ground students in understanding how sports are involved in the issue. Then, to specifically focus on cheerleading, the sport depicted in Johnston's novel, teachers could ask students to read articles about the lives of NFL cheerleaders. For example, Belson (2018) detailed the lifestyle expectations of cheerleaders that include rules for how they dress, when they can take water breaks during games, and what content they can post to social media. As well, Macur and Branch (2018) shared stories from NFL cheerleaders about the rampant sexual harassment and rape culture they too often face.

Responding with Dual-Entry Reading Logs

While reading independently, students may also benefit from maintaining reading logs, records of their individual responses to the story, which will prepare them for their reading groups or literature circles. An effective strategy for a reading log is to use a dual-entry strategy, particularly when reading literature with scenes that could evoke strong emotional reactions. One way Mark Lewis, one of the authors of this book, has structured this type of reading log with his own students is to follow a protocol in which students record quotations from the novel that they deem important in the left-hand column. Then, in the right-hand column, they record what they "thought, wondered, felt" about each quotation (see Figure 7.1). In this way, the students embrace a co-character stance in which they connect their thoughts and emotions directly to the thoughts and emotions of the character (Lewis, 2014). Making these connections can work to raise the empathy that students have for Hermione as she grapples with her varied reactions and feelings in the aftermath of her attack.

Direct quotation from text	What I thought, wondered, felt
"I've never seen Polly's face so white. I've never felt this rough waking up, either. I can't remember what we did, why she's so worried, but it must be awful. I hope we don't get expelled. Also, I am going to vomit" (p. 51).	I felt horrible for Hermione, especially since she can't remember what happened at the party. I wondered if she will ever remember and if she would even want those memories to return.
"'I don't want to be afraid,' I say. 'You might have to be,' he says. 'But I have faith in you. You seem like the type who eats fear for breakfast'" (p. 147).	I thought that it was interesting how Dr. Hutt already understood Hermione's personality from only one therapy session. I felt glad that she had a good psychiatrist to talk to.

FIGURE 7.1: Dual-Entry Reading Log Example

Conducting Character Analyses

To deepen character analyses, we recommend students focus on the divergent ways different characters react to Hermione's rape and aftermath. Essential characters to include in the analysis are Polly, Leo, the entire cheerleading team, Hermione's parents, and Coach Caledon. For each reading group, teachers can assign one of these characters or a set of characters (e.g., the team or her parents). As part of their discussions, students collect scenes and moments when their assigned character reacts to or judges, either through words or actions, Hermione's tragic situation. We imagine a character log in which each student would record the page number of the scene, note the character's words or actions, and include the group's analysis for why the characters said or acted in the way they did (see Figure 7.2). Using a jigsaw protocol, teachers could then regroup the students so one representative from each reading group can share their character analysis, and all characters are discussed in the new groups.

Coach Caledon	
Character's words and actions	**Reading group analysis**
Caledon watches Hermione to make sure she doesn't have a panic attack when they begin discussing future practices. She wants to know if Hermione will quit but doesn't want to push her into making a quick decision (pp. 71–72).	Caledon treats her athletes as people rather than a means to an end. Some coaches would push Hermione to stay on the team because she is the best player and all the coach cares about is winning.
Caledon shares with Hermione the story of her own pregnancy at a young age (pp. 123–124).	Caledon rarely gets personal with her athletes but is willing when they need to hear a story that helps them with their own troubles.

FIGURE 7.2: Character Log Example

All of these formative assignments should include opportunities for students to think about their answers to the focal essential questions, so remind them daily to consider those questions when responding to discussion prompts and recording their ideas in each log. As well, these instructional activities should prepare students to complete the chosen culminating task.

Voices from the Field
Discussing Sexual Assault in the Classroom: A Difficult Necessity

Shannon McLeod Mound
English Teacher and Reading Specialist, Albemarle County Public Schools, Virginia

While teaching adolescents, it is important to recognize that many students have either been the victim or the perpetrator of some kind of sexual violence. Still, many educators are afraid of broaching the subject in the classroom. I myself have been discouraged by a supervising administrator from teaching the award-winning YA novel *Speak* by Laurie Halse Anderson (1999) because the book addresses sexual violence, though explicit details of rape in the novel are unspoken. Even with administrative support, some teachers fear backlash from parents for bringing the subject of sexual assault into the classroom. Yet the fact that the topic is often unaddressed in classrooms and other adult-monitored spaces puts young people at greater risk. The lack of open communication and education about sexual assault only leaves victims more ashamed, afraid, and stigmatized, and it leaves potential perpetrators in greater ignorance of what constitutes sexual assault and the lifelong harm such violations create.

Granted, sexual assault is difficult subject matter. For this reason, I like to bring my school social worker into the classroom for co-teaching support during such lessons. Frontloading the topic of sexual assault so that students have a common language, clear understanding of facts, and a chance to dispel misconceptions can lead to a safer, more productive environment in which to explore this topic in literature such as *Speak* (Anderson, 1999) or *Exit, Pursued by a Bear* (Johnston, 2016). As well, *Safe Dates* (Foshee, 2021) is an excellent program, introduced to me several years ago by my school's social worker. Safe Dates is a secondary school-based program intended to stop or prevent dating violence among teens. The program includes nine lessons centering on topics such as "Defining Caring Relationships," "Defining Dating Abuse," "Helping Friends," and "Preventing Sexual Assault." Before Hermione is the victim of sexual assault in the novel *Exit, Pursued by a Bear,* her relationship with fellow cheerleader and boyfriend Leo brings up concerns for the reader. They have an unhealthy dynamic that may raise red flags for some readers yet go unnoticed for readers unfamiliar with what makes a relationship healthy. Throughout the novel, Leo is possessive and controlling. He tries to pressure Hermione into sex by planting condoms in her bag after she has said she does not want to engage in intercourse, and he later shames her as a victim, as though her flirting with boys at camp brought on her sexual assault. All of these are perhaps more subtle symptoms of rape culture than rape itself, but they play into a norm of victimizing and shaming women that helps perpetuate sexual violence. Reading these passages in conjunction with Safe Dates lessons can help students discuss and better understand unhealthy relationship dynamics to help stop them.

When discussing traumatic experiences such as sexual assault with adolescents who may have dealt with the same, it is also important for teachers to connect students with resources for support. In addition to programs like *Safe Dates* and organizations like RAINN (2023) and Planned Parenthood (2023), support can also come in the form of students' personal allies. *Exit, Pursued by a Bear* is an excellent example of a novel depicting a sexual assault victim who has an array of supportive people in her life and chooses to seek them out. Reading the book provides an opportunity for students to reflect on the caring people in their lives they could safely reach out to in times of crisis. Young people often struggle to identify healthy relationships. So, discussions of not only healthy *romantic* relationships, through lessons like the ones provided in Safe Dates, but also healthy friendships and mentoring relationships are also important. Hermione cites many "superheroes" in the book: the people who helped her by providing emotional support, safeguarding her from secondary trauma, and seeking justice on her behalf, such as Polly, her parents, Officer Plummer, Coach Caledon, and even Reverend Rob. In her author's note, E. K. Johnston says it was important to her to provide a strong support system for her protagonist, which not all victims experience. Building on the concept of real-life "superheroes," teachers might consider pairing this text with an assignment in which students write about their own real-life superheroes. This could give students a chance to think about trusted allies in their lives to seek out in the event of such a violation or similar trauma. Ending the unit of study with a reflective personal writing assignment would also be a means of self-empowerment.

References

Anderson, L. H. (1999). *Speak*. Farrar, Straus and Giroux.

Foshee, V. (2021). *Safe dates: A teen relationship abuse prevention curriculum* (3rd ed.). Hazelden.

Johnston, E. K. (2016). *Exit, pursued by a bear*. Dutton Books for Young Readers.

Planned Parenthood. (2023). https://www.plannedparenthood.org/

Rape, Abuse & Incest National Network. (2023). https://www.rainn.org/

Shannon McLeod Mound has a B.A. in English Language and Literature from the University of Michigan and an M.Ed. in Literacy from James Madison University. She has been teaching in different capacities for over a decade: as a secondary English teacher, a youth slam poetry coach, a creative writing teacher, and an elementary reading specialist. She became a National Writing Project teacher consultant in 2013. She is the author of the collection Nature Trail Stories *(Thirty West Publishing, 2023) and the novella* Whimsy *(Long Day Press, 2021).*

Culminating Tasks after Reading the Novel

We believe it is important to create culminating tasks that ask students to address the essential questions of the unit, challenge their literacy skills and knowledge, and afford opportunities to be creative.

Creating Public Service Announcements

One possibility would be to assign each reading group to create a public service announcement (PSA) about sexual violence in sports culture. Each group could be given a different audience to target for their PSA so they can consider what specific messages they would want to include. For example, a PSA for first-year college football players would have different content than a PSA for an audience of coaches. To begin, teachers can provide PSAs for students to peruse, such as ones from RAINN's PSA library (2023), which include television, radio, and print examples. When showing examples, teachers might invite students to share what they noticed about the characteristics and the content of the PSAs, which will help them build familiarity with the genre, as Turner and Hicks (2016) advised. Then, students would need time to explore different video-making, audio-recording, and/or graphic-designing platforms so they can become comfortable using the technology. We suggest requiring each group to submit a script for their PSA, providing time parameters for the length of the PSA (for video and radio formats), and asking students to independently write a brief reflection explaining how their PSA accounts for one or more of the essential questions. To both encourage and support students to take action, teachers can organize a screening night for parents and community members and/or find outlets to distribute the students' PSAs.

Writing Multimodal, Hypertext Essays

Another appropriate summative assignment is an inquiry-based multimodal, hypertext essay (Lutkewitte, 2013) in which students address one or more essential questions in relation to a specific topic related to sexual violence. This type of essay asks students to include images and hyperlinks throughout to resemble more of a website than a traditional essay, which supports students to practice employing the viewing and visually representing domains of literacy in addition to the traditional domains of reading and writing. For example, multimodal projects include several modes of communicating a message. While a traditional essay usually uses text as a single mode, a multimodal project would include a combination of text, images, motion, and/or audio. Also, hypertext essays include text linked to either internal or external resources that augment the arguments, claims, ideas, and/or opinions stated in the text. These links can send the reader to an internal section of the essay (e.g., link an in-text citation to the bibliographic citation in the reference section) or to an external resource (e.g., a website). Writers should intentionally use these links to direct readers how to engage with the content of the essay. Finally, students could also insert images that are "clickable" to take the reader to the image's original internet-based source, or the hyperlinked URL could be included below the image as a caption.

Each student would choose a research topic for their inquiry related to the essential questions. Possible topics include researching incidents of sexual violence in middle and high school, college, and/or professional sports programs; investigating how rape victims and perpetrators are often treated by the police, defense attorneys, and district prosecutors; evaluating several safety and prevention programs conducted at the middle and high school level and at the college level; and analyzing the efficacy of the various policies of professional sports organizations aimed at curbing and penalizing athletes who are accused and/or convicted of sexual misconduct, assault, or violence. The final product would include links to relevant websites related to their topic and research, as well as inserted images with captions to enhance the narrative. Due to the content of these essays and relevant resources, it would be important for teachers to discuss appropriate content from the resources students should include in their essays and provide some examples of resources to use, such as those from RAINN and SSAIS.

CONCLUSION

In conjunction with reading E. K. Johnston's (2016) *Exit, Pursued by a Bear,* these literacy-based activities give students multiple opportunities to grapple with the unit's essential questions as well as their own perspectives about sexual violence and rape culture in sports and society. The hope is that after experiencing this curriculum, youth would have reasoned reactions to stories about athletes engaged in sexual violence, assault, and harassment.

Options for Book Clubs

Teachers looking to facilitate book clubs in which students explore issues related to sexual violence can incorporate *Exit, Pursued by a Bear* alongside titles like the following:

Canary (Alpine, 2013)
Kate's father is the basketball coach at an elite prep school, and she starts dating one of the players. The basketball team feels entitled because the town residents place them on pedestals. For example, they host alcohol-infused parties that the police ignore. When another player on the team begins sexually harassing Kate, nothing is done to intervene or protect her due to his privileged status, so his harassment eventually leads to assault.

Speak (Anderson, 1999)
Anderson's award-winning novel remains a bestseller and there is now a twentieth-anniversary edition and a graphic novel adaptation. The protagonist, Melinda, is assaulted, which leads to her self-isolation, and she stops speaking in response to the trauma. This selection provides an option that is not sports-related.

Swagger (Deuker, 2013)
Due to his father's change in jobs, Jonas Dolan must move to a new city and school and away from his championship-level basketball team. He quickly befriends Levi Rawdon, a member of the basketball team at his new high school, and hopes Levi can help him not only make the team but also earn a college basketball scholarship. Levi's personality shifts and his performance on the court declines after he is sexually abused by a trusted adult.

Inexcusable (Lynch, 2005)
Keir is a high school football star who believes he is a "good guy." Yet he refuses to take responsibility for his actions. On the football field, he horribly injures an opponent with a questionable hit. Off the football field, he is infatuated with Gigi, and one night when her boyfriend does not show up, Keir allegedly assaults her. Lynch's story slowly reveals the truth, keeping the reader guessing exactly what happened until the end of the novel.

Options for Film Study

Teachers looking to incorporate film study to help students explore issues related to sexual violence can consider the following options:

Athlete A (Cohen & Shenk, 2020)
This documentary addresses the sexual abuse endured by female gymnasts at the hands of Larry Nassar, a doctor for USA Gymnastics, and the investigative reporting that broke the story. Focusing on Nassar and other adults who failed so many young gymnasts, as opposed to abuses carried out by athletes, the film offers another angle for consideration as students explore the intersections of sports culture and sexual violence.

The Hunting Ground (Dick, 2015)
Although controversial and criticized for its portrayal of certain colleges (see Yoffe, 2015, for a critical review), this documentary focuses on the story of two victims who filed a Title IX complaint for how their university handled their sexual assault cases. It explores how university administrators handle cases involving athletes differently than cases involving non-athletes. It also shares stories of men who are victims of sexual assault, which are reported at an even lower rate than incidents of violence against women.

#MeToo, Now What? (Kim & Hayward, 2018)
In this five-part PBS series, host Zainab Salbi examines how our society enables sexual harassment in the workplace, ways our society views women, problems with hyper-masculinity, and determining possible solutions. The series also asks viewers how best to bring men into the discussion so that women are not solely responsible for change.

Roll Red Roll (Schwartzman, 2018)
This award-winning documentary examines the "boys will be boys" culture that contributes to the normalization of sexual violence. The film focuses specifically on the rape of a teenage girl in Steubenville, Ohio, a crime that was perpetrated by members of the local high school football team, and the collusion of teens and adults—including teachers, administrators, parents, and coaches—that followed. In the classroom, the film stands to support critical questioning of rape culture, popular notions of masculinity, and the prioritization of male athletes over others in schools and society.

Young Adult Literature

Alpine, R. (2013). *Canary.* Medallion Press.

Anderson, L. H. (1999). *Speak.* Farrar, Straus and Giroux.

Deuker, C. (2013). *Swagger.* Houghton Mifflin Harcourt.

Draper, S. (2006). *Copper sun.* Atheneum Books for Young Readers.

Johnston, E. K. (2016). *Exit, pursued by a bear.* Dutton Books.

Lynch, C. (2005). *Inexcusable.* Atheneum Books for Young Readers.

Other Texts for Classroom Use

Cohen, B., & Shenk, J. (Directors). (2020). *Athlete A* [Film]. Actual Films.

Dick, K. (Director). (2015). *The hunting ground* [Film]. The Weinstein Company.

Kim, G., & Hayward, S. (Executive Producers). (2018). *#MeToo, now what?* [TV series]. PBS.

Schwartzman, N. (Director). (2018). *Roll red roll* [Film]. Sunset Park Pictures.

REFERENCES

Balingit, M. (2020, October 15). Sexual assault reports sharply increased at K–12 schools, numbering nearly 15,000, Education Department data shows. *The Washington Post.* https://www.washingtonpost.com/education/2020/10/15/sexual-assault-k-12-schools/

Beaver, W. (2019). College athletes and sexual assault. *Society, 56*(6), 620–624.

Belson, K. (2018, April 2). No sweatpants in public: Inside the rule books for N.F.L. cheerleaders. *The New York Times.* https://www.nytimes.com/2018/04/02/sports/nfl-cheerleaders.html

Cantor, D., Fisher, B., Chibnall, S., Harps, S., & Townsend, R. (2020). *Report on the AAU campus climate survey on sexual assault and sexual misconduct.* Association of American Universities. https://www.aau.edu/sites/default/files/AAU-Files/Key-Issues/Campus-Safety/Revised%20Aggregate%20report%20%20and%20appendices%201-7_(01-16-2020_FINAL).pdf

Charles, A. (2019). Sexual assault and its impacts in young adult literature. *Criterion: A Journal of Literary Criticism, 12*(2), 97–103.

Cleveland, E., & Durand, E. S. (2014). Critical representations of sexual assault in young adult literature. *The Looking Glass: New Perspectives on Children's Literature, 17*(3). https://ojs.latrobe.edu.au/ojs/index.php/tlg/article/view/545

Colantonio-Yurko, K. C., Miller, H. C., & Cheveallier, J. (2018). "But she didn't scream": Teaching about sexual assault in young adult literature. *Journal of Language & Literacy Education, 14*(1), 1–16.

Coleman, M. (2021, March 26). Here's what we know about the lawsuits facing Deshaun Watson. *Sports Illustrated.* https://www.si.com/nfl/2021/03/26/deshaun-watson-tony-buzbee-lawsuits-summary

Crosset, T., Benedict, J., & McDonald, M. (1995). Male student-athletes reported for sexual assault: A survey of campus police departments and judicial affairs offices. *Journal of Sport & Social Issues, 19*(2), 126–140.

Daniels, H. (2002). *Literature circles: Voice and choice in book clubs & reading groups.* Stenhouse Publishers.

DeMatteo, D., Galloway, M., Arnold, S., & Patel, U. (2015). Sexual assault on college campuses: A 50-state survey of criminal sexual assault statutes and their relevance to campus sexual assault. *Psychology, Public Policy, and Law, 21*(3), 227–238.

Diaz, J. (2021, October 28). *Kyle Beach reveals he is the player suing the Chicago Blackhawks over sex assault.* NPR. https://www.npr.org/2021/10/28/1049910345/kyle-beach-reveals-chicago-blackhawks-coach-assaulted-him

Draper, K. (2022, October 3). Report details "systemic" abuse of players in women's soccer. *The New York Times.* https://www.nytimes.com/2022/10/03/sports/soccer/us-soccer-abuse-nwsl.html

Grant, B. J., Wilkerson, S. B., Pelton, d., Cosby, A., & Henschel, M. (2017). *A case study of K–12 school employee sexual misconduct: Lessons learned from Title IX policy implementation.* National Institute of Justice. https://www.ncjrs.gov/pdffiles1/nij/grants/252484.pdf

Green, L. (2018, February 5). *#MeToo: Future impact on sexual harassment litigation involving schools, athletic programs.* National Federation of State High School Associations. https://www.nfhs.org/articles/metoo-future-impact-on-sexual-harassment-litigation-involving-schools-athletic-programs/

Jackett, M. (2007). Something to *Speak* about: Addressing sensitive issues through literature. *English Journal, 96*(4), 102–105.

Jacoby, K. (2019, December 16). College athletes more likely to be disciplined for sex assault. *USA Today.* https://www.usatoday.com/in-depth/news/investigations/2019/12/12/ncaa-athletes-more-likely-disciplined-sex-assault/4379153002/

Lewis, M. A. (2014). Co-characters in an immigration story: Sixth grade students' narrative interpretations of literature and life. *Middle Grades Research Journal, 9*(1), 19–34.

Lutkewitte, C. (2013). *Multimodal composition: A critical sourcebook.* Bedford/St. Martin's.

Lyndon, A. E., Duffy, D. M., Smith, P. H., & White, J. W. (2011). The role of high school coaches in helping prevent adolescent sexual aggression: Part of the solution or part of the problem? *Journal of Sport and Social Issues, 35*(4), 377–399.

Macur, J., & Branch, J. (2018, April 10). Pro cheerleaders say groping and sexual harassment are part of the job. *The New York Times.* https://www.nytimes.com/2018/04/10/sports/cheerleaders-nfl.html

Malo-Juvera, V. (2014). *Speak:* The effect of literacy instruction on adolescents' rape myth acceptance. *Research in the Teaching of English, 48*(4), 407–427.

Markus, N., Brown, A., Reynolds, C., & Bhardwaj, D. (2023, July 8). Former NU football player details hazing allegations after coach suspension. *The Daily Northwestern.* https://dailynorthwestern.com/2023/07/08/top-stories/former-nu-football-player-details-hazing-allegations-after-coach-suspension/

McCray, K. L. (2019). Sexual assault and intercollegiate athletes. In W. O'Donohue & P. Schewe (Eds.), *Handbook of sexual assault and sexual assault prevention* (pp. 733–744). Springer.

McMahon, S., & Farmer, G. L. (2011). An updated measure for assessing subtle rape myths. *Social Work Research, 35*(2), 71–81.

Morgan, R., & Oudekerk, B. (2019). *Criminal victimization, 2018.* Bureau of Justice Statistics. https://www.bjs.gov/content/pub/pdf/cv18.pdf

Pennepacker, P. (2019, September 17). *Proposed Title IX regulations: Effect on K–12 schools.* National Federation of State High School Associations. https://www.nfhs.org/articles/proposed-title-ix-regulations-effect-on-k-12-schools/

Rape, Abuse & Incest National Network. (2023). *Public service announcements.* https://www.rainn.org/PSAs

———. (2023). *Victims of sexual violence: Statistics.* https://www.rainn.org/statistics/victims-sexual-violence

Stop Sexual Assault in Schools. (2023). https://stopsexualassaultinschools.org/

Suarez, E., & Gadalla, T. M. (2010). Stop blaming the victim: A meta-analysis on rape myths. *Journal of Interpersonal Violence, 25*(11), 2010–2035.

Thelan, A. R., & Meadows, E. A. (2021). The Illinois rape myth acceptance scale—subtle version: Using an adapted measure to understand the declining rates of rape myth acceptance. *Journal of Interpersonal Violence, 37*(19–20), NP17807–NP17833. https://doi.org/10.1177/08862605211030013

Turner, K. H., & Hicks, T. (2016). *Argument in the real world: Teaching adolescents to read and write digital texts.* Heinemann.

Yoffe, E. (2015, June 1). *How* The hunting ground *blurs the truth.* Slate. https://slate.com/news-and-politics/2015/06/the-hunting-ground-a-closer-look-at-the-influential-documentary-reveals-the-filmmakers-put-advocacy-ahead-of-accuracy.html

Young, B-R., Desmarais, S. L., Baldwin, J. A., & Chandler, R. (2017). Sexual coercion practices among undergraduate male recreational athletes, intercollegiate athletes, and non-athletes. *Violence Against Women, 23*(7), 795–812.

Yung, C. R. (2015). Concealing campus sexual assault: An empirical examination. *Psychology, Public Policy, and Law, 21*(1), 1–9.

8

Grappling with Death and Dying through Sports

I'd lost all hope of seeing any of my family alive again. There was no god for me anymore.

—*Harry Haft,* The Boxer *(Kleist, 2014, p. 44)*

For Hertzko (Harry) Haft, life as a Jewish child and teenager in 1930s Poland was difficult. His father died when he was a boy, forcing his family to split for financial reasons, so he watched his sisters move away. At school, he experienced antisemitism, which was rampant before the Second World War. Harry was fourteen when the Germans invaded Poland, and he quickly became a smuggler, carrying banned goods across the border into the "occupied zone," even getting shot on one of his excursions. Eventually, he joined millions of other Jews interned in Nazi concentration camps, where he was forced to fight to the death in boxing matches to entertain German officers. As he expresses in this chapter's epigraph, due to all the loss he had endured, Harry lost hope in both ever seeing his family again and his religious faith. Clearly, Harry witnessed death and dying throughout his life, and it is a focal theme of *The Boxer: The True Story of Holocaust Survivor Harry Haft,* Reinhard Kleist's (2014) graphic biography.

Though central to Kleist's (2014) award-winning story and other works of Holocaust literature, death and dying is not reserved for wartime genocide; it is a part of life. Consider the following stories about the death of athletes in and outside the arena:

- Four NCAA women athletes died by suicide in the first half of 2022, stressing ongoing mental health issues amongst college athletes (Darnay, 2022; Dodd, 2022).
- A Connecticut high school hockey player died from an on-ice collision during an interscholastic game (Helsel, 2022).

- Nine people died, including seven members of the University of the Southwest's golf teams returning home from a tournament, when their team passenger van was hit by a truck (Mayer, 2022).
- A University of Utah football player was shot and killed less than one year after a former teammate also died in a gun-related incident (Bonagura, 2021).

In all of these stories, we not only read about the tragedy of those who died but also about how the communities, families, friends, and teammates dealt with their ensuing grief. Death and grief affect us all, so talking about these issues with youth is not only important but inevitable for secondary teachers. This instructional unit incorporating *The Boxer* provides one avenue for such discussions.

THE SOCIAL CONCERN OF DEATH AND DYING

Death is omnipresent. We might not think about it from moment to moment, but it is there, and it often reminds us of its presence unexpectedly. The sudden death of a loved one is perhaps the most jarring. Or, as the COVID-19 pandemic reminded everyone in the early 2020s, death and dying can move to the forefront of most everyone's thoughts on a daily basis. The issue, then, is not how to avoid death and dying; rather, it is how to grapple with its omnipresence and the ensuing grief a death might cause.

By August 2023, over three years into the COVID-19 pandemic, almost seven million people had died from the disease (World Health Organization, 2023). This massive amount of death is not something we have seen, either nationally or globally since the 1918–1919 flu pandemic, and there have been consequences spanning from the economic and political spheres to communal health. For individuals and societies, one of the most important consequences has been finding ways to productively grieve for this extreme loss of life and honor those who died. Hauser (2022) outlined some of the ways people tried to address their grief, including a memorial of over 700,000 white flags surrounding the Washington Monument, the half-mile of painted hearts along the River Thames in London, and over 46,000 white remembrance ribbons installed outside a church in Bedfordview, South Africa. These memorials served as more than symbols of an event; rather, each flag, heart, and ribbon was the memory of an individual whom someone loved. And, for the still-evolving memorial along the River Thames, when another heart is added, it is a reminder that the tragedy is ongoing.

Educators and other adults who work directly with children must recognize the impact the pandemic continues to have on children and youth. In August 2022, the Imperial College of London estimated that 263,000 children in the US had lost a primary or secondary caregiver during the pandemic. The US has not seen this amount of caregiver loss since the AIDS crisis in the 1980s (Kamenetz, 2022). Teachers need to be prepared to support students as they grieve because tragedies will continue to happen. We hope this instructional unit for *The Boxer* provides one way to begin addressing this concern.

Voices from the Field
Death and Grief in the Classroom

Erin Denby
Former Classroom Teacher,
Fluvanna County Public Schools, Palmyra, VA

One hundred percent of the human population will die at some point in their lives. This is an unavoidable fact. Of the hundreds of thousands of children's and young adult books, only a small percentage of them discusses the very human process of dying and, depending on the depth of love, the grief that follows. In 2022, one in thirteen people under the age of eighteen will experience the death of a parent or sibling (Judi's House, 2023). Classroom teachers everywhere strive to connect to all their students because the best learning comes from strong relationships. Shared experiences are one way we can connect with others; therefore, one might assume that the most certain and final human experience, death, would lend itself to making connections. However, when faced with teaching about and through a death experience, fewer than one in ten teachers say they are prepared to deal with the conversations, behaviors, and coping strategies that young people can experience with the death of a loved one (Heath, 2017). Statistics suggest that teachers, whether they are comfortable or not, will be forced to create relationships with grieving students. Because of teachers' access to children, they can come alongside students who are grieving and provide support, insight, and compassion for their grief, as well as provide examples of the growth that can occur through the grieving process.

Children's and young adult literature is an effective way to reach and help the children who have experienced bereavement and to normalize the human experience of grief. However, young adult literature does not always tell a representative story of death and grief (Heath, 2017), so teachers' discernment when choosing what literature to share with youth is important and can play a crucial role by helping inexperienced grievers create an understanding of their grief and facilitate post-traumatic growth. Books that successfully deal with death and grief include the reasons for grief, the emotions of grief, the time grieving takes, and the growth that can happen to the griever. I suggest that teachers use their school's counselor and the child's at-home supports when dealing with a recent loss or an acute grief situation. Hospice facilities can also provide recommendations and supports.

In Waves, AJ Dungo's 2019 graphic memoir, uses the historical evolution of surfing to explore his own grief and growth during the terminal illness and death of his girlfriend. Dungo explains and shares his own adaptive coping strategies, such as remembrance and receiving emotional support from others when facing the loss of a loved one, which teachers could discuss with students. Mirra (2018) reminds us that grief can take many forms and not only involve the commonly expressed emotions of sadness, tears, and depression, but a whole range of other acceptable emotions. Teachers can introduce students to universal tasks of grieving, including accepting, processing, adjusting, and remembering (Worden, 2018), and can invite students to take them up through reading, responding in conversations, and writing. Following Mirra, I argue that teachers have a responsibility to allow students the opportunity to examine and express their losses and create opportunities for others to share empathy for their classmates.

Dungo's memoir shows that the process of grieving can start before someone we love dies. Many deaths are due to prolonged illnesses and are not sudden at all. The opportunity to grieve with an individual who is dying is a chance to process personal grief but also to support the dying. Sharing ways that young adults can help their dying loved ones can be valuable to their own grief tasks. Helping someone who is dying can involve providing physical support, but it may also include writing letters, songs, or poems and remembering with or retelling stories to the dying.

Literature and writing can remind us all, even if we haven't experienced loss, that grief can be an isolating experience because of the uniqueness of each person's relationship with the deceased. We know, too, that "loss is a difficult topic to write about but is one that invites personal, authentic writing" (Witte & Dail, 2021, p. 39). Death and loss are also full-body sensory experiences. Therefore, using our senses to process grief can help us through the devastation. The action of writing and drawing can be a release for the body. Crafting poems, lyrics, letters, or prose, and, in Dungo's case, drawing and creating graphics attend to the physical nature of death and grief.

Creating a curriculum to introduce and respond to the topic of death and grief is difficult, but with gentle, grace-filled, and discriminating book choices and reader-response activities, we can address the final chapter of every life with love and dignity.

References

Dungo, AJ. (2019). *In waves*. Nobrow.

Heath, M. (2017). Grief-themed literature for elementary school children. *The Utah Journal of Literacy*, *20*(1), 5–14.

Judi's House. (2023). *Childhood bereavement estimation model*. Judi's House/JAG Institute. https://judishouse.org/research-tools/cbem/

Mirra, N. (2018). *Educating for empathy: Literacy learning and civic engagement*. Teachers College Press.

Witte, S., & Dail, J. S. (2021). "The grief that fills one's heart": Pairing loss narratives and graphic young adult literature. In N. Sieben & S. A. Shelton (Eds.), *Humanizing grief in higher education: Narratives of allyship and hope* (pp. 38–48). Routledge.

Worden, J. W. (2018). *Grief counseling and grief therapy: A handbook for the mental health practitioner* (5th ed.). Springer.

Erin Denby is mother to two daughters, Kara (11) and Sadie (9), widow to Ty, businesswoman, former teacher, and Master of Education candidate at James Madison University. Through her grief journey, she has read and listened to thousands of words regarding death and grief that have brought comfort and inspiration and taught her that grief is the price we pay for love.

DEATH AND DYING IN SPORTS

Frequently, death and dying in sports is sudden, as the examples opening this chapter indicate. This suddenness tends to be more jarring when the athlete is actively playing, which communicates a sense of overall health and wellness, than when the public knows that an athlete, often older and retired, is ill. When a sudden death occurs in sports, players, fans, and organizations tend to celebrate the athlete through various forms of mourning, from attending a memorial to wearing armbands to building statues. Sometimes the circumstances around an athlete's death result in national mourning, such as in the US when MLB player Lou Gehrig died in 1941 and the country was enduring the Second World War or when a national icon like Argentine soccer star Diego Maradona died in 2020. Media outlets respond with their own version of memorials, often in the form of a video essay narrated by a sportswriter while images of the athlete reaching achievements in the arena play on the screen. In contemporary society, messages of mourning are posted across social media outlets, building a digital memorial honoring the athlete.

Any discussion on death, dying, and grief in sports is not complete without consideration of the Holocaust, for many Jewish athletes lost their lives during that horrific event. In an appendix, *The Boxer* includes a report by Martin Krauss about "Boxing in Concentration Camps" (pp. 185–193), in which he briefly shares the stories of other boxers who fought—and died—while interned. Survivors also engaged in sports while living in the "displaced persons" camps that served as transitional spaces after liberation at the end of the Second World War. Soccer and boxing were the two most prominent sports, and Krauss quotes journalist Eric Friedler to answer the question on why boxing was so popular: The boxer was "'for many people an image of the rekindled Jewish strength and therefore became a symbol for a future life in dignity and freedom'" (p. 193). In this way, Harry Haft's story is a memorial for the millions of Jews killed, so using his story to support youth in grappling with death, dying, and grief continues to honor Harry's life and the countless lives lost in the Holocaust.

FOCAL YA TEXT: *THE BOXER* BY REINHARD KLEIST

Hertzko (Harry) Haft was sixteen years old when he was interned in Auschwitz by the Nazis for being a Polish Jew. As Kleist (2014) illustrates in his biography, Harry endures personal tragedy—he witnesses his baby niece murdered by a German soldier, and he is separated from his fiancée—along with communal tragedy of the persecution of his fellow Jews. Harry makes difficult decisions to survive in captivity, including agreeing to search dead internees for valuables and trading them to one of the Schutzstaffel (SS) officers, Schneider, for privileges that other internees do not receive, such as whiskey, easier work, and extra rations. Schneider, recognizing Harry's strength and will to survive, turns him into a boxer to fight in a series of death matches for the amusement of other Nazi officers. Harry eventually escapes, posing as a German officer, but he ends up killing a man during the process, another forced decision of violence that haunts Harry for the rest of his life. After the Second World War ends, Harry immigrates to the US and becomes a successful professional boxer, wearing proudly on his boxing gear the same Jewish star he was forced to don in the concentration camps. He also uses his fame to search for and briefly reunite with the fiancée he lost during the war. However, Harry is never able to shed the atrocities he experienced in the camps and during the war, and the long-lasting effects of what he endured continue to impact his familial relationships throughout his life. Kleist details Harry's experiences with death and dying in stark imagery, providing readers graphic insight into the Holocaust and its horrors.

The Boxer was listed as a 2015 YALSA Great Graphic Novels for Teens and has received positive public reception, including starred reviews from *Publishers Weekly* and *Library Journal.* Kleist and his graphic biography were also honored with the Deutscher Jugendliteraturpreis (German Youth Literature Award) for nonfiction, which is Germany's premier award for children's and young adult literature, and the Best German Book at the 2013 Munich Comic Festival.

INCORPORATING *THE BOXER* INTO THE SECONDARY ELA CLASSROOM

Teaching about the Second World War and the Holocaust has long been addressed in secondary education, both in English language arts and social studies classrooms, and the breadth of resources are too numerous to review in a single chapter. For teachers interested in including *The Boxer* in an instructional unit with this focus, we suggest reviewing the teaching ideas and instructional resources provided by the US Holocaust Memorial Museum (2023) and Bosmajian (2002).

Beyond teaching about the Second World War and the Holocaust, which are topics not to be ignored, our focus for this literature unit is on the sociopolitical topic of death and dying. Therefore, three essential questions guide the following instructional tasks for incorporating *The Boxer* into the secondary ELA classroom:

- How is death and dying discussed in our society?
- What does Harry Haft's story reveal about death and grieving?
- How can we support ourselves and others to grapple with grief?

From a culturally responsive pedagogical perspective, it is essential to recognize that students grow up within different cultural spaces and, therefore, will hold divergent traditions and beliefs related to death and dying practices. A way to honor this broad diversity is for teachers to provide an overview of death and dying practices from around the world. During this overview, teachers could include opportunities for students to share their particular cultural and familial traditions but should not require students to do so in order to both honor their privacy and to avoid singling them out as "representative" of a particular tradition, which could be construed as tokenism. It would also be important for teachers to communicate with students' parents and guardians about the focus of this literature unit to ensure that all traditions are honored and that no single tradition is privileged as "better" or "correct." Student-friendly resources include Kerrigan's (2017) *The History of Death* and Applebury's (2020) review of traditions. Teachers could create rotating stations for students to explore these resources.

However, in our contemporary global society, children no longer solely learn about death and dying through parental communication or direct experiences. Media portrayals are also prominent, such as focused episodes on children's programming like *Sesame Street* and media reports broadcast on television or online (Longbottom & Slaughter, 2018). Reading about death and dying in children's and young adult literature in K–12 classrooms is another common medium through which youth learn about this topic (Lewis, 2018; Rossi & Lewis, 2021; Šubrtová, 2009). Moreover, not only are youth not shielded from stories about death and dying, they are also quite capable of discussing such topics with respect and often display hope during such conversations. The activities included in this chapter begin with this assumption about youth's capability for complex conversations about death and dying.

Prior to Teaching the Biography

There are many distinctive aspects of *The Boxer* for teachers to address before exploring Harry Haft's story with students. First, his story is told in graphic form, so students who have not had prior experiences with this medium will need preparation for fully comprehending graphic literature. We suggest teachers consider using activities we share in Chapter 4 with *Spinning* (Walden,

2017), including "identifying artistic features in graphic novels" and "image and metaphor sketch journals," as part of a literature unit on *The Boxer.* Second, Kleist is a biographer who employs particular literary elements in telling Harry's story, some of which are unique to nonfiction and some which are similar to fiction. Finally, this story focuses on death, dying, and grieving, so students will need to be prepared for reading about and sensitively discussing this sociopolitical issue. The following two activities are aimed at addressing these latter aspects of *The Boxer.*

Defining Nonfiction Elements

For students who are unfamiliar with reading nonfiction, reviewing the similarities and differences between fiction and nonfiction can be a useful prereading activity. As well, there are two primary types of nonfiction—informational and literary—so comparing and contrasting these two types along with fiction might also be helpful for students. Taking this step is particularly useful when students are exploring "science-based" fiction that provides a large amount of factual scientific information, such as in *The Way of the Hive* (Hosler, 2021). This story follows the life of an anthropomorphized honeybee, so it is fiction, but some students might label it nonfiction because the author includes a large amount of biological information about bees. We suggest beginning with a classroom brainstorm in which students can add ideas about the features of each. For example, teachers could divide the whiteboard into three columns: one for fiction, one for informational nonfiction, and one for literary nonfiction. After thinking about elements or characteristics of each, students can then take turns adding their ideas to the corresponding columns on the whiteboard. A whole-class discussion could follow with the teacher highlighting accurate features of each type by underlining or circling students' contributions.

Then, teachers can provide small groups of students with (a) a compare/contrast chart that resembles the three columns on the whiteboard and includes definitions of the three types and (b) three books, each an example of one of the three types. For this study on a graphic biography, we suggest using graphic versions of each text. Figure 8.1 provides some possible options with key elements and definitions of fiction, informational nonfiction, and literary nonfiction. Students can use the examples to identify features of each type of text, completing their own compare/contrast charts. These group-generated charts can be posted in the classroom for future reference as students read *The Boxer.*

Type	Definition	Elements, Features, and Characteristics	Graphic Novel Options for Analysis
Fiction	A story that has been created by the author that does not refer to any actual people or event. A story with fictionalized or anthropomorphized characters that relates factual information.	Epigraph and Acknowledgments Characters Setting Plot Dialogue Author Bio	*The Way of the Hive* (Hosler, 2021) *The Magic Fish* (Nguyen, 2020)
Informational Nonfiction	A collection of facts about people and events told to relay information.	Table of Contents Diagrams, Tables, Graphs, and Figures Terminology and Definitions References and Resources Author Bio	*Brief Histories of Everyday Objects* (Warner, 2016) *This Land Is My Land* (Warner & Dam, 2019)
Literary Nonfiction	A story about real people and actual events told to entertain.	Characters Setting Plot Historical Accuracy Realistic Events Terminology and Definitions References and Resources Author Bio	*I Was Their American Dream* (Gharib, 2019) *Astronauts* (Ottaviani, 2020)

FIGURE 8.1: Fiction and Nonfiction Elements

Exploring Death, Dying, and Grief

As we have suggested with sociopolitical issues discussed across other chapters, providing time for a school counselor or other professional to visit the classroom and discuss death, dying, and grief could be a vital first step prior to teaching *The Boxer* or any literary story with this thematic focus. We also suggest reviewing resources from the National Association of School Psychologists (2015) and Schonfeld and Quackenbush (2021) that outline specific steps for discussing death with youth and supporting grieving students, including being straightforward with language (rather than relying on euphemisms), acknowledging but not forcing students to express their feelings, and offering supports such as alternative instructional tasks. Mark Lewis, one of the authors of this book, shared how he used "affective response journals" to discuss grief in Chapter 5, and we would suggest using the same activity in this literature unit.

Another way Mark has explored grief with older students is to analyze scenes from the award-winning illustrated novel *A Monster Calls* (Ness, 2011). In the story, Conor O'Malley's mother is dying of cancer, and he is moving through typical emotions related to grief, including denial, anger, bargaining, depression, and acceptance. The "monster" is a yew tree that comes to life and visits Conor, mostly when he is acutely grieving and expressing one (or more) of these emotions, and it uses three tales (see pp. 52–64, 99–110, and 146–152) to help Conor understand what he is feeling and experiencing in response to his mother dying. Ness's novel was adapted for film (see "Options for Film Study"), and Mark uses excerpts from that adaptation for this activity. (The film adaptations of the three tales are readily available through online video-streaming services.) After reviewing the definitions of each emotion and how they are related to grief, along with a brief synopsis of Conor's story, students view the film version of each tale, stopping to write a quick response to the following prompts:

- What message about death and dying is the monster trying to communicate to Conor?
- What feelings related to grief is Conor experiencing?

Once students have viewed all three tales and finished their written responses, they can share their thoughts within small groups prior to a whole-class discussion about the two prompts. The aim of the discussion is for students to understand that there are not "good" or "bad" ways to react to death and dying nor "appropriate" ways to grieve. Teachers can then conclude the discussion with a preview of *The Boxer* and ask students to identify the ways Harry experiences death and dying, and expresses his grief, as they read.

As Students Read the Biography

These two during-reading activities are aimed at supporting students' overall comprehension of the graphic biography and developing their answers to the second essential question focusing on what Harry's story reveals about death, dying, and grief.

Responding through Duo-Journals

The Boxer is graphic in two senses of the word: Kleist shares Harry's story through illustrations, and he vividly depicts the violence Harry experiences. Openly discussing reactions to such violence can be difficult for many readers, so teachers need to provide safer spaces for students to engage and express their reactions. One way to provide a safer space is through writing because of the distance it provides between the author and the audience. Another way teachers can build safety is to pair students with "trust buddies" or dyads in which both partners can rely on each other to maintain privacy and not to ridicule or demean the other's thoughts, opinions, beliefs, or ideas. Of course, teachers need to have an acute understanding of students' relationships to create these dyads successfully. For the "duo-journal" activity, teachers identify student dyads and collect a set of materials for each dyad, including two journaling notebooks and two writing utensils of different colors.

To introduce the ongoing reader-response activity, teachers explain that the students will work in a partnership to share their reactions to Harry's story through the use of a "duologue and duotone journal" or a "duo-journal." Most likely, students will need a definition for the journal title. Teachers can explain that this specific type of journal is both a duologue, or a conversation exclusively held between two individuals, and a duotone, or an artistic creation that only uses two colors. After explaining the definition of the duo-journal, teachers identify the student dyads and ask students to find a shared space to write in the classroom. Students then select their writing utensil color and if they would use the left-hand or right-hand page of the open notebook. At this point, teachers can outline the parameters of using the duo-journal:

- Each partner only uses their side of the notebook and writes/draws in their chosen color in every duo-journal entry.
- Each partner should both share their reactions to the story and respond to their partners' reactions.
- Duo-journal entries should include both writing and drawing.
- Each partner should complete every duo-journal entry begun by the other partner.
- Partners should share the responsibility of starting new duo-journal entries.
- Partners agree to maintain privacy of their journal's content.

We recommend teachers reinforce the final parameter about privacy to establish the journal as a safer space to share personal reactions to the content of *The Boxer.* It is also important for teachers to remind students that they will also read their journal entries and that they must follow mandatory reporting guidelines for all teachers. The first task for students could be to create a cover for their duo-journals. The cover design could include both students' stylized names, self-portraits, and/or boxing-related images. For students hesitant to add their own drawings, teachers can mitigate those hesitations by encouraging the use of "stick figures," symbology, shapes, arrows, etc. It is important to remind students that only two colors can be used in their cover creation and that each partner should use their assigned color for their names and depictions. This duotone approach is meant to provide a visual distinction between the two student-writers, and it will be used again in the other during-reading activity included in this chapter.

Teachers can decide how often they want students to complete a duo-journal entry, but we recommend three times per week to establish a consistent writing routine. We also suggest providing time for students to create open-ended entries, in which students decide what to write and draw about in reaction to the story, and directed entries, in which students respond to teacher-identified plot events and/or journaling prompts. Figure 8.2 provides suggested plot events from *The Boxer* and associated prompts that directly connect to the framing essential questions. While the primary aim for the duo-journal is to create a safer, semi-private space for students to express their reactions to Harry's story, it is also meant to provide sufficient material for students to use in small-group and whole-class discussions. During these discussions, it will again be important to remind students that they only have to share what they are comfortable sharing and that duo-journal partners should never prompt their partner to share a particular entry. As noted in Chapter 7, we recommend using a discussion protocol that outlines discussion norms and expectations for conversations that involve sensitive content.

***The Boxer* Scene Synopsis**	**Writing Prompt**	**Drawing Prompt**
Hertzko describes his father's work, death, and what happens to his family after his father died (pp. 13–14).	What do you think Hertzko learns about life due to his father's death at a young age?	Draw your own family, including everyone living in your house.
Hertzko finds a way to get a letter to his fiancée, Leah, who writes back to him (pp. 40–41).	Describe the ways Hertzko finds hope in the work camp.	Leah is not pictured in this scene. Draw what you imagine she would look like when she receives Hertzko's letter.
Schneider tells Hertzko about the "high stakes" fight with a new challenger (p. 68).	Describe what you think Hertzko might be thinking and feeling about the upcoming fight.	Depict Hertzko the night before the big fight in a way that shows his thoughts and feelings.
Harry arrives in the US and tries to find information about Leah (pp. 120–121).	Why do you think Hertzko chose to change his name to Harry? How do you think he feels about changing his name?	Sketch the scene when Harry and the German Heavyweight Champion meet in the ring.
Harry fights Rocky Marciano (pp. 152–160).	Why do you think Kleist juxtaposes images of Harry fighting in the concentration camps with images of Harry fighting Marciano?	Imagine if Harry won the fight and draw his facial expressions as he looks at Marciano, his manager, the crowd, and/or the men who told him to take a dive.

FIGURE 8.2: Teacher-Directed Duo-Journal Entries

Illustrating Plot Elements

Kleist chose to use black-and-white illustrations in his graphic biography of Harry Haft, and his artwork is incredible for its use of specific artistic elements, including chiaroscuro, shading, and negative space, to create action and emotion. For example, rather than solely relying on narration and dialogue, Kleist uses these artistic elements in drawing Harry's facial expressions to reveal what he is thinking and feeling throughout his ordeal in wartime Poland and in the Auschwitz concentration camp during the Second World War. Yet for students less experienced with reading graphic novels, they might either overlook how the illustrations contribute to the mood and tone of the story or misconstrue the particular thoughts and emotions Kleist is attempting to disclose through his artwork. As *The Boxer* is drawn without color, this graphic novel offers an opportunity for students to use artistic elements to support their comprehension of the plot elements of characterization, setting, and conflict through their own colorization. To be clear, we are not arguing that Kleist's novel needs color to improve or to enhance his work; it is an award-winning artistic creation, after all. Rather, we are offering a possible scaffold for students who need extra comprehension support and, like any scaffolding strategy, we would also recommend that teachers stop asking readers to use it once they have become proficient in using the artistic elements in *The Boxer* to build their comprehension.

The Boxer begins with a short prelude (pp. 5–7) that introduces Harry as an older man, apparently taking his son on an important trip. A narrative bubble on the opening page tells the reader they are in Miami in 1963, indicating that the Second World War is long over. The reason behind the trip is unclear, and the reader must infer that the older man is Harry and the younger boy is his son through the bubbles clearly narrated by the boy. The faces of Harry, his (implied) wife, and his son express various emotions in the three pages of this prelude. We suggest using the prelude as an introduction to this activity on illustrating plot events. Students could be placed into small groups and provided copies of the prelude, along with a set of coloring pencils. The overarching task is for the students to add coloration to depict the different emotions expressed in the characters' faces. After reading the prelude, the students could discuss what they believe is occurring in this short vignette, including identifying the three people and the exact setting. They could then also identify the emotions expressed, using the coloring pencils to shade artistic features that express certain emotions. For example, Harry, who is driving the car, is apparently distressed and then angrily directs his son to turn off the radio, so students could use red coloring to shade features of Harry's face to show that distress and anger. Meanwhile, his son looks glum or bored, so students could use blue coloring to shade features of his face to show those emotions. Once all the groups have completed their coloration of illustrated emotions, a quick share and discussion with the entire class could follow.

While it is impractical to provide copies of the entire graphic biography for students to follow this protocol, teachers could ask small groups to discuss what colors they might use to highlight characters' emotions, key plot events, and action scenes after a whole-class reading session. For students who need the additional scaffold, teachers could provide copies for them to color as needed. Students could also re-create key images in their duo-journals, using their chosen color to highlight aspects they want to write about and discuss with their duo-journal partner.

Culminating Tasks after Reading the Biography

These two suggestions for culminating tasks are meant to focus on life while acknowledging the reality of death, dying, and grief.

Creating "Celebration of Life" Biographical Essays

The Boxer is a story about death and dying. It is also a story about life and living. Most biographies, as public narratives, are meant to celebrate someone's life so others can learn about their successes and their struggles. These public stories also present possibilities for how we might live our own lives and create our own productive relationships. In that vein, asking students to create their own "Celebration of Life" biographies of Jewish athletes could provide opportunities for them to research the lives of distant and diverse others and to make statements about the lessons we can learn from those lives.

In addition to supporting students as they progress through the steps of a research project, we recommend providing students with some biography examples, particularly the brief stories of "Forgotten Champions" from the concentration camps included in Krauss's report in the back matter of *The Boxer.* Other examples could come from photo and video essays ESPN and other sports media outlets put together to honor recently deceased athletes (e.g., "A Look Back at Jim Brown's Life and Legacy in Photos" [ESPN, 2023]) and graphic short biography collections like *Survivors of the Holocaust: True Stories of Six Extraordinary Children* (Shackleton, 2019) or *Black Heroes of the Wild West* (Smith, 2020). Teachers could determine parameters for the subjects of the biographies, and, for this particular instructional unit, we recommend identifying several Jewish athletes as possible subjects. Both the US National Jewish Sports Hall of Fame and the International Jewish Sports Hall of Fame are good resources for lists of accomplished athletes. Also, websites like Bleacher Report and Ranker provide lists of "great" Jewish athletes that could be used to pique students' interests. Finally, we suggest asking all students to draft a biographical essay detailing the lives of their chosen athlete and the lessons others can learn from their athlete's experiences. Then, teachers could allow students to choose how they want to present their biographical essays. For example, students could create videos in which they narrate the athlete's story over a photo slideshow, or they could storyboard their own graphic biography to include with their biographical essay.

Researching Resources

As students read *The Boxer,* they might express many thoughts either through their duo-journals or in-class discussions about how Harry needed support from family and friends to grapple with his grief after the Second World War. The students might wonder if or how his life might have been different if he had sought out more help or if those in his life could have provided the help he seemed to need. With the aim of students connecting these discussions with their own lives, which is the focus of the third essential question framing this instructional unit, teachers could ask students to conduct research into local groups that support youth who have experienced a death and/or are grieving (PBS, 2000). Students could be asked to summarize the focus (or mission) of each group, the resources each group offers, and how people in the community can gain access to those resources (i.e., cost and availability). Students could prepare a report on their findings through a brochure to distribute in the school. Teachers could also invite speakers from these groups to visit the classroom and/or school.

CONCLUSION

Harry Haft's story has much to teach us. In stark depiction, it reveals the horrors of war and prejudice, it illustrates the lifelong effects of experiencing violence, and it shows how the inner strength of one human can endure. We hope reading and discussing his story can support youth to consider how death, dying, and grief affect us all.

Options for Book Clubs

Teachers looking to facilitate book clubs in which students explore death and dying can incorporate *The Boxer* alongside titles like the following:

Firekeeper's Daughter (Boulley, 2021)
Daunis Fontaine is greatly looking forward to going to college. She hopes it will be a new

beginning to her life because she never really found a fit in her high school or on her Ojibwe reservation. Unfortunately, a family tragedy changes those plans, and she must postpone her college plans. A new member of her brother's hockey team, however, might present an unexpected relationship.

The Canyon's Edge (Bowling, 2021)
On the one-year anniversary of her mother's death, Nora and her father take a canyoneering trip, a sport all three enjoyed as a family, to honor her memory. As the trip progresses, readers learn more about the circumstances surrounding her mother's death and how Nora and her father have been struggling in the ensuing year.

Lucy in the Sky (Brinkman, 2021)
Lucy Stillete's grandmother has cancer, and her treatment has sapped her usual energy that Lucy has come to rely on throughout her childhood. As she copes with her grandmother's illness, she also discovers her father's old vinyl records, including the entire Beatles oeuvre. This discovery leads to new musical interests, new friends, and, perhaps, new ways to bond with her family. This graphic novel selection provides an option that is not sports-related.

In Waves (Dungo, 2019)
In his moving graphic memoir, AJ Dungo shares his longtime girlfriend's struggle with bone cancer and how he grapples with his grief, including using surfing as a salve for his internal pain.

Options for Film Study

Teachers who want to use films to augment students' discussions about death and dying can incorporate *The Boxer* alongside titles like the following:

A Monster Calls (Bayona, 2016)
This film is the adaptation of Patrick Ness's (2011) young adult novel that shares Conor O'Malley's (Lewis MacDougall) story of grief caused by his mother's prolonged illness. Conor is visited by a monster (voiced by Liam Neeson), the yew tree in his backyard that has come to life, who tells him three tales about death and dying.

Hillsborough (Gordon, 2014)
In 1989, Liverpool was scheduled to play Nottingham Forest in a FA Cup semifinal, a major tournament in professional British football. A decision aimed at easing overcrowding at an entrance gate had the opposite result, causing 97 deaths and over 700 injuries. This documentary tells the history behind the tragedy, reviews the years-long investigation, and interviews survivors and others involved.

The Survivor (Levinson, 2021)
This film also tells the story of Harry Haft (Ben Foster), and, like *The Boxer*, is also based on Alan Scott Haft's (2006) biography of his father. It accounts for Haft's life prior to the Second World War, his imprisonment in Nazi concentration camps, his boxing career in New York, and his post-ring years, a time when he confronts his nightmarish past.

I Kill Giants (Walter, 2017)
This film adaptation of the graphic novel by Joe Kelly and Ken Niimura (2014) shares the story of Barbara (Madison Wolfe), who has created a fantasy world built around *Dungeons & Dragons* and a former Philadelphia Phillies pitcher. Barbara's fantasy creation is her way of deflecting the reality of her mother's illness.

Young Adult Literature

Boulley, A. (2021). *Firekeeper's daughter.* Henry Holt and Company.

Bowling, D. (2021). *The canyon's edge.* Little, Brown Books for Young Readers.

Brinkman, K. (2021). *Lucy in the sky* (S. Chiki, Illus.). First Second.

Dungo, AJ. (2019). *In waves.* Nobrow.

Gharib, M. (2019). *I was their American dream: A graphic memoir.* Clarkson Potter.

Hosler, J. (2021). *The way of the hive: A honey bee's story.* HarperAlley.

Kelly, J. (2014). *I kill giants* (K. Niimura, Illus., 5th ed.). Image Comics.

Kleist, R. (2014). *The boxer: The true story of Holocaust survivor Harry Haft.* SelfMadeHero.

Ness, P. (2011). *A monster calls.* Candlewick Press.

Nguyen, T. L. (2020). *The magic fish.* Random House Graphic.

Ottaviani, J. (2020). *Astronauts: Women on the final frontier* (M. Wicks, Illus.). First Second.

Shackleton, K. (Ed.) (2019). *Survivors of the Holocaust: True stories of six extraordinary children* (Z. Whittingham, Illus.). Sourcebooks Explore.

Smith, J. O. (2020). *Black heroes of the wild west.* TOON Books.

Walden, T. (2017). *Spinning.* First Second.

Warner, A. (2016). *Brief histories of everyday objects.* Picador.

Warner, A., & Dam, S. L. (2019). *This land is my land: A graphic history of big dreams, micronations, and other self-made states.* Chronicle Books.

Other Texts for Classroom Use

Applebury, G. (2020, June 15). *Different cultural beliefs on death and dying practices.* Love to Know. https://www.lovetoknow.com/life/grief-loss/different-cultural-beliefs-death-dying-practices

Bayona, J. A. (Director). (2016). *A monster calls* [Film]. Participant Media; River Road Entertainment; Apaches Entertainment; Telecino Cinema; La Trini.

ESPN. (2023, May 19). *A look back at Jim Brown's life and legacy in photos.* https://www.espn.com/nfl/story/_/id/30116359/photos-jim-brown-cleveland-browns-running-back-died

Gordon, D. (Director). (2014). *Hillsborough* [Film]. ESPN; BBC.

Kerrigan, M. (2017). *The history of death.* Amber Books.

Levinson, B. (Director). (2021). *The survivor* [Film]. Bron Studios; New Mandate Films; Creative Wealth Media; Endeavor Content; USC Shoah Foundation.

Walter, A. (Director). (2017). *I kill giants* [Film]. 1492 Pictures; Ocean Blue Entertainment; XYZ Films; uMedia.

REFERENCES

Bonagura, K. (2021, October 26). *Utah to honor Ty Jordan, Aaron Lowe by retiring no. 22 during UCLA game.* ESPN. https://www.espn.com/college-football/story/_/id/32481446/utah-honor-ty-jordan-aaron-lowe-retiring-no-22-ucla-game

Bosmajian, H. (2002). *Sparing the child: Grief and the unspeakable in youth literature about Nazism and the Holocaust.* Routledge.

Darnay, M. (2022, May 4). *Mental health and the sudden surge in suicides among NCAA women's athletes.* CBS News Pittsburgh. https://www.cbsnews.com/pittsburgh/news/mental-health-college-womens-sports-suicides/

Dodd, D. (2022, August 12). *As another football season begins, a mental health crisis gnaws at the fabric of college sports.* CBS Sports. https://www.cbssports.com/college-football/news/as-another-football-season-begins-a-mental-health-crisis-gnaws-at-the-fabric-of-college-sports/

Haft, A. S. (2006). *Harry Haft: Survivor of Auschwitz, challenger of Rocky Marciano.* Syracuse University Press.

Hauser, C. (2022, August 9). How we mourn COVID's victims. *The Seattle Times.* https://www.seattletimes.com/nation-world/how-we-mourn-covids-victims/

Helsel, P. (2022, January 9). *Connecticut high school hockey player dies after on-ice collision.* NBC News. https://www.nbcnews.com/news/us-news/connecticut-high-school-hockey-player-dies-ice-collision-rcna11309

Imperial College London. (2022). *COVID-19 orphanhood.* https://imperialcollegelondon.github.io/orphanhood_calculator/#/country/United%20States%20of%20America

Kamenetz, A. (2022, August 22). What grieving children need from the grown-ups in their lives. *TIME.* https://time.com/6202983/children-grief-covid-19-pandemic-bereavement/

Lewis, M. A. (2018). Disruption of adolescent-adult and death-life binaries: The experiences of Elizabeth Hall in *Elsewhere.* In M. Falter & S. Bickmore (Eds.), *Moving beyond personal loss to societal grieving: Discussing death's social impact through literature in the secondary ELA classroom* (pp. 3–12). Rowman & Littlefield.

Longbottom, S., & Slaughter, V. (2018). Sources of children's knowledge about death and dying. *Philosophical Transactions of the Royal Society B: Biological Sciences, 373*(1754). https://doi.org/10.1098%2Frstb.2017.0267

Mayer, C. (2022, March 16). University of the Southwest teams in fatal bus crash, multiple people dead. *Newsweek.* https://www.newsweek.com/deaths-college-bus-crash-usw-texas-1688438

National Association of School Psychologists. (2015). *Addressing grief: Tips for teachers and administrators.* https://www.nasponline.org/resources-and-publications/resources-and-podcasts/school-safety-and-crisis/mental-health-resources/addressing-grief/addressing-grief-tips-for-teachers-and-administrators

PBS. (2000). *Grief and healing*. https://www.pbs.org/witheyesopen/mourning_teachers_612.html

Rossi, M., & Lewis, M. A. (2021). Teaching *The Harlem Hellfighters*: A Great War counter-narrative. *English Journal, 111*(1), 56–64.

Schonfeld, D. J., & Quackenbush, M. (2021). *The grieving student: A guide for schools* (2nd ed.). Brookes Publishing.

Šubrtová, M. (2009). When children die in war: Death in war literature for children and youth. *Bookbird: A Journal of International Children's Literature, 47*(4), 1–8.

United States Holocaust Memorial Museum. (2023). *Teach.* https://www.ushmm.org/teach

World Health Organization. (2023). *WHO coronavirus (COVID-19) dashboard.* https://covid19.who.int/

9

Disrupting Bullying Behaviors in Schools, in Sports, and in Society

"I'm not going to cower or allow ignorance to run my life. I'm going to be me, whether you like it or not."

—*Bijan Majidi,* Here to Stay *(Farizan, 2018, p. 245)*

Though many might associate bullying with elementary school playgrounds, the reality is that bullying—behavior in which an aggressor who is perceived to hold power repeatedly intends to cause harm to their victim (American Psychological Association, 2017)—is not restricted to the playground nor is it limited to children. Rather, people carry out this kind of interpersonal violence in the home, in the workplace, in the classroom, and in digital spaces. Sometimes it plays out as hazing, a distinct form of aggressive behavior that involves established members of a group (e.g., a fraternity, a marching band) intentionally and repeatedly causing harm to an individual before welcoming that person into the group (Jonas, 2017). Unfortunately, bullying and hazing also permeate sports culture and are exhibited at all levels of sport.

Bullying in the realm of sport can transpire between teammates, between coaches and the players in their charge, between head and assistant coaches, and even within the administration of professional sports franchises. That much is evident from news stories like the following:

- New Mexico State University canceled the 2022–2023 men's basketball season, fired head coach Greg Heiar, and settled a lawsuit with players following an investigation into allegations of hazing among teammates (Pells, 2023).
- Football coaches at Canton McKinley High School (OH) were fired for allegedly forcing a player to eat pizza that contained pork, despite knowing the player's beliefs as a Hebrew Israelite restricted him from eating it (Weir, 2021).

- The women's basketball coach at Syracuse University, Quentin Hillsman, resigned amid allegations of bullying female coaches and staff members (Vasudevan, 2021).
- An investigation into the workplace culture of the NFL's Washington franchise determined that employees experienced bullying and intimidation, as well as sexual harassment, prompting the league to levy a $10 million fine (Jackson, 2021; see Chapter 7 for discussion of sexual violence and sports).

In light of such stories, this chapter is intended to help disrupt bullying behaviors that are so pervasive in the sports world and beyond. To that end, we share ideas for helping students interrogate bullying behaviors using sports-related young adult literature and other relevant texts.

THE SOCIAL CONCERN OF BULLYING

Bullying is a long-standing concern in schools across the United States. The cause for concern is reflected in national data indicating that 22 percent of students between the ages of twelve and eighteen reported being bullied at school in the previous twelve months (Irwin et al., 2021). The types of bullying students reported enduring at school included physical (e.g., pushed, shoved, tripped, or spit on), verbal (e.g., made fun of, called names, or insulted), and social (e.g., excluded from activities on purpose or subject of rumors). According to Irwin et al. (2021), reporting varied with student and school characteristics. For instance, a higher percentage of students who identified as two or more races (37 percent) reported bullying victimization than pupils who identified as White (25 percent), Black (22 percent), or Asian (13 percent). Grade level was a factor as well, as higher percentages of students in grades six, seven, and eight (27–28 percent) reported being bullied than their peers in grades nine, ten, and twelve (16–19 percent). Considering school characteristics, a higher percentage of students attending schools in rural locales (28 percent) reported being bullied at school than their counterparts in other settings (21–22 percent). The data are concerning—and even more so when recognizing that bullying is not limited to school grounds. Bullying occurs in digital spaces, too.

Electronic bullying or cyberbullying involves elements associated with bullying in a more traditional sense—aggressive behavior, repetition, and intent to cause harm—but it occurs through electronic or digital media (Tokunaga, 2010). As Tokunaga (2010) noted, cyberbullying is unique in its reach; it may occur at school, but it commonly occurs off school property and beyond the hours of the school day. Plus, given the affordances of online communication, victims of cyberbullying may or may not know the perpetrator's true identity. It comes as little surprise, then, that students in grades 9–12 also reported being bullied via electronic means. According to Irwin et al. (2021), approximately 16 percent of students reported being victimized by bullies online in the previous twelve months. Again, reporting varied based on student characteristics. For instance, a higher percentage of female students (20 percent) reported enduring cyberbullying than male students (11 percent). As well, a higher percentage of students who identified as gay, lesbian, or bisexual (27 percent) reported suffering cyberbullying than their peers identifying as heterosexual (14 percent) or not sure about their sexual identity (19 percent). So, though technological advancements and increased online access come with many benefits for students, reducing instances of bullying is not one of them.

The prevalence of bullying in the lives of youth is significant because research has shown that bullying victimization may have immediate and long-term consequences. For instance, as Arseneault et al. (2010) explained in a review of empirical evidence, being bullied is associated with severe symptoms of mental health problems in childhood and adolescence, including social isolation, depression, anxiety, self-harm, and suicidal ideations. Moreover, the negative ramifications of bullying victimization can be long-lasting. Conducting a longitudinal study, Evans-Lacko et al. (2017) found that adults who were frequently bullied in childhood were more likely than those who were not to use mental health services in childhood, in adolescence, and in midlife. The short- and long-term consequences of bullying victimization justify the efforts schools nationwide continue making to prevent bullying behaviors.

BULLYING AND HAZING IN SPORTS CULTURE

We know that bullying does occur in sports settings, and some athletes are more vulnerable than others. Students who identify as sexual or ethnic minorities, for example, are at greater risk of being bullied in sports settings than their peers who do not (Demers, 2010; Jarvie, 2003). Further, research indicates that athletes who identify as male are more likely to perpetrate bullying, and athletes with male coaches report higher rates of bullying compared to athletes with female coaches (Evans et al., 2016). Still, there is evidence to suggest that sports participation protects against bullying victimization. For instance, Merrill and Hanson (2016) reported that playing on one or more sports teams in the previous twelve months was associated with significantly lower bullying victimization. But bullying is distinct from hazing, which also transpires in sports settings.

Another form of interpersonal violence, hazing is often conceptualized as a type of initiation—one way people new to a team earn full acceptance from established members (Waldron, 2020). Researchers recognize a spectrum of behaviors that qualify as hazing, from those Waldron (2014) categorized as "harmless fun," such as cursing at the victim or making the victim wear embarrassing clothing, to acts of physical and/or sexual violence. Research suggests that the incidence of hazing in interscholastic sports varies based on grade level, ranging from 5–17 percent in middle school up to 17–48 percent in high school (Diamond et al., 2016; Fields et al., 2010; Gershel et al., 2003). Even those numbers may downplay the issue's prevalence because some experts believe hazing in sports settings is underreported. For instance, teen athletes may not recognize hazing when they see it, or they may opt not to report hazing for fear of retribution (Waldron & Kowalski, 2009).

Given the prevalence of bullying and hazing in sports culture and beyond, some athletes have shared their experiences—as bullies, as victims, and as bystanders—with the aim of reducing bullying behaviors. In an essay published by *The Players' Tribune*, NFL quarterback Russell Wilson (2014) lamented bullying behaviors he exhibited as a kid. In an essay of his own, NFL running back David Johnson (2016) described the anguish he felt as a child just anticipating the bullying to come. And NBA player Tyson Chandler (2015) conveyed regret reflecting on instances in elementary school when he was a bystander to bullying behaviors, never speaking out or standing up to bullies who victimized others. Together, these pieces offer multiple perspectives on bullying as perpetrated, experienced, or witnessed by pro athletes in their youth. Teachers can incorporate the study of sports-related young adult literature alongside such texts to begin disrupting bullying behaviors in schools, in sports, and in society.

FOCAL YA TEXT: *HERE TO STAY* BY SARA FARIZAN

Here to Stay (Farizan, 2018) is narrated by Bijan Majidi, a young man of Iranian Jordanian heritage who is thrust into the spotlight at the Boston-area private school he attends when, as a back-up on loan from the JV squad, he makes a clutch shot to help the varsity basketball team, the Granger Gunners, advance in the state playoffs. Bijan's newfound celebrity coincides with a campaign to change the school's mascot to something less violent, a movement he supports to get closer to his crush Elle Powell. However, he is soon subject to Islamophobic cyberbullying, as an image photoshopped to frame him as a terrorist is sent anonymously to the entire school. Despite the support of his single mother, some of his peers, and school faculty, Bijan struggles with the idea of being the face of efforts to halt racism and bullying. He has enough on his plate between playing basketball, crushing on Elle, and going to school.

Anonymous acts of Islamophobic bullying follow Bijan into the locker room, and his resistance to speaking out fades once a similar act of homophobic cyberbullying targets two of his friends, who are lesbians. In fact, Bijan is moved to take a public stand on more than one occasion—he challenges his coach, who to that point had never spoken his name, to acknowledge him, and he addresses the student body to let them know he is a typical teenager, not a terrorist. The bully is eventually revealed by the novel's end, and humor is threaded throughout the story, often in the form of commentary on Bijan's life delivered in the voices of NBA commentators Reggie Miller and Kevin Harlan, which more or less serves as an interior monologue.

Since its publication in 2018, *Here to Stay* has earned recognition from multiple outlets and organizations. The novel was first honored by *Booklist* as one of the 2018 Top 10 Sports Books for Youth. Additionally, *Here to Stay* was lauded among titles on the 2019 Rainbow Book List, a distinction established by ALA's Rainbow Round Table to aid readers in identifying and selecting books with content that supports LQBTQ+ inclusion. Bijan's story was also included in CCBC Choices 2019, the Cooperative Children's Book Center's annual listing of the best books for children and teenagers, and it was recognized among YALSA's 2020 Quick Picks for Reluctant Readers. These accolades stand to bolster any case for including *Here to Stay* in the ELA curriculum.

INCORPORATING *HERE TO STAY* INTO THE SECONDARY ELA CLASSROOM

Farizan's (2018) novel includes various incidents of bullying (e.g., physical, verbal, cyber). These incidents include individuals singling out others for their ethnicity and for their sexuality. But such behavior is met with resistance. Accordingly, the activities detailed in this section are intended to support students in critically examining cultures of bullying that permeate sports and other facets of life and/or in considering appropriate responses to injustice as they read *Here to Stay* and other relevant texts. Each activity presented is designed to support students as they consider one or more of the following essential questions:

- What drives bullying behaviors?
- How do stereotypes inform our views of others in the world around us?
- How should one respond in the face of injustice?

Prior to Teaching the Novel

Before beginning a whole-class reading of *Here to Stay*, teachers can facilitate various activities to support students as they prepare to discuss serious topics that include bullying, Islamophobia, and stereotypes. The activities we present involve welcoming a counselor into the classroom, understanding Islamophobia through Muslim athletes' experiences, and writing about related problems.

Welcoming a Counselor into the Classroom

As addressed previously, bullying—no matter the type, be it physical, verbal, or social, in person or cyber—has significant consequences. Again, research indicates that being bullied is associated with anxiety, depression, self-harm, and suicidal ideations (Arseneault et al., 2010). Considering the serious nature of the matter, teachers might find it helpful to tap the expertise of counseling professionals when introducing the topic. Hosting a counselor with expertise on the issue can help to establish the matter as one to be taken seriously, which is especially important in contexts where students are inclined to make light of bullying behaviors. In addition to conveying the severity of the issue, a counselor can also help students identify and distinguish between different types of bullying and learn what steps to take if someone attempts to bully them or if they are a witness to bullying behaviors. The knowledge about bullying students can build during a counselor's visit is applicable to discussions of *Here to Stay*, and it is relevant to their lives beyond the ELA classroom as well.

Understanding Islamophobia through Muslim Athletes' Experiences

In *Here to Stay*, the cyberbullying Bijan endures involves a gross play on the dangerous stereotype that men of Middle Eastern heritage are Muslim terrorists, so it is appropriate to spend time with students building understandings about Islamophobia, which Bleich (2012) defined as "indiscriminate negative attitudes or emotions directed at Islam or Muslims" (p. 182). Shaker Samman's (2021) article titled "'Things Are Going to Be Different Now'" is one that, through the prism of sport, can help students better understand the prejudice Muslim athletes and those who may be perceived to be Muslim, like Bijan, experienced in the twenty years following the terrorist attacks on September 11, 2001. For instance, the article accounts for the experiences of Bilqis Abdul-Qaadir, Massachusetts's 2009 Gatorade Player of the Year, who was harassed for playing basketball in a hijab, both in high school and college. What Abdul-Qaadir experienced—game stoppages to remove fans hurling Islamophobic hate speech from the stands—is akin to what Bijan endures in Chapter 20 of *Here to Stay*. To gauge students' comprehension of the article and to facilitate discussion about relevant topics, teachers might use prompts like those included in Figure 9.1.

Topic	Questions to Discuss
Islamophobia	Based on Samman's article, how do you understand Islamophobia? How does Islamophobia affect people, including practicing Muslims and those perceived as such?
Life post-9/11	Samman wrote, "The lost story of September 11 is the story of September 12, the day Muslims in America woke up to a new reality. One that's continued each morning since." What has been the reality for Muslim Americans since September 12, 2001?
Identity	Samman described Bilqis Abdul-Qaadir being viewed as "*the Muslim basketball player*—a caricature, not a fully formed person." Have you ever experienced that, where others define you in just one way? How is the narrow focus on a singular aspect of your identity limiting?
Fighting Islamophobia	Samman described the growing acceptance of the hijab in sports settings as "part of what [Ibtihaj] Muhammad says has been a concerted effort by Muslims to combat Islamophobia." How does the mere presence of a hijab in sports settings help to challenge Islamophobia?
Perception and reality	Basketball hall-of-famer Hakeem Olajuwon described feeling compelled to defend his faith as a Muslim and "shape the perception of what Islam really is." What misconceptions do people hold about Islam? What is it, really?
Faith and sport	Considering the experiences of athletes like Abdul-Qaadir, Muhammad, Olajuwon, and Husain and Hamza Abdullah, what obstacles do Muslim athletes encounter when staying true to their faith while competing in their respective sports?

FIGURE 9.1: Potential Questions for Discussing "'Things Are Going to Be Different Now'" (Samman, 2021)

To extend discussions about Islamophobia in the real world, teachers might also share excerpts from a book written by one of the Muslim athletes featured in Samman's (2021) article. Ibtihaj Muhammad, a fencer and the first female Muslim American to medal at the Olympics, wrote *Proud: My Fight for an Unlikely American Dream*, a memoir published in 2018. In the book, she details her experiences as the lone African American Muslim hijabi in the schools she attended and in the arenas she entered. Excerpts from the book can provide a glimpse at the faith-based bullying she experienced growing up. For example, the third chapter of *Proud* opens with abhorrent words a middle-school bully uttered to disparage Muhammad and her hijab: "Why are you wearing a tablecloth on your head?" (p. 26). In the chapter, Muhammad goes on to question why wearing a scarf to cover her hair was so bothersome to others, to clarify misunderstandings about Islam, and to share other acts of cruelty she experienced from her peers. Reading a chapter like this one stands to expand students' understandings of the Muslim faith, to challenge the othering of Muslim women, and to help students begin to consider ways of disrupting Islamophobic bullying like those presented in Muhammad's memoir and in *Here to Stay*.

Reflecting on Personal Experiences with Stereotypes

Given the story told in *Here to Stay*, another way of helping students connect with the novel prior to reading it is by inviting them to reflect in writing on their own experiences with stereotyping. For instance, teachers might use the following protocol:

> We'll soon be reading a story in which a dangerous stereotype is involved in the central conflict. Before we start reading, we are going to reflect on our own knowledge of and experiences with stereotypes. Take some time to write in response to each of the following prompts:
>
> - What is a stereotype?
> - Where do stereotypes come from, and why do they persist?
> - Describe an instance in which you or someone you knew was unfairly judged based on a stereotype. Then, drawing from that situation, explain what problems you see with judging others based on a stereotype alone.
>
> Please be prepared to share your writing with your peers.

Through reflection, students stand to begin making personal connections with Farizan's (2018) novel. Moreover, as students read the book, they can consider how Bijan's experience being stereotyped is similar to or distinct from their own.

As Students Read the Novel

There are numerous activities that could benefit students as they read *Here to Stay*. Among them are creating identity charts, reconsidering injustices and (in) actions via rotating small-group stations, and examining microaggressions and coach-athlete relationships. In the subsections that follow, we describe how such activities might take shape in the ELA classroom.

Creating Identity Charts

An identity chart is a tool for documenting the qualities that make someone—real or fictional—who they are. Commonly, an identity chart includes the subject's name in the center with lines jutting out from there, each connecting to a relevant descriptor (see Figure 9.2). Creating an identity chart can support a teacher's self-reflection (Kleinrock, 2021), but when reading literature, students can create identity charts to solidify their knowledge about characters while also advancing their understanding about the traits that make characters unique. When studying a novel in which stereotypes, prejudice, and related issues come into play, creating identity charts can be especially useful. That is, they can help students see there is more to an individual character than the narrow vision other characters may have of them. Moreover, identity charts create opportunities for considering intersectionality, or how the interconnectedness of an individual's various identity markers (e.g., gender, race, nationality, age) shape them and their lived experiences (Crenshaw, 1991; Tefera et al., 2018). Stereotype-laden cyberbullying, the story's central conflict, comes into play at the end of Chapter 5 in *Here to Stay*. Therefore, creating an identity chart at that point in the reading becomes a particularly valuable activity for students.

Because Bijan Majidi is the stereotyped victim of the initial cyberbullying incident in Farizan's (2018) novel, he is the character for whom an identity chart is most pressing. However, creating identity charts for other characters as well could help students make predictions about the identity of the anonymous cyberbully. Regardless, whether focusing strictly on Bijan or considering other characters as well, we recommend modeling the process when introducing the concept of an identity chart. Teachers might think aloud as they add the first couple of entries on a chart for Bijan before inviting students to continue on independently, or they might opt to model the process using a completely different character central to the story like, say, Will Thompson III. Will is not the victim of stereotyping, but establishing his traits would be time well spent. Following the teacher's model, students should use evidence from the text to support them in creating an identity chart driven by one focused question: "Who is Bijan Majidi?" As contexts dictate, teachers can provide mini-lessons on direct and indirect characterization to help students locate relevant evidence from the text. Figure 9.2 presents an example identity chart complete with information about Bijan introduced through the first two chapters of *Here to Stay*.

Once students have made an identity chart for Bijan, they should have the opportunity to reflect on what they have created—it is through reflection that students will really reap benefits from this activity. To that end, teachers might present prompts like the following:

- Which characteristics most closely reflect how Bijan sees himself?
- Which characteristics most closely reflect how others see Bijan?
- How might the intersection of various characteristics shape how others see Bijan?

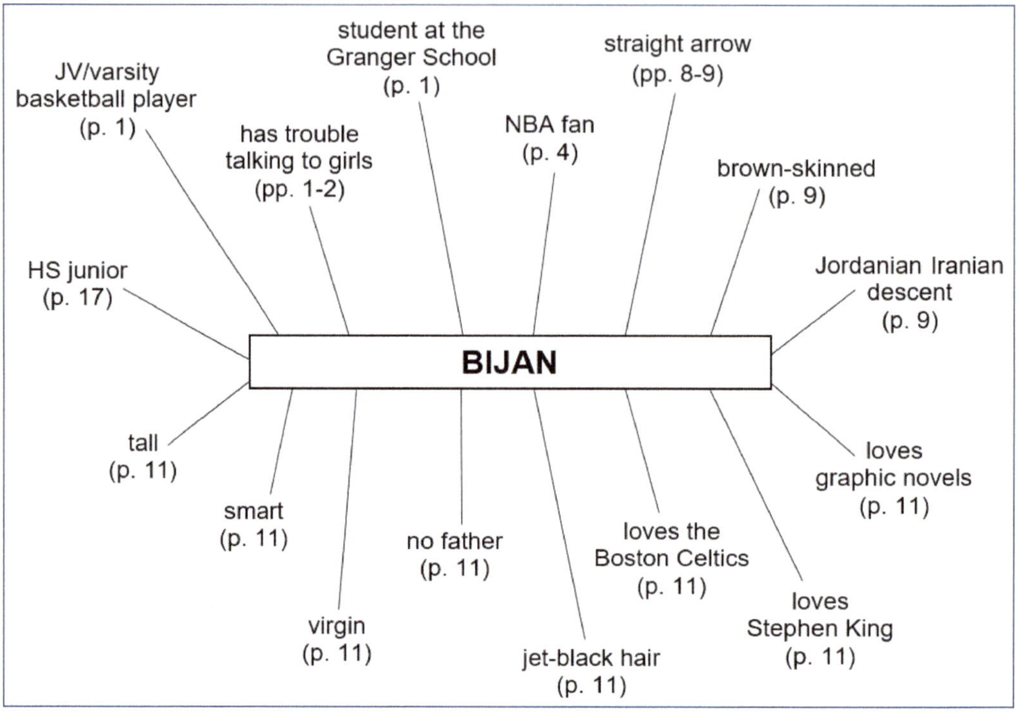

FIGURE 9.2: An Example Identity Chart

- How do you explain the difference in how Bijan sees himself and how others see him?
- Which characteristics are fixed or will forever remain unchanged?
- Which characteristics are subject to change, say, in a different context or at a later time?
- Speaking of context, which characteristics define Bijan as an athlete? As a student?

By considering such questions, students stand to see a more complete picture of Bijan while advancing their understanding that identities are complex, informed by context and other factors, some static and some dynamic.

Finally, to help students make those all-important text-to-self connections, teachers can invite students to chart their own identities and reflect in a similar fashion. Doing so should help students consider how they see themselves and how others see them, as well as recognize that, like Bijan, they are far more dynamic than the narrow perceptions others may have of them.

Reconsidering Injustices and (In)Actions via Rotating Small-Group Stations

Facilitating rotating small-group stations is an effective method for generating small-group discussion around a range of topics in relatively short order. Setup is largely context-dependent, but it often involves placing open-ended prompts around the classroom on large pieces of butcher paper or sheets from an easel pad that allow space for numerous written responses—these prompts mark the stations. When facilitating this activity in his own classroom, Luke Rodesiler, one of the authors of this book, has found it helpful to divide students into groups of approximately four or five. He gives each group a marker of a different color to help him distinguish responses for the purposes of formative assessment and directs each group to begin at a different station. In the first round, students read the prompt posted at their station, discuss it amongst themselves, and then write their answers beneath the prompt. Then, on Luke's signal, students leave the prompt but take their marker as they rotate clockwise to the next station. During the second round and those thereafter, students begin by reading the prompt and the answers provided by the previous group or groups. After discussing the ideas posted, students are expected to complicate or affirm the ideas as warranted before adding their own original thoughts to what has been shared. The process continues until each group has had a chance to address each prompt. In closing, Luke facilitates a whole-class review of what the class came up with in response to each prompt.

With the structure of rotating small-group stations in mind, teachers can invite discussion around *Here to Stay* with the aim of examining issues of injustice and (in)action. For example, teachers might consider using open-ended questions like those presented in Figure 9.3. These questions invite students to contemplate why bullying persists, to weigh appropriate responses to bullying behaviors, to consider issues of personal concern, and more. Whether teachers adopt the questions in Figure 9.3 or create their own, students will benefit most from prompts that support exploration of the established essential questions more broadly while also inviting students to delve deeper into their reading of Farizan's (2018) novel specifically.

Examining Microaggressions and Coach-Athlete Relationships

As current or former participants in organized athletics, many students have personally experienced coach-athlete relationships. Most students who have never participated in sports have probably still been introduced to coach-athlete relationships, real and fictional, through broadcasts of live sporting events, popular movies, and television shows. Other students may have been

Topic	Questions to Discuss
Bullying's persistence	There are multiple incidents of bullying in *Here to Stay* and, unfortunately, it happens in various facets of our world as well. Why do you think bullying persists? And what, if anything, do you think could be done to stop it?
Types of bullying	We previously learned about different types of bullying, including the verbal, physical, social, and cyber varieties. How would you categorize the various incidents of bullying we've seen in *Here to Stay*? Do you think some types are more hurtful than others? Why or why not?
Bijan's response	Consider Bijan's response to the initial cyberbullying incident. To what degree do you think his reaction was appropriate? What more, if anything, could he have done in response? Would those alternative responses have been helpful or hurtful?
Granger's response	In your estimation, have the Granger School administrators done enough to address the initial Islamophobic cyberbullying incident? If so, what makes you think so? If not, why not? And what more, if anything, could be done to make things right?
Social causes	Stephanie Bergner is passionate about social causes, as suggested by her efforts to change the Granger School's mascot from the Gunners to something nonviolent and culturally sensitive. What social causes are you passionate about? And what actions might you take to bring about change for those causes?
Tradition	Bijan explained that people challenging Stephanie's mascot petition—people like Will Thompson's grandfather—framed it as disrespecting tradition. What place, if any, does tradition have in society? What dangers, if any, do you see in blindly following tradition? What traditions would you like to see changed, if any?
Motivations	Bijan joined Stephanie's campaign to change the Granger School's mascot, but he did so to be closer to Elle Powell. Does it matter *why* someone supports a social cause, or is it simply enough that they support it, regardless of their motivation? What difference, if any, does one's motivation make?

FIGURE 9.3: Potential Questions for Use in Rotating Small-Group Stations

introduced to coach-athlete relationships by reading sports-related YAL. Some of those fictional coaches have redeeming qualities—think of Coach Brody in *Ghost* (Reynolds, 2016) or Coach Wilcox in *Foul Trouble* (Feinstein, 2013)—yet other coaches do not operate with athletes' best interests in mind: consider Coach Brigs in *Leverage* (Cohen, 2011) or Coach Carney in *All American Boys* (Reynolds & Kiely, 2015; see Chapter 3 for more on *All American Boys*). In *Here to Stay*, the depiction of Bijan's relationship with Coach Johnson, the varsity boys' basketball coach at the Granger School, provides opportunities for examining coach-athlete relationships and introducing the concept of *microaggressions*.

Presenting an analysis of award-winning and recommended works of sports-related YAL, Rodesiler and Lewis (2019) established five distinct types of relationships between athletic coaches and youth-athletes: (a) coach-athlete, (b) mentor-protégé, (c) counselor-client, (d) victor-victim, and (e) master-puppet. Figure 9.4 includes a breakdown of each relationship type, as well as examples of where they can be found in YAL and in popular movies. Teachers might invite students to reflect on the relationships they have personally built with coaches before introducing the five established types of relationships. When introducing these relationships, teachers can share excerpts from relevant novels and/or show clips from relevant films to help students see the concepts in action (Rodesiler et al., 2021). Then, having established understandings of each relationship type, students can weigh the dynamic between Coach Johnson and Bijan and which label(s) apply, if any. Johnson's microaggressions are pertinent to such analysis.

Relationship	Definition	Example in YAL	Example in Popular Movies
Coach-Athlete	The coach is focused primarily on supporting the athletic development of the athlete(s).	Coach Kyrokowski & Jessica Carlisle, *The Running Dream* (Van Draanen, 2011)	Coach Dale & the Hickory Huskers, *Hoosiers* (Anspaugh, 1986)
Mentor-Protégé	The coach taps their knowledge and experience to mentor the athlete(s) in life beyond the arena.	Coach Franzen & Liam Bergstrom, *Box Out* (Coy, 2008)	Coach Boone & Louie Lastik, *Remember the Titans* (Yakin, 2000)
Counselor-Client	The coach intimately counsels the athlete(s) through emotional hardships in their personal lives.	Coach Caledon & Hermione Winters, *Exit, Pursued by a Bear* (Johnston, 2016)	Coach Carter & Timo Cruz, *Coach Carter* (Carter, 2005)
Victor-Victim	The coach ranks winning in the arena so highly that it is detrimental to the athlete(s) competing.	Coach Carney & Quinn Collins, *All American Boys* (Reynolds & Kiely, 2015)	Sensei Kreese & Cobra Kai, *The Karate Kid* (Avildsen, 1984)
Master-Puppet	The coach prioritizes personal beliefs or benefits over the interests or concerns of the athlete(s).	Coach Stephenson & Terrell Jamerson, *Foul Trouble* (Feinstein, 2013)	Coach Cotton & Michael Oher, *The Blind Side* (Hancock, 2009)

FIGURE 9.4: Relationships between Coaches and Youth-Athletes Defined, Plus Examples

Microaggressions are defined as "everyday verbal, nonverbal, and environmental slights, snubs, or insults, whether intentional or unintentional, that communicate hostile, derogatory, or negative messages to target persons based solely upon their marginalized group membership" (Sue, 2010, p. 3). In *Here to Stay*, Johnson has multiple interactions with Bijan that can be categorized as microaggressions. For example, at the end of Chapter 3, after talking with Bijan about playing the rest of the season with the varsity team, Johnson begins writing him a note so he can grab some lunch before heading to class. Bijan spells his last name for the coach, who asks, "That an Irish name?" (Farizan, 2018, p. 38). Though perhaps Johnson spoke in jest, benign intent does not excuse microaggressions, and readers quickly learn how the joke played with Bijan: "[Coach Johnson] stood up and patted me on the shoulder before he left the cafeteria. I wasn't so hungry anymore" (Farizan, 2018, p. 39). Also, through most of the story, Johnson calls Bijan "B" instead of using his actual name. It is a repeated microaggression that Bijan eventually addresses mid-game in Chapter 20, when he refuses to continue playing until the coach says his name.

By facilitating the critical analysis of Coach Johnson's relationship with Bijan, teachers can position students to consider what is appropriate and what is not in such relationships. These are valuable lessons students can apply to their own lives as athletes. Moreover, critically analyzing the fictional relationship creates opportunities for students to consider other matters, including whether bullying is limited to interactions between peers, how power differentials factor into bullying behaviors, and what to do if a coach directs microaggressions at them.

Voices from the Field
Benching Bullying Behaviors

Kristen M. Black
English Teacher,
Fort Wayne,
Indiana

Olivia Anderson
Administrator,
Toledo, Ohio

Recently, I, Olivia, taught a summer school session for seventh-grade students. The heat brings students outside or, within a school, to the gym to run off their post-winter energy. The students I taught didn't have established relationships with one another, and it wasn't long before they were teasing each other. At first it was minimal, but it soon became more frequent than I anticipated. I had to build a community with students who, at this point, had only ever played dodgeball in the gym together. I hoped sharing the experience of reading a YA novel might help us establish a sense of community during the summer months.

Over the summer, we read *The Crossover* (Alexander 2014), a sports-related YA novel about a boy who plays basketball with his twin brother. After some time, students were remembering the exact pages on which the main character was questioning his brother's allegiance, like a fellow teammate who switches sides during dodgeball. In discussion, students shared personal experiences of deep hurt they had endured while playing sports, from teammate betrayal to skill hazing and peer ostracizing that involved students being told they didn't have the skill level to join a pick-up game. Students equated those experiences to feelings of hurt for a lost loved one. They explained that, in these instances, the relationship cannot continue as it had previously. Looking to expound upon that teaching moment, I explained that, with us sharing the same learning environment and spending so much time together, we are now a team with a shared allegiance, and teasing only creates hurt feelings like the painful ones they had just described. Sports literature created space for us to talk candidly, to strengthen our bonds, and to disrupt bullying behaviors.

Like Olivia, I, Kristen, have witnessed an array of oppressive and intimidating behaviors among children who try to fit in by putting others down. Some involve sports settings, where such behaviors have been notoriously normalized. For example, I taught a teenage boy who struggled to feel confident in his evolving sexual identity. His classmates did not appear to cause him discomfort or embarrassment, but when he tried out for the school's basketball team, he ran into myriad complications with the established social group. His eagerness to improve his athletic skills was squashed beneath unfair assumptions and hurtful comments from the very teammates he was expected to trust. At one point, he revealed to me that even though he successfully acquired the jersey he dreamt of having, he felt as if he would never truly be accepted. By the time this conversation took place, there was no amount of encouragement I could offer to convince him to see it through. Instead of playing, he opted to be the team's manager, which temporarily satisfied his desires to be involved in extracurricular activities. Following this, I found it extremely troubling to know that there were other kids in the same position; I recognized how important it was to address bullying behaviors in my curriculum.

When approaching the subject of bullying, there are a few practices to help students learn in authentic ways that they can apply to situations throughout their lives. As Olivia described, literature can help us have those tough conversations that many people, including most of the middle schoolers I teach, wish to avoid. By integrating materials that speak to the subjects surrounding their daily lives, we can make a world of a difference for the ones who most need to be seen and heard. Going beyond reading a chapter of a book and taking a quiz, a well-rounded curriculum with the right reading materials can be the most powerful tool for making an impact. Another proactive method can be carried out by empowering students to "call foul." That is, teachers can set expectations that students will call out peers who are not displaying good citizenship toward others. When the classroom environment becomes one in which everyone feels comfortable enough to speak, even with the potential to be perceived as inferior, students know they have a room full of "referees" who will hold one another accountable and foster a positive environment that is conducive to learning.

Reference

Alexander, K. (2014). *The crossover*. Clarion Books.

Kristen M. Black, a middle school language arts teacher in Fort Wayne, Indiana, has a B.S. in Secondary English Education from Indiana University. She has also served as a tutor for Boys and Girls Club of America, a Social-Emotional Learning (SEL) liaison, an advisor for Gay-Straight Alliance (GSA) Club, a mentor for eSports Club, a member of Quality Improvement Team, and a participant in district curriculum development.

Olivia Anderson earned a Master of Science in Educational Leadership from Purdue University Fort Wayne. She has enjoyed filling various roles while working in economically diverse, urban school districts for a decade. Currently, she is a school district administrator working with students in Toledo, Ohio.

Culminating Tasks after Reading the Novel

Following extensive exploration of bullying, stereotyping, and responding to injustice, the study of *Here to Stay* could culminate in various ways. For instance, students might write and deliver speeches to celebrate their individuality and to disavow the stereotypical views people may have of them, or they could write original narratives about characters standing up and speaking out against forms of injustice the characters encounter in Farizan's (2018) novel, such as bullying, Islamophobia, and homophobia.

Developing and Delivering "Here to Stay" Speeches

Teachers eager to sharpen students' speaking and listening skills might draw inspiration from Bijan's powerful speech at the school assembly in Chapter 22. The speech is Bijan's attempt to set the record straight, to let his peers and others in the Granger School community know things about him that they could not possibly gather just by looking at him (e.g., his favorite sport, what he reads for fun, the food he enjoys, his future plans). During the speech, Bijan undercuts the stereotypical views so many people hold of those who look like him and, ultimately, declares that he is "here to stay" (Farizan, 2018, p. 245). Using Bijan's speech as a springboard, teachers can invite students to write their own "here to stay" speeches as a way to celebrate the unique qualities of each individual in the class. Just as Bijan did, students can help their classmates learn things about them that could not be gleaned simply from their appearance. With their speeches, students can disrupt the stereotypical views that others hold of them, as Bijan did, and they can declare their intentions to unabashedly be themselves.

How students deliver their speeches will likely depend on context. Teachers might opt to have students deliver their speeches in person, whether in the classroom or on a stage. Alternatively, some teachers might take a page from Dawn Reed, a veteran English teacher in mid-Michigan, by aiding students in recording their speeches digitally and publishing them online as podcasts for an authentic virtual audience (Reed & Hicks, 2009). Beyond positioning students to hone their writing and speaking skills, such an approach stands to support students in developing digital literacies as well, a worthwhile endeavor in an increasingly technological world.

Writing Narratives of Resistance

High school students are often tasked with reading fiction, yet rarely are they given the opportunity to write fiction (Smagorinsky et al., 2010). However, as Newkirk (2021) argued, students who glean insights from the writerly moves they make while crafting fiction can apply those understandings to the fiction they read. Moreover, the ability to generate narratives is one that students can apply to the writing of nonfiction as well, whether they seek to argue or inform (Prather, 2019). Accordingly, crafting original stories of resistance is one culminating task teachers might choose to facilitate following the study of *Here to Stay*. Given the focus of the novel and the established essential questions, students might write and share stories, sports-related or otherwise, about characters standing up in the face of bullies, pushing back against hazing rituals, or resisting other forms of injustice—or perhaps wishing they had.

The type of story that teachers invite students to generate will surely depend on context. For instance, if short on time, teachers could focus on teaching the craft of writing microfiction, a strikingly short story that still includes standard narrative elements (Nobis, 2016). Alternatively, if schedules allow, teachers might position students to write with a younger audience in mind as they create picture books of resistance. When Luke was teaching English at a high school in mid-Michigan, he collaborated with an art teacher on a picture-book project—students in the English class wrote original narratives, and students in the art class created the accompanying visuals—that culminated with students reading their stories to children at a nearby elementary school. Though that partnership required some flexible scheduling, a similar audience seems apt for the stories of resistance that students would generate after reading *Here to Stay*. And actually sharing students' stories of resistance aligns with a dimension of critical literacy Lewison et al. (2002) advanced: "taking action and promoting social justice" (p. 382).

No matter what type of text students create or for what audience they choose to write, students are sure to benefit from examining relevant mentor texts, engaging in mini-lessons that account for various narrative elements (e.g., plot, setting, point of view), and participating in conferences to enrich and enhance their writing. For example, if students are crafting picture books of resistance, then Muhammad's (2019) *The Proudest Blue: A Story of Hijab and Family* can serve as a valuable mentor text. Inspired by the aforementioned Olympian's personal experience being bullied for the way she showed her faith, the acclaimed book works to "show other little girls wearing hijabs to school that it's okay" (Mosley, 2019). Examining Muhammad's picture book can help students see ways of drawing from personal experience to inform their own respective narratives, ways of depicting bullies without boosting them, and the power of nonviolent resistance.

Depending on the kind of narrative students are writing, teachers might also consider helping students incorporate color commentary as Farizan (2018) did when writing *Here to Stay*. The color commentary that Bijan pretends Reggie Miller and Kevin Harlan, a pair of NBA commentators, offer about the developments unfolding in his life is one unique feature of the novel. To add a bit of levity to what could otherwise be some heavy stories, students can use *Here to Stay* as a mentor text while incorporating imaginary color commentary into their own narratives. If following Farizan's lead, students need not stick with the commentary tandem of Miller and Harlan. Rather, students could incorporate the voices of their favorite in-game broadcast team, be it the NFL's Mike Tirico and Cris Collinsworth, MLB's Joe Buck and John Smoltz, the NBA's Doris Burke and Beth Mowins, or whomever they prefer. Regardless of students' preferences, they should strive to capture the commentators' voices and, as appropriate, incorporate their catchphrases, from Mike Breen's "Bang!" to Gus Johnson's "Pure!"

CONCLUSION

Beyond its humor and sheer entertainment value, Sara Farizan's (2018) *Here to Stay* offers teachers and students a powerful vehicle for critically examining bullying behaviors, including those marked by Islamophobic and homophobic hate. Given the significant damage to an individual's health and well-being that bullying can cause, whether it transpires in the locker room, in the classroom, or in digital spaces, *Here to Stay* makes for a valuable addition to any ELA curriculum. Moreover, with a diverse mix of strong teenage characters who advocate for themselves, for others, and for the justice-oriented causes in which they believe, the story is one that provides models teenage readers can emulate with the aims of rejecting lazy or prejudicial stereotypes and disrupting cultures that normalize bullying behaviors of any kind, from the verbal and physical sort to the cyber variety.

Options for Book Clubs

Teachers eager to employ book clubs as students explore bullying and hazing in sports culture can incorporate *Here to Stay* and other titles that include the following:

Michigan vs. the Boys (Allen, 2019)
Suggested as a book-club option in Chapter 2, this novel can also support the critical study of bullying. When Michigan earns a starting position on the boys hockey team, some of her new teammates take to bullying and hazing, which devolves into sexual assault.

Leverage (Cohen, 2011)
Danny, a gymnast, and Kurt, the school's new football star, narrate this story in which the unlikely pair share knowledge about a bullying incident stemming from a clash between the gymnasts and football players that resulted in a teen's tragic suicide.

Gutless (Deuker, 2016)
Brock, a sure-handed soccer goalie, could be a varsity-level receiver, but he shies away from the physical contact football requires. Brock's penchant for avoiding conflict is tested when Richie, his friend and soccer teammate, becomes the target of the quarterback's bullying.

Game Changer (Greenwald, 2018)
This multigenre novel, suggested as a book-club option in Chapter 6, can also be used to explore hazing in sports settings. As Teddy's family tries to understand how he ended up in critical condition, football players contemplate speaking up about an annual hazing ritual.

Stick (Harmon, 2015)
Stick is a star receiver with a bright future in football, but his passion for the sport is waning, and it is extinguished further by his teammates' bullying of Preston, a freshman outcast. When Preston tutors Stick, they help one another see themselves for who they really are.

Options for Film Study

Teachers looking to extend students' exploration of bullying and hazing in sports culture and beyond might consider screening one of the following films:

The Karate Kid (Avildsen, 1984)
After moving from Newark to Reseda, teenager Daniel LaRusso (Ralph Macchio) is bullied by members of the local karate dojo and sets out to defend himself by learning karate from Mr. Miyagi (Pat Morita), who works at the apartment complex where the teen resides.

Bully (Hirsch, 2011)
Though not specific to bullying in the world of sport, this film documents the lives of five students who have endured bullying in US schools. In that way, it offers opportunities to consider what some students endure and the devastating consequences of bullying behaviors.

Triumph (Leonard, 2021)
This feature film tells the story of Mike (RJ Mitte), a teen living with cerebral palsy, who endures bullying from some of his peers at school and vies to compete as a member of the wrestling team led by Coach Cutter (Terrence Howard).

Submit the Documentary: The Virtual Reality of Cyberbullying (Muhammad, 2013)
This documentary focuses on the dangers of cyberbullying by telling the stories of children and families who have endured it. The film considers various perspectives on the issue, from educators and researchers to legislators and law enforcement officials.

Young Adult Literature

Allen, C. S. (2019). *Michigan vs. the boys*. Kids Can Press.

Cohen, J. (2011). *Leverage*. Dutton Books for Young Readers.

Coy, J. (2008). *Box out*. Scholastic Press.

Deuker, C. (2016). *Gutless*. HMH Books for Young Readers.

Farizan, S. (2018). *Here to stay*. Algonquin Young Readers.

Feinstein, J. (2013). *Foul trouble*. Knopf Books for Young Readers.

Greenwald, T. (2018). *Game changer*. Amulet Books.

Harmon, M. (2015). *Stick*. Knopf Books for Young Readers.

Johnston, E. K. (2016). *Exit, pursued by a bear*. Dutton Books.

Reynolds, J. (2016). *Ghost*. Atheneum/Caitlyn Dlouhy Books.

Reynolds, J., & Kiely, B. (2015). *All American boys*. Atheneum/Caitlyn Dlouhy Books.

Van Draanen, W. (2011). *The running dream*. Knopf Books for Young Readers.

Other Texts for Classroom Use

Anspaugh, D. (Director). (1986). *Hoosiers* [Film]. Hemdale Pictures.

Avildsen, J. G. (Director). (1984). *The karate kid* [Film]. Delphi II Productions.

Carter, T. (Director). (2005). *Coach Carter* [Film]. MTV Films.

Chandler, T. (2015, October 23). *Bully*. The Players' Tribune. https://www.theplayerstribune.com/articles/bullying-awareness-tyson-chandler

Hancock, J. L. (Director). (2009). *The blind side* [Film]. Alcon Entertainment.

Hirsch, L. (Director). (2011). *Bully* [Film]. Cinereach; Where We Live Films.

Johnson, D. (2016, November 8). *Let's talk about bullying*. The Players' Tribune. https://www.theplayerstribune.com/articles/david-johnson-cardinals-bullying

Leonard, B. (Director). (2021). *Triumph* [Film]. Digital Ignition Entertainment.

Muhammad, I., & Ali, S. K. (2019). *The proudest blue: A story of hijab and family*. Little, Brown Books for Young Readers.

Muhammad, I., & Tharps, L. L. (2018). *Proud: My fight for an unlikely American dream*. Legacy Lit.

Muhammad, M. (Director). (2013). *Submit the documentary: The virtual reality of cyberbullying* [Film]. Plat4m Studios.

Samman, S. (2021, September 10). "Things are going to be different now." *Sports Illustrated*. https://www.si.com/nba/2021/09/10/muslims-in-sports-after-9-11-daily-cover

Wilson, R. (2014, October 3). *Let's talk about it*. The Players' Tribune. https://www.theplayerstribune.com/articles/lets-talk-about-it

Yakin, B. (Director). (2000). *Remember the Titans* [Film]. Walt Disney Pictures; Jerry Bruckheimer Films.

REFERENCES

American Psychological Association. (2017). *Bullying and school climate*. https://www.apa.org/advocacy/interpersonal-violence/bullying-school-climate

Arseneault, L., Bowes, L., & Shakoor, S. (2010). Bullying victimization in youths and mental health problems: "Much ado about nothing"? *Psychological Medicine, 40*(5), 717–729.

Bleich, E. (2012). Defining and researching Islamophobia. *Review of Middle East Studies, 46*(2), 180–189.

Crenshaw, K. (1991). Mapping the margins: Intersectionality, identity politics, and violence against women of color. *Stanford Law Review, 43*(6), 1241–1299.

Demers, G. (2010). Homophobia in sport: Fact of life, taboo subject. In S. Robertson (Ed.), *Taking the lead: Strategies and solutions from female coaches* (pp. 73–96). University of Alberta Press.

Diamond, A. B., Callahan, S. T., Chain, K. F., & Solomon, G. S. (2016). Qualitative review of hazing in collegiate and school sports: Consequences from a lack of culture, knowledge and responsiveness. *British Journal of Sports Medicine, 50*(3), 149–153.

Evans, B., Adler, A., Macdonald, D., & Côté, J. (2016). Bullying victimization and perpetration among adolescent sport teammates. *Pediatric Exercise Science, 28*(2), 296–303.

Evans-Lacko, S., Takizawa, R., Brimblecombe, N., King, D., Knapp, M., Maughan, B., & Arseneault, L. (2017). Childhood bullying victimization is associated with use of mental health services over five decades: A longitudinal nationally representative cohort study. *Psychological Medicine, 47*(1), 127–135.

Fields, S. K., Collins, C. L., & Comstock, R. D. (2010). Violence in youth sports: Hazing, brawling and foul play. *British Journal of Sports Medicine, 44*(1), 32–37.

Gershel, J. C., Katz-Sidlow, R. J., Small, E., & Zandieh, S. (2003). Hazing of suburban middle school and high school athletes. *Journal of Adolescent Health, 32*(5), 333–335.

Irwin, V., Wang, K., Cui, J., Zhang, J., & Thompson, A. (2021, July). *Report on indicators of school crime and safety: 2020*. National Center for Education Statistics. https://bjs.ojp.gov/sites/g/files/xyckuh236/files/media/document/iscs20.pdf

Jackson, W. (2021, July 1). NFL fines Washington $10 million after investigation into workplace culture. *Sports Illustrated*. https://www.si.com/nfl/2021/07/01/nfl-fines-washington-10-million-workplace-investigation

Jarvie, G. (Ed.). (2003). *Sport, racism and ethnicity*. Routledge.

Jonas, J. (2017, September 6). *Hazing in high school athletics*. National Federation of State High School Associations. https://www.nfhs.org/articles/hazing-in-high-school-athletics

Kleinrock, L. (2021). *Start here, start now: A guide to antibias and antiracist work in your school community*. Heinemann.

Lewison, M., Flint, A. S., & Van Sluys, K. (2002). Taking on critical literacy: The journey of newcomers and novices. *Language Arts*, *79*(5), 382–392.

Merrill, R. M., & Hanson, C. L. (2016). Risk and protective factors associated with being bullied on school property compared with cyberbullied. *BMC Public Health*, *16*, 1–10.

Mosley, T. (2019, September 30). *Olympic fencer Ibtihaj Muhammad turns bullying experiences into new children's book*. WBUR. https://www.wbur.org/hereandnow/2019/09/30/ibtihaj-muhammad-childrens-book-hijab

Newkirk, T. (2021). *Writing unbound: How fiction transforms student writers*. Heinemann.

Nobis, M. (2016). Writing sports fiction to build empathy and understanding. In A. Brown & L. Rodesiler (Eds.), *Developing contemporary literacies through sports: A guide for the English classroom* (pp. 67–72). National Council of Teachers of English.

Pells, E. (2023, June 28). *New Mexico State agrees to pay $8M to settle basketball players' sex assault, hazing lawsuit*. Associated Press. https://apnews.com/article/new-mexico-state-aggies-lawsuit-sexual-hazing-a1e0b79c62c3032ec877bdf9035d7636

Prather, L. (2019). *Story matters: Teaching teens to use the tools of narrative to argue and inform*. Heinemann.

Reed, D., & Hicks, T. (2009). From the front of the classroom to the ears of the world: Multimodal composing in speech class. In A. Herrington, K. Hodgson, & C. Moran (Eds.), *Teaching the new writing: Technology, change, and assessment in the 21st-century classroom* (pp. 124–139). Teachers College Press.

Rodesiler, L., & Lewis, M. A. (2019). "I thought coaches were supposed to set an example": Coaches' divergent roles in young adult literature. *The ALAN Review*, *46*(2), 27–39.

Rodesiler, L., Lewis, M. A., & Brown, A. (2021). Relationships between youth-sports coaches and athletes: Messages from the "best" sports-related films. In K. Garland, K. S. Dredger, C. L. Beach, & C. Leogrande (Eds.), *Stories of sports: Critical literacy in media production, consumption, and dissemination* (pp. 49–69). Lexington Books.

Smagorinsky, P., Johannessen, L. R., Kahn, E. A., & McCann, T. M. (2010). *The dynamics of writing instruction: A structured process approach for middle and high school*. Heinemann.

Sue, D. W. (2010). Microaggressions, marginality, and oppression: An introduction. In D. W. Sue (Ed.), *Microaggressions and marginality: Manifestation, dynamics, and impact* (pp. 3–22). Wiley.

Tefera, A. A., Powers, J. M., & Fischman, G. E. (2018). Intersectionality in education: A conceptual aspiration and research imperative. *Review of Research in Education*, *42*(1), vii–xvii.

Tokunaga, R. S. (2010). Following you home from school: A critical review and synthesis of research on cyberbullying victimization. *Computers in Human Behavior*, *26*(3), 277–287.

Vasudevan, A. (2021, August 2). Syracuse women's basketball head coach Quentin Hillsman resigns amid bullying allegations. *The Daily Orange*. http://dailyorange.com/2021/08/syracuse-womens-basketball-head-coach-quentin-hillsman-resigns

Waldron, J. J. (2014). A post-structuralist approach to hazing in sport. In R. Schinke & K. McGannon (Eds.), *The psychology of sub-culture in sport and physical activity: Critical perspectives* (pp. 31–47). Routledge.

———. (2020). Degrading and harming new teammates during hazing: "Athletes will be athletes." In M. Lang (Ed.), *Routledge handbook of athlete welfare* (pp. 119–127). Routledge.

Waldron, J. J., & Kowalski, C. L. (2009). Crossing the line: Rites of passage, team aspects, and ambiguity of hazing. *Research Quarterly for Exercise and Sport*, *80*(2), 291–302.

Weir, K. (2021, June 1). Canton McKinley High School football player says he was forced to eat pork against religious beliefs. *The Canton Repository*. https://www.cantonrep.com/story/news/2021/06/01/mckinley-football-player-sue-canton-schools-religious-violation/5290290001

10 Questioning Messages about Masculinity in Sports and Other Popular Cultures

I swear, Dad should write a book called *How to Be an Average Chump* because his definition of "man" is way off.

—*David Espinoza,* The New David Espinoza *(Aceves, 2020, p. 141)*

In sports and other popular cultures, men are often celebrated for their physical prowess. Subsequently, men are commonly expected to be strong and muscular, to be aggressive and dominant in whatever they pursue. Living under such expectations, some men commit to succeeding at all costs, even if it means illicitly enhancing their physical makeup and performance. Over time, high-profile sports figures and actors have admitted to abusing steroids and taking other shortcuts to boost their performance in athletic competition or their appearance on the screen. Consider, for example, the following stories about prominent athletes and entertainers coming clean in years past:

- Lance Armstrong, an American cyclist who survived testicular cancer and proceeded to win seven Tour de France titles, admitted to using steroids and taking other prohibited measures to secure victory (Carroll, 2013).
- Major League Baseball star Alex Rodriguez admitted to using performance-enhancing drugs and manipulating drug tests while playing for the New York Yankees (Gregory, 2014).
- World's Strongest Man champion Hafþór Júlíus Björnsson, who played "The Mountain" Gregor Clegane in *Game of Thrones*, admitted to taking steroids during his journey to best all other strongmen he competed against (Williams, 2019).
- Arnold Schwarzenegger admitted to taking steroids as a bodybuilder who won seven Mr. Olympia titles, success he parlayed into a notable acting career and, eventually, two terms as California's governor (Schuler, 2018).

Would athletes and entertainers like these feel compelled to use drugs that enhance their performance and/or appearance if masculinity was not widely conceptualized in such narrow terms? Moreover, the consequences for taking shortcuts varied among the figures noted above. For instance, Armstrong was stripped of his Tour de France titles and banned from competitive cycling, yet Schwarzenegger faced no official sanctions. Regardless, these men knew they were cutting corners to maximize their gains. That raises the question: What, if anything, does one lose when taking shortcuts to the top, be it in athletics, entertainment, or any other field? In this chapter, we present ideas for exploring with students this question and others as they reconsider messages about masculinity in sports and other popular cultures.

THE SOCIAL CONCERN OF TRADITIONAL MASCULINITY IDEOLOGY

As explained by Pleck et al. (1993), the concept of *masculinity ideology* frames masculinity not as a biological or psychological characteristic but as a cultural construct. That is, from a social constructionist perspective, masculinity is viewed as a band of expectations and convictions regarding the standards for men's behavior and appearance in a particular context. Conceptualized as a cultural construct, masculinity can take various forms, and experts contend that masculinities (Connell, 1995) are "continuously being constructed and contested" (Addis & Cohane, 2005, p. 640). While there are diverse masculinity ideologies, the embrace of *traditional masculinity ideology* is common (Levant & Richmond, 2007). Traditional masculinity ideology is associated with eschewing femininity; striving for success; shunning displays of weakness; and engaging in risky behavior (American Psychological Association, 2018). Mahalik et al. (2003) argued that adhering to this vision of masculinity can be beneficial in some contexts. For instance, they explained that being aggressive or taking risks may support acceptance within a peer group, and achieving success in various realms of life may contribute positively to a sense of worth. But in other contexts, problems can come with enacting traditional masculinity ideology.

Enacting traditional masculinity ideology can be detrimental to the well-being of men and boys—and to that of others. Behaviors that support men's health, including taking measures to aid self-care, seeking preventative treatments, and pursuing psychological support, have historically been deemed "feminine" or "weak" (Salgado et al., 2019). Such thinking puts the enactment of traditional masculine norms in opposition to an individual's health and well-being. Likewise, studies have documented associations between the endorsement of traditional masculine gender norms and behaviors that put one's health at risk, such as high rates of alcohol consumption (Monk & Ricciardelli, 2003) and the abuse of steroids (Parent & Bradstreet, 2018). Beyond damaging one's own quality of life, consideration must also be given to how embracing traditional views of masculinity stands to affect others. For instance, according to Smith et al. (2015), adherence to traditional views of masculinity can be linked to increased sexual aggression toward intimate partners. Such findings support critically examining the traditionally narrow conceptualization of masculinity.

The work of disrupting traditional masculinity ideology has been taken up in recent years by the American Psychological Association (APA). Recognizing the harm caused by embracing dominant masculine ideals, the organization issued *APA Guidelines for Psychological Practice with Boys and Men* in 2018. Informed by research published over more than 40 years, the *Guidelines* offer clinicians several points of advice. These include, among others, recognizing the constructed nature of masculinities; seeing how power, privilege, and sexism influence the development of boys and men; and helping boys and men take up healthful behaviors. Teachers are not clinicians, but we contend that traditional masculinity ideology is yet another text to be read critically in the secondary ELA classroom. Plus, doing this work stands to support the health and well-being of the young men teachers serve. Therefore, in this chapter, we promote activities that support critically reading messages about masculinity that students encounter in sports culture, in young adult literature, and in popular media.

TRADITIONAL MASCULINITY IDEOLOGY AND SPORTS CULTURE

The perceived importance of adhering to traditional masculinity ideology stands to negatively affect the health and well-being of youth who participate in sports. For some male athletes, the dangers of traumatic brain injuries are less concerning than the risk of being perceived as weak for seeking the medical attention they need. In a study conducted by Wallace et al. (2017), male and female high school athletes were found to have similar knowledge of sports-related concussions, yet male athletes were four to eleven times more likely to not report a concussion for reasons tied to how they would be perceived by others. Concerns cited included teammates and coaches thinking that they were weak. In other words, numerous male athletes participating in Wallace et al.'s study deemed it better to suffer a traumatic brain injury in silence—and to risk doing greater damage by continuing to compete—than to have their masculinity called into question. (See Chapter 6 for ideas about using YAL to explore the dangers of brain trauma suffered through sports participation.)

One need not compete in the arena to sustain traditional norms of masculinity; rather, simply consuming sports media may also play a role. Studies suggest that viewing sports-related television programming and adhering to traditional notions of masculinity go hand in hand. For instance, examining associations between time spent watching TV and views regarding masculine gender roles, Scharrer and Blackburn (2018) found that the viewing of sports programming on television was positively associated with more traditional views of masculinity, regardless of sex. Their findings were in line with Giaccardi et al.'s (2017) study, which found an association between adherence to masculinity ideology and sports television viewing. Considering the popularity of televised sporting events and the potential harm of masculinity ideology, such findings are concerning. However, incorporating select works of sports-related young adult literature can support teachers in facilitating the critical study of masculinity ideology and sports culture. *The New David Espinoza* (Aceves, 2020) is one such text.

FOCAL YA TEXT: *THE NEW DAVID ESPINOZA* BY FRED ACEVES

As its title suggests, *The New David Espinoza* (Aceves, 2020) is about seventeen-year-old David Espinoza, the story's narrator and title character, who seeks to reinvent himself. After a video of David being assaulted by a classmate goes viral, he is convinced that he can change how others see him if he puts on more muscle mass by dedicating himself to a strict diet and a disciplined workout regimen. With that goal in mind and with inspiration from Hollywood stars who quickly bulk up for blockbuster action roles, David begins working out at a local gym, where he becomes enamored with massive bodybuilders, men he believes are shown proper respect due to their immense proportions. Before long, though, David grows increasingly frustrated with the pace of his own physical development.

Eager to accelerate his muscle gains—even if they come through unnatural means—David seeks assistance from Alpha, the gym's owner and a professional bodybuilder. Under Alpha's tutelage, he begins taking steroids and seeing rapid growth, but not without costs. As David increasingly gains muscle, he spends more and more time working out at the gym with Alpha and his crew or otherwise obsessing about his physical appearance. That leaves him little time for nurturing relationships with those to whom he had been closest previously, including his father, his sister, and his girlfriend. David grows larger as his senior year approaches, but is he strong enough to overcome his fixation on being a "real" man?

The New David Espinoza, Fred Aceves's second novel, has received recommendations from reputable outlets and organizations. The recommendations began with a starred review from *School Library Journal* prior to the book's February 2020 publication. Then, in March of that year, the story was recognized as a Junior Library Guild selection in the "Sports High" category, which accounts for sports-related works of fiction and nonfiction. Later, in November 2020, the novel was included among thirty titles selected for the Chicago Public Library Best Teen Fiction list. Such recognition frames *The New David Espinoza* as a book of interest for secondary readers.

INCORPORATING *THE NEW DAVID ESPINOZA* INTO THE SECONDARY ELA CLASSROOM

The activities described in this chapter can support teachers as they incorporate Aceves's novel into the secondary ELA classroom. Given the events that unfold in the story, there are various ways a teacher could approach it and still explore sociopolitical issues, from focusing on bullying behaviors and their repercussions (as presented in Chapter 9) to examining the rippling effects of drug abuse (as proposed in Chapter 11). However, for this chapter, we opted to concentrate primarily on the issue of traditional masculinity ideology. Accordingly, the activities that follow are intended to advance students' thinking as it relates to four overarching essential questions:

- What does it mean to be a man in today's society?
- What do models of masculinity in sports and other popular cultures convey?
- How does media—both social media and the more traditional variety—inform one's perceptions of self and others?
- What, if anything, does one lose when taking shortcuts to the top, be it in athletics, entertainment, or any other field?

These questions and more can be explored through the close study of *The New David Espinoza* and other relevant texts.

Prior to Teaching the Novel

Before students begin reading Aceves's (2020) novel, teachers can facilitate activities that introduce them to the big ideas that emerge in the story, including how sports and other popular cultures commonly frame men, the expectations we as a society have for men—whether we are consciously aware of them or not—and the implications of "reinventing" oneself. Such activities include establishing the mixed messages that surround the concept of masculinity, frontloading with images, and making predictions about the novel based on peritextual analysis.

Establishing Mixed Messages about Masculinity

Framing the study of *The New David Espinoza* as an exploration into the issue of traditional masculinity ideology, teachers can begin by establishing students' understandings of what it means to be a man and underscoring the mixed messages men receive. To do that, teachers might draw inspiration from an article published in *The New York Times*. Bennett (2015) began "A Master's Degree in . . . Masculinity?" by describing an exercise employed by Dr. Michael Kimmel, director of Stony Brook University's Center for the Study of Men and Masculinities. According to Bennett, Kimmel first asked students, "What does it mean to be a good man?" After receiving puzzled looks, Kimmel gave the example of someone saying at a funeral, "He was a good man," and asked the class, "What does that mean to you?" Students responded, suggesting the statement describes a man who was honest, caring, and put the needs of others before their own, and Kimmel wrote their thoughts in a column under the heading "Good Man." As Bennett explained, Kimmel then asked what it means "to be a *real man*" (italics in original). Needing no further prompting, students framed a "real man" as someone who is authoritative, takes risks, suppresses weakness, and does not cry—ever. Kimmel added these thoughts to a separate column labeled "Real Man." Then, Kimmel closed the exercise by prompting students to notice disparities between the two columns and to consider how an American man might have trouble discerning what traits they ought to embody.

In a unit anchored by *The New David Espinoza*, an introductory activity like that which Bennett (2015) described serves multiple purposes. First, it positions students to consider the initial essential question presented in this chapter: What does it mean to be a man in today's society? Second, it documents students' initial thoughts on the issue, establishing ideas the class can revisit as the unit unfolds. Moreover, an activity like Kimmel's uses students' own words to underscore the mixed messages that surround the concept of masculinity in American society. Finally, the exercise also sets the stage for suggested activities presented later in this chapter. These include activities that invite critically examining cultural resources that inform students' (and literary characters') thinking about what it means to be a man and tasks that require developing extended definitions of masculinity.

Frontloading with Popular Cultural Images

David Espinoza's image of a "real" man, which is also the vision he holds for his future self, is shaped in part by the media he consumes. For instance, he finds inspiration in the six-month physical transformation that actor Van Nelson underwent to prepare for a blockbuster action role (Aceves, 2020). Considering David's relationship with popular media, teaching for critical media literacy, which includes helping students examine the values and ideologies represented in and absent from media messages (Kellner & Share, 2019), is apt. To help students begin contemplating popular media's role in shaping one's thinking about body image and what it means to be a man, teachers can start by prompting students to examine select images from sports and other popular cultures and the messages they convey. Visuals for students' consideration include advertisements, album covers, movie posters, promotional stills, and screenshots from movies, television shows, and/or music videos, among others.

When projecting an image, teachers can simply invite students to share what they notice about it. For example, if projecting the first teaser poster (Wolters, 2018) for Stephen Caple Jr.'s (2018) film *Creed II*, students might immediately notice the muted color of the black-and-white poster. Students are also likely to notice the musculature of actor Michael B. Jordan in the role of Adonis Creed, who stands shirtless with his shoulders square, his well-defined torso glistening. As well, students may notice the stern expression on the actor's face, the slight bend in his hard-muscled arms, and the boxing gloves on his hands, a clear indication that he is prepared to trade blows at a moment's notice. Likewise, if projecting a still from "Leg Day in the Iron Paradise" (The Rock, 2019), an advertisement for athletic apparel company Under Armour's "Project Rock" collection, students may recognize muscle-bound pro wrestler-turned-movie star Dwayne "The Rock" Johnson in a weight room. They may notice an expression of exertion on the actor's face, his bald head shining with perspiration, an oversized silver chain draped over his shoulders to add greater resistance still, and his veins bulging as his massive quads flex mid-lunge. The *Creed II* poster and a still from the Under Armour advertisement are sound examples for this activity because they limit their focus to widely recognizable male figures, creating accessible opportunities for discussing the messages they send about masculinity.

After presenting students with a handful of relevant images to observe, teachers can invite students to look across them and contemplate what they suggest about being a man. For instance, teachers might ask students to reflect in writing using the following exercise:

> In light of what you observed when viewing select images from sports and other popular cultures, consider what they say collectively about being a man in the world today.
>
> - What do these images suggest a man is? What makes you say so?
> - What do these images suggest a man is not? What makes you say so?
> - Of course, these are just a handful among countless images. What other messages about being a man do you see in the popular media with which you engage?
> - How, if at all, does popular media shape your thinking about "being" in this world? Explain.
>
> Please be prepared to share your thinking with your peers.

A reflection exercise like this invites students to begin contemplating issues central to *The New David Espinoza* before they ever crack open the novel.

Making Predictions Based on Peritextual Analysis

Making predictions while reading helps students set expectations, which they can then trace to see if and how the text meets them (Daniels & Zemelman, 2014). By analyzing a book's peritext, the elements "around the text, in the space of the same volume" (Genette, 1991, p. 263), students can make predictions about plot and theme before reading commences (Hill, 2019). Gross and Latham (2017) detailed different types of peritext, including production-related and promotional. Production-related peritext helps to identify the text. It includes elements such as the book's title and the author's name. Promotional peritext, which interfaces between the book and potential readers, includes endorsements, synopses, and more. Analysis of such elements can support students in making predictions about a given text.

When introducing the 2020 HarperTeen edition of *The New David Espinoza*, peritextual analysis might begin with study of the spine, where the title is fully displayed. Asking students what they notice about the title is sure to draw attention to the word "New," which appears in a red font and stands out from the other words in the title. That creates opportunities to discuss the idea of becoming a "new" person and to invite inferences informed by the title. For example, teachers might pose follow-up questions like these:

- How does one go about becoming a "new" person?
- Why might someone want to become a "new" person?
- What can you infer about this book based on the title?

Next, students should analyze the front cover. When facilitating discussion about the cover, teachers can begin with author Adi Alsaid's endorsement, which reads as follows: "Powerful, raw, and honest. A gripping and realistic tale of body image and toxic masculinity." Alsaid's endorsement invites questions like the following:

- What is "body image"?
- What is "toxic masculinity"?
- How does toxic masculinity inform views of body image?
- In light of Asiad's endorsement and the title, now what can you infer about the book?

Additional analysis of the front cover should account for the line below the title (i.e., "No Pain, No Gain . . . Right?") and the cover image depicting the title character's physical transformation.

Once students have analyzed the book's peritext, teachers can invite them to make predictions about the novel's plot and themes using a prompt like the following:

> Now that you've had a chance to analyze the spine, front and back covers, and inside flaps of *The New David Espinoza*, let's make some predictions. Take some time to respond to the following questions:
>
> - How do you think the plot will unfold in *The New David Espinoza*? What makes you think so?
> - Considering the plot you predicted, what themes do you expect to encounter in *The New David Espinoza*? What makes you think so?
>
> Please note that you will be invited to share your thoughts with the class.

After facilitating a prereading activity like this, it is only appropriate for students to revisit their predictions while reading, so we encourage teachers to allot time for reflection on their original predictions as the unit unfolds.

As Students Read the Novel

While students are reading *The New David Espinoza*, teachers can facilitate activities to extend students' thinking as it relates to issues raised in the novel and the essential questions presented elsewhere in this chapter. Suggested activities involve embodying the protagonist's relationships through tableaux, considering other visions of masculinity, and building understandings of muscle dysmorphia, a condition with which the protagonist struggles. We describe these activities in the subsections that follow.

Embodying David Espinoza's Relationships through Tableaux

The plot of *The New David Espinoza* revolves around David's body and his desire to reshape it in a way that conforms to traditional, narrowly conceived notions of masculinity. This desire is informed by various factors, including David's interactions with his peers, with social media, and with texts associated with sports and other popular cultures. Further, David's desire to transform his body ends up altering relationships in his life, including those with his family, his friends, and even himself. Given the emphasis on the shape of David's body, it seems fitting to use enactment strategies (Wilhelm, 2008) to facilitate exploration of what is transpiring in the story.

Enactment strategies position students to use their bodies in ways that help them make meaning of written texts while becoming texts to be read by others. As Wilhelm (2008) explained, enactment strategies can take various forms, including analogy dramas and dramatic play, yet no props or acting chops are necessary. When teaching high school English in southeast Michigan, Luke Rodesiler, one of the authors of this book, occasionally facilitated the creation of tableaux. That is, he engaged students in using intentional body positioning, gestures, and expressions to create silent frozen scenes to be read by the rest of the class. The activity supported the exploration of a given text, for small groups of students were challenged (a) to determine shared understandings about a central idea, theme, or relationship in the text; (b) to embody those understandings for their peers; and (c) to articulate their thinking verbally by clarifying their intentions and citing textual support. Teachers can use a similar approach to facilitate exploration of David Espinoza's various relationships in the novel.

As Figure 10.1 indicates, there are several relationships in *The New David Espinoza* that students can examine and embody. Contemplating questions like those provided in the figure, students can work together in small groups to develop their thinking, communicate their ideas to the class through tableaux, and then offer verbal reflections that clarify what they aimed to convey with their embodiments. Depending on the time available for the unit, teachers might opt to have all groups work to embody select relationships at different points in the book (e.g., all groups work to embody David's relationship with social media after Chapter 4), or teachers might opt to assign each group of students a different relationship to embody after the class has covered more ground in the novel. Either way, teachers can also take photos of the students' tableaux to provide points of reference that they can revisit as the class progresses through the remainder of the story and examines the evolution of David's relationships with social media and with other characters over time.

Relationship to Embody	Questions to Consider
David's relationship with social media	- What role does social media play in how David sees himself? - What textual evidence supports your thinking? - How can you embody David's relationship with social media?
David's relationship with pop culture	- What popular cultural texts inform how David sees himself? How so? - What textual evidence supports your thinking? - How can you embody David's relationship with pop culture?
David's relationship with Alpha	- How has David's relationship with Alpha shaped his self-perception? - What textual evidence supports your thinking? - How can you embody David's relationship with Alpha?
David's relationship with his family	- How has David's fixation on redefining himself affected his familial relationships? - What textual evidence supports your thinking? - How can you embody David's relationship with his family?
David's relationship with his friends	- How has David's obsession with his body affected his relationships with his friends? - What textual evidence supports your thinking? - How can you embody David's relationship with his friends?
David's relationship with himself	- How has David's obsession with his body affected how he feels about himself? - What textual evidence supports your thinking? - How can you embody David's relationship with himself?

FIGURE 10.1: Relationships and Questions to Guide Students in Creating Tableaux

Considering Other Visions of Masculinity

When reading *The New David Espinoza* and exploring the issue of traditional masculinity ideology, teachers can invite students to consider how others have conceptualized the matter. Works of nonfiction can be helpful in this regard. Take, for example, *Season of Life: A Football Star, a Boy, and a Journey to Manhood* (Marx, 2004). The book is a work of narrative nonfiction about Joe Ehrmann, a volunteer football coach at a high school in Baltimore, Maryland. Following a career playing in the National Football League during the 1970s and 1980s, Ehrmann became an ordained minister and began supporting youth on the gridiron and off. In the classroom, *Season of Life* can support students in critically analyzing traditional concepts of masculinity, for it disrupts commonplace notions (Rodesiler, 2021b). Such critical analysis is supported by Ehrmann problematizing *false masculinity*, which he associates with three faulty indicators of manhood: athletic ability, sexual conquest, and economic success (p. 36). Alternatively, Ehrmann promotes *strategic masculinity*, a vision that frames building meaningful relationships and living for a cause beyond oneself as more apt markers of manliness (p. 36).

After reading about the concepts Ehrmann introduces, students can use them as lenses to examine *The New David Espinoza* and their own school culture. For instance, teachers might pose questions like the following:

- Who in David's life, if anyone, promotes indicators associated with what Joe Ehrmann calls "false masculinity"? How so? Provide textual evidence to support your thinking.
- How, if at all, does the media David consumes promote indicators associated with false masculinity? Provide textual evidence to support your thinking.
- How, if at all, does David himself promote false masculinity? Provide textual evidence to support your thinking.
- What models for "strategic masculinity," if any, does David have in his life? How do they reflect that concept? Provide textual evidence to support your thinking.
- Consider the culture of our school. If you had to choose, would you say it promotes false masculinity or strategic masculinity? What makes you say so?

Engaging with such prompts, both in writing and in discussion, can help students consider how particular notions of masculinity are perpetuated in David Espinoza's world as well as in their own. An activity like this is particularly apt for inclusion near the halfway point of the novel, around Chapter 15, when David is entrenched with Alpha's crew at the Iron Life gym and reflecting on his ongoing efforts to prove himself as a man (Aceves, 2020, p. 166). Moreover, the work involved in this activity stands to help students develop an extended definition of masculinity, which can be especially beneficial if students are going to complete the corresponding culminating task presented later in this chapter.

Building Understandings about Muscle Dysmorphia

In Chapter 23, after getting the sense that David is not satisfied with his appearance despite massive gains in the weight room, Rogelio, a member of Iron Life who is not caught up in its steroid culture, tells David about his own previous struggles with *muscle dysmorphia*, which he explains as "this idea some people, mostly guys, get in their heads that they don't look good enough" (Aceves, 2020, p. 255). To help students better understand muscle dysmorphia as they read about David's struggles with the disorder, teachers can invite students to read "What Is 'Bigorexia'?" (Hawgood, 2022). The piece, an article from *The New York Times*, explores the pressure to build muscle that some teenage boys feel after engaging with content on social media.

Hawgood's (2022) article stands to aid students in examining Aceves's novel and their own experiences with muscle-worshiping social media. For example, teachers can use prompts like the following to help students make text-to-text connections between the article and *The New David Espinoza*:

- What is "bigorexia," according to Hawgood? What contributes to the disorder, and what are the symptoms?
- What textual evidence in the novel itself suggests that David Espinoza is afflicted with bigorexia or some other form of muscle dysmorphia?
- Hawgood describes a "beefcake-saturated culture," citing examples that include "the hypermasculine video games [boys and young men] play" and "the mesomorphic superheroes in the movies they watch," which are steeped in "C.G.I.-enhanced masculine clichés." What role does popular media play in shaping David Espinoza's body image? How so? What textual evidence supports your thinking?
- The article describes the research of Dr. Veya Seekis, who found that "exposure to images of archetypal masculine physiques was linked to low body esteem in young men and an increased desire to become more muscular." What models of masculine physiques does David Espinoza seek to emulate? How do these models affect his self-esteem and desires for muscularity? Cite textual evidence to support your thinking.

Teachers can also use prompts like the following to aid students in making connections between the article and their own lived experiences:

- What kind of muscle-promoting popular media have you encountered in recent years? Whether it is social media or more traditional media (e.g., movies, video games), describe the content you've seen that promotes the kind of muscle worship Hawgood described.

- How, if at all, has your own body image been informed by the popular media you consume? How does your experience compare to what teens described in Hawgood's article?
- Given what you know about bigorexia, the perspectives shared by teens in Hawgood's article, and your own experiences with muscle-worshiping content via social media and/or more traditional media platforms, how might we combat the issue in productive ways?

For additional perspectives on Hawgood's (2022) article and social media's contributions to muscle dysmorphia, teachers can share "What Students Are Saying about How Social Media Affects Their Body Image" (The Learning Network, 2022). The piece includes comments from students across the country (and beyond) who read the article and responded to it by addressing relevant topics, including the influence social media can have on one's body image and self-esteem, the unique pressures men and boys face when it comes to body image, and the value of consuming body-positive content.

Voices from the Field
The Courage to Grow: Reflections of an English Teaching Football Coach

Steven J. Arenas
Assistant Principal,
Phoenix Union High School District, Arizona

I have a six-year-old son named Gabriel. Gabriel is kind, smart, talented, and, like most six-year-olds, incredibly curious. And when he says things like "Boys don't do cheerleading," my wife and I carefully remind him there are many things that both boys and girls can do together. Admittedly, this took some practice on my part. The dynamic between a Chicano (Mexican American) father and son is nuanced. It's a delicate balance between cultural conditioning, internalized assimilation, socialization, and *machismo*.

Take my father, for example. He is the product of a single-parent household, raised by a single mother in the downtown neighborhoods of Phoenix. He did well in school, played sports, and became a first-generation college graduate. He soon after became a husband and father and committed his professional career to serving students as an educator for over 30 years. Today, despite conscious efforts my younger brother and I made to forge our own paths, we are also proud college graduates, high school teachers, and football coaches.

Thankfully, my father always encouraged me to be "well-rounded." In my elementary years, I played sports, but I also played trumpet in the school band and participated in school theater performances. Each time, my father played the role of proud parent. However, in middle school, the pressure to fit in became too much of a tightrope despite my father's support. I had to choose between athletics and the arts; the two could not co-exist in my adolescent world. Now, as a father, I ask myself: How do I teach Gabriel to be Gabriel? As a teacher, I ask myself: How do I create a space where all students are safe to be themselves? As a head football coach, I ask myself: How do I disrupt sports culture to allow student-athletes to explore multiple aspects of their identity?

In 2021, I began teaching a course new to our district and my campus: Culturally Relevant English 7–8 from a Mexican American/Chicanx Perspective. I shared my personal anecdote with students in the class as we prepared to read Matt de la Peña's (2008) *Mexican WhiteBoy* for our opening unit on racial identity. I modeled for students all the identities I identify with, and together we brainstormed the social factors that help us define ourselves. Using my anecdote as an example, we questioned how societal norms shape our identity in negative and positive ways. We used this conversation as a way to analyze how Danny's identity is constantly being informed throughout de la Peña's novel. This sort of activity requires vulnerability, but it provides students with an opportunity to navigate the intersections of their identity.

Embracing vulnerability is something I also try to impress upon the athletes I coach. For example, take Carlos Mejia (pseudonym). The young man is every bit of 6'3" and 275 pounds. He is an incredibly gifted football player with an opportunity to use the sport to earn a college education. Carlos is notably insightful and kind despite his intimidating stature. During Carlos's senior year, he was voted one of the team captains. He understood the expectations and responsibilities of this role, so it was surprising that he was frequently absent from my class. After one of our team meetings, Carlos hung around my classroom longer than normal. He shuffled around some of his papers before throwing on his backpack and slowly inching toward my desk.

"Hey, Coach . . . I want to apologize," he muttered. Wanting him to be more direct, I asked, "For what, Carlos?"

Carlos nervously began to explain that he had been missing my class because he had been attending family therapy with his mother. He was embarrassed, and worst of all he was ashamed as he lowered his head, fighting back tears. Me, on the other hand, I was beaming with pride. He shared that he and his single mother were having "problems," and at her request, they sought out professional help. I handed Carlos a tissue and explained how fortunate he is to have a mother who is willing to support their relationship in this way. I continued to share how proud I was that he was brave enough to seek help and let him know that even football coaches need the professional help of a therapist. I wanted Carlos to know that it's okay for boys and men to be vulnerable and to ask for help when they need it; it's a message I hope my son is courageous enough to embrace as he grows older as well.

Reference

de la Peña, M. (2008). *Mexican whiteboy*. Delacorte Press.

Steven Arenas is a former English teacher and head football coach. He currently serves as an assistant principal in the Phoenix Union High School District.

Culminating Tasks after Reading the Novel

In light of the aforementioned essential questions and activities, a culminating task for students might involve writing an extended definition essay or conducting a critical media analysis.

Writing an Extended Definition Essay

To close out a unit anchored by *The New David Espinoza*, teachers looking to go a more traditional route with their writing instruction might opt to facilitate the writing of an extended definition essay. For example, given the materials and activities described in this chapter, it would be apt for students to define what it means to be a man in the modern day. When establishing a definition, students could cite characters from the story (e.g., David, his father, Alpha) and figures featured in other relevant texts included in the unit for illustrative purposes, whether presenting them as supporting or contrasting examples. Further, students could draw ideas from previous discussions to formulate clear and unambiguous criteria by which they would define, say, the concept of a "real" man and relate their supporting and contrasting examples.

Depending on students' needs, teachers might scaffold instruction so that students have opportunities to practice the kind of work required to complete the writing task. For example, teachers might invite students to collaborate as they define a separate concept like, say, "sport." Together, students could formulate criteria that support classifying an activity as "sport," identify an example that meets the established criteria, and explain the example's alignment with those criteria. For instance, as described in *Bringing Sports Culture to the English Classroom* (Rodesiler, 2022), a criterion for "sport" might include "participants engage in competition," and students might choose "competitive cheerleading" as an example, explaining that it satisfies the "competition" criterion because participating cheerleaders are judged in competition against others. Then, students could continue by identifying a non-example, something that stands in contrast to the example, and explaining how it illuminates the criteria's bounds. For instance, if competition helps to define an activity as "sport," then students might choose "sideline cheerleading" as a non-example. Students might explain how, though sideline cheerleading is like competitive cheer in that it requires physical exertion, the "competition" criterion distinguishes the two, for sideline cheer does not involve judging or any other competitive element. Such scaffolding stands to support students when independently writing an extended definition essay about what it means to be a man in today's world.

In addition to advocating for scaffolding, we also encourage teachers to support students in developing their ideas through one-to-one conferences and mini-lessons as warranted. Further, we recommend *The Dynamics of Writing Instruction* (Smagorinsky et al., 2010) for detailed activities teachers can use to support students at each point in the process of crafting an extended definition essay.

Conducting a Critical Media Analysis

Alternatively, teachers might choose to facilitate a critical media analysis. Building on the idea of students critically examining depictions of female athletes in popular media (Rodesiler, 2021a), teachers can facilitate a critical media analysis that positions students to explore how popular media—sports-related or otherwise—perpetuate traditional masculinity ideology. Such work falls in line with a focus on the role that sports and other popular cultures play in shaping one's perception of masculinity.

Drawing from Mahalik et al.'s (2003) research, teachers can first introduce students to the idea of "masculinity scripts" (p. 123), the various ways people perform or enact traditional masculinity ideology. As noted in Figure 10.2, these include the tough-guy script, the "give-'em-hell" script, the playboy script, the homophobic script, the winner script, and the independent script. Students can apply their understanding of masculinity-as-performance when examining

Masculinity Script	Description
Strong and silent	This script is all about remaining stoic and suppressing feelings, despite extensive research indicating that restricting emotions has significant consequences for one's mental health.
Tough guy	This script perpetuates the idea that masculinity is marked by aggressiveness, fearlessness, and the willingness to take up extreme behaviors—even to one's own detriment.
"Give-'em-hell"	This script promotes conforming to norms of violence, despite research showing that embracing such standards is associated with violence against domestic partners.
Playboy	This script limits one's connection with or care for intimate partners, despite research indicating that such norms are associated with hostility and a preference for inequitable social relationships.
Homophobic	This script involves the ridicule or avoidance of anything that could be construed as feminine or homosexual (e.g., close relationships with other men) for fear it threatens one's masculinity.
Winner	This script emphasizes being competitive and successful as markers of masculinity, despite research showing that related qualities (e.g., high drive for achievement) are linked to coronary health issues.
Independent	This script reflects conformity to norms of self-reliance, despite research indicating that such behavior is related to psychological distress and an unwillingness to seek psychological help.

FIGURE 10.2: Masculinity Scripts Identified by Mahalik et al. (2003)

popular media. The texts students choose to analyze may vary widely. Live broadcasts of sporting events, select episodes of a television series, and feature films are fair game. Podcasts, video games, and social media generated by prominent figures in the sports world would also be appropriate for analysis. Likewise, stories published in newspapers or magazines, as well as biographies and memoirs or even works of fiction, could be used in a project like this.

To carry out the project, students can follow the steps commonly associated with content analysis. First, students must identify the media they will be analyzing. This involves setting parameters for the work. For instance, if a student is intent on analyzing the Instagram posts of a professional athlete or a sports franchise, then they would need to establish how deep into the feed they are going to go (i.e., set an established time period or a specific number of posts). Next, students need to collect their data. The shape this step takes will vary, depending on the media students choose to analyze. For example, if a student is analyzing a podcast, they would need to download episodes. Yet if a student is analyzing articles posted on a newspaper's website, they may need to use the media center to get behind the newspaper's paywall and then download or copy-and-paste articles into a word processor for future access. With data collected, students can begin coding or carrying out a recursive process of sorting, categorizing, and interpreting their data, specifically with Mahalik et al.'s (2003) masculinity scripts in mind. At this stage, and for illustrative purposes, teachers purposes, teachers can work with students to analyze *The New David Espinoza* (Aceves, 2020) in light of Mahalik et al.'s masculinity scripts and to create a codebook students can use as they code their chosen texts. Figure 10.3 provides an example of the shape a codebook might take. By analyzing their codes and categories, students can then construct the thematic messages about masculinity that are communicated through the media they examined.

In a move toward social action, students can share the findings of their critical media analyses. This might take the shape of poster presentations, in which students create and placard posters that describe the research they conducted, including but not limited to their methods of data collection, their methods of data analysis, their findings, and the implications stemming from the research. Audience members, whether from the student body or the local community, can circulate from poster to poster and hear more about the research from the presenters themselves. In the event that many students choose to critically analyze multimodal texts, a multimedia presentation format that allows students to play specific, illustrative clips for their audience would also be apt.

Code	Definition	Example
strong and silent	Instances in which a character restricts emotions, promotes the idea of doing so, or criticizes another for not doing so.	"'You two are pathetic,' I say, but the truth is it feels good to be higher on the guy scale for once. I'm manlier than them" (p. 125).
tough guy	Instances in which a character displays aggressiveness, shows fearlessness, or carries out extreme behavior.	"'Do you know where I can buy steroids?'" (p. 91).
give-'em-hell	Instances in which a character perpetrates violence against another or otherwise embraces violent behavior.	"I rush at him, gripping his shirtfront with my fists and keep rushing. I slam him against the wall" (pp. 183–184).
playboy	Instances in which a character resists relational intimacy or experiences sex as lust with no emotional attachment.	"Alpha has been saying, 'More girls than you'll know what to do with, bro,' and maybe he's right" (p. 206).
homophobic	Instances in which a character rejects any association with femininity and/or homosexuality.	"I'm just not comfortable around male nudity" (p. 270).
winner	Instances in which a character demonstrates a highly competitive spirit and an intense drive for success.	"You're really going to do this, David. For the next three months you'll eat clean and be all about your goal. You'll become so unrecognizable that people won't even believe you were that scrawny kid in the slap video" (p. 45).
independent	Instances in which a character pushes for independence or promotes people solving problems on their own.	"It's so ridiculous, this chump trying to tell me what to do. . . . Who needs Culler High? Who needs this bullshit?" (p. 243).

FIGURE 10.3: Sample Codebook with Examples from *The New David Espinoza* (Aceves, 2020)

CONCLUSION

Study of *The New David Espinoza* (Aceves, 2020) and relevant texts can support the important work of critically reading messages about masculinity in the world today. The title character's feelings—his admiration of celebrities based on their appearance and his desire to become something more than he currently is—are the sort with which many teenagers can surely relate. The media messages they, like David Espinoza, receive from advertisements, popular music, blockbuster movies, and sports culture often suggest that to be a man is to be muscular and to never accept the slightest sign of disrespect. Conceptualizing masculinity in such ways contributes to David abusing steroids and alienating loved ones as he reinvents himself over the course of a summer. But it is through the critical analysis of sports and popular media that students can begin conceptualizing masculinity in new ways, reinventing what it means to be a man in contemporary society.

Options for Book Clubs

Teachers looking to facilitate book clubs in which students explore through literature conceptualizations of masculinity can incorporate *The New David Espinoza* alongside titles like the following:

Michigan vs. the Boys (Allen, 2019)
A suggested book-club option in Chapters 2 and 9, this novel can also support the critical study of masculinity. The mistreatment of Michigan, the lone girl on the boys' hockey team, invites critical analysis of the culture that fuels such behavior.

Leverage (Cohen, 2011)
This novel, suggested as a book-club option in Chapter 9, can also be a vehicle for examining masculinity. From the coaches to the players, the culture surrounding the football program is toxic, and the framing of masculinity as a show of brutish dominance has tragic results.

Gut Check (Kester, 2019)
A suggested book-club option in Chapter 6, this novel can also support a study of masculinity. Grayport's football team is engulfed in toxic masculinity, yet Wyatt sees making the team as his last chance to connect with his brother, the star quarterback, before he graduates.

Losers Take All (Klass, 2015)
Though Jack's father and brother were football stars, Jack has no affinity for sports. But when the principal at "Muscles" High requires all seniors to join a sports team, Jack and some of his like-minded peers field a soccer team that upends the school's toxic sports culture.

Manning Up (Walsh, 2019)
In this verse novel, Jack is a star running back, but he fears disappointing his family, living and dead, and struggles with body dysmorphia. Driven by his self-perceived need to "man up," he starves himself and takes steroids, leading to an on-field collapse, therapy, and rehab.

Options for Film Study

Teachers eager to incorporate film study to extend students' exploration of conceptualizations of masculinity might consider screening one of the following documentary films:

*Bigger, Stronger, Faster** (Bell, 2008)
Beyond looking at the history of performance-enhancing drugs in the US, this documentary creates opportunities for questioning conceptualizations of masculinity that drive men in America to strive for domination at any cost, even if it means taking shortcuts to victory.

Tough Guise 2: Violence, Manhood & American Culture (Earp, 2013)
This documentary based on the work of anti-violence educator Jackson Katz explores how limited depictions of manhood in various forms of popular media, from advertising and movies to video games and sports, contribute to antiquated views of masculinity in the US.

You Throw Like a Girl: The Blind Spot of Masculinity (Hutchison & Sabean, 2020)
Drawing from his own lived experiences, Don McPherson, a former NFL quarterback, scrutinizes popular notions of masculinity and considers how everyone, regardless of gender, suffers when society embraces narrow views of manliness.

The Bro Code: How Contemporary Culture Creates Sexist Men (Keith, 2011)
In this documentary examining how contemporary culture reinforces misogyny, sexism, and violence against women, Dr. Thomas Keith calls for viewers to challenge narrow conceptualizations of masculinity and embrace a more humanizing vision of manhood.

The Mask You Live In (Newsom, 2015)
This documentary examines popular perceptions of masculinity and the harm done by narrow conceptualizations of manhood, including stereotypes that eschew the expression of emotions beyond anger and rage.

Young Adult Literature

Aceves, F. (2020). *The new David Espinoza*. HarperTeen.

Allen, C. S. (2019). *Michigan vs. the boys*. Kids Can Press.

Cohen, J. (2011). *Leverage*. Dutton Books for Young Readers.

Kester, E. (2019). *Gut check*. Farrar, Straus and Giroux.

Klass, D. (2015). *Losers take all*. Farrar, Straus and Giroux.

Walsh, B. (2019). *Manning up*. West 44 Books.

Other Texts for Classroom Use

Bell, C. (Director). (2008). *Bigger, stronger, faster** [Film]. BSF Film.

Caple, S. (Director). (2018). *Creed II* [Film]. Metro-Goldwyn-Mayer; New Line Cinema.

Earp, J. (Director). (2013). *Tough guise 2: Violence, manhood & American culture* [Film]. Media Education Foundation.

Hawgood, A. (2022, March 5). What is "bigorexia"? *The New York Times*. https://www.nytimes.com/2022/03/05/style/teen-bodybuilding-bigorexia-tiktok.html

Hutchison, P. D., & Sabean, L. (Directors). (2020). *You throw like a girl: The blind spot of masculinity* [Film]. Eat the Moon Films.

Keith, T. (Director). (2011). *The bro code: How contemporary culture creates sexist men* [Film]. Media Education Foundation.

Marx, J. (2004). *Season of life: A football star, a boy, a journey to manhood*. Simon & Schuster.

Newsom, J. S. (Director). (2015). *The mask you live in* [Film]. The Representation Project.

The Rock. (2019, March 14). *Leg day in the Iron Paradise* [Video]. YouTube. https://www.youtube.com/watch?v=rwMFUgUhhls

REFERENCES

Addis, M. E., & Cohane, G. H. (2005). Social scientific paradigms of masculinity and their implications for research and practice in men's mental health. *Journal of Clinical Psychology, 61*(6), 633–647.

American Psychological Association. (2018). *APA guidelines for psychological practice with boys and men*. https://www.apa.org/about/policy/boys-men-practice-guidelines.pdf

Bennett, J. (2015, August 8). A master's degree . . . in masculinity? *The New York Times*. https://www.nytimes.com/2015/08/09/fashion/masculinities-studies-stony brook-michael-kimmel.html

Carroll, R. (2013, January 18). Lance Armstrong admits doping in Oprah Winfrey interview. *The Guardian*. https://www.theguardian.com/sport/2013/jan/18/lance-armstrong-admits-doping-oprah-winfrey

Connell, R. W. (1995). *Masculinities*. University of California Press.

Daniels, H., & Zemelman, S. (2014). *Subjects matter: Exceeding standards through powerful content-area reading* (2nd ed.). Heinemann.

Genette, G. (1991). Introduction to the paratext (M. Maclean, Trans.). *New Literary History, 22*(2), 261–272.

Giaccardi, S., Ward, L. M., Seabrook, R. C., Manago, A., & Lippman, J. (2017). Media use and men's risk behaviors: Examining the role of masculinity ideology. *Sex Roles, 77*, 581–592.

Gregory, S. (2014, November 5). The stream is over: A-Rod admits to manipulating drug tests. *TIME*. https://time.com/3559856/a-rod-urine-steroids

Gross, M., & Latham, D. (2017). The peritextual literacy framework: Using the functions of peritext to support critical thinking. *Library & Information Science Research, 39*(2), 116–123.

Hill, C. (2019). Peritextual bridges: Predicting plot and theme in *Boxers & Saints*. In S. Witte, D. Latham, & M. Gross (Eds.), *Literacy engagement through peritextual analysis* (pp. 31–40). American Library Association; National Council of Teachers of English.

Kellner, D., & Share, J. (2019). *The critical media literacy guide: Engaging media and transforming education*. Brill Sense.

Levant, R. F., & Richmond, K. (2007). A review of research on masculinity ideologies using the male role norms inventory. *The Journal of Men's Studies, 15*(2), 130–146.

Mahalik, J. R., Good, G. E., & Englar-Carlson, M. (2003). Masculinity scripts, presenting concerns, and help seeking: Implications for practice and training. *Professional Psychology: Research and Practice, 34*(2), 123–131.

Monk, D., & Ricciardelli, L. A. (2003). Three dimensions of the male gender role as correlates of alcohol and cannabis involvement in young Australian men. *Psychology of Men & Masculinity, 4*(1), 57–69.

Parent, M. C., & Bradstreet, T. C. (2018). Sexual orientation, bullying for being labeled gay or bisexual, and steroid use among US adolescent boys. *Journal of Health Psychology, 23*(4), 608–617.

Pleck, J. H., Sonenstein, F. L., & Ku, L. C. (1993). Masculinity ideology: Its impact on adolescent males' heterosexual relationships. *Journal of Social Issues, 49*(3), 11–29.

Rodesiler, L. (2021a). Controversies, rivalries, and representation: Sports culture as a site for research and inquiry. *Journal of Adolescent & Adult Literacy, 65*(1), 55–63.

———. (2021b). Focusing on sociopolitical issues in a secondary sports literature class: Opportunities and experiences. *English Teaching: Practice & Critique, 20*(3), 341–353.

———. (2022). *Bringing sports culture to the English classroom: An interest-driven approach to literacy instruction*. Teachers College Press.

Salgado, D. M., Knowlton, A. L., & Johnson, B. L. (2019). Men's health-risk and protective behaviors: The effects of masculinity and masculine norms. *Psychology of Men & Masculinities, 20*(2), 266–275.

Scharrer, E., & Blackburn, G. (2018). Cultivating conceptions of masculinity: Television and perceptions of masculine gender role norms. *Mass Communication and Society, 21*(2), 149–177.

Schuler, L. (2018, October 10). How Arnold became Arnold: The *Men's Health* legends interview with Arnold Schwarzenegger. *Men's Health*. https://www.menshealth.com/entertainment/a23621596/arnold-schwarzenegger-bodybuilding-interview

Smagorinsky, P., Johannessen, L. R., Kahn, E. A., & McCann, T. M. (2010). *The dynamics of writing instruction: A structured process approach for middle and high school*. Heinemann.

Smith, R. M., Parrott, D. J., Swartout, K. M., & Tharp, A. T. (2015). Deconstructing hegemonic masculinity: The roles of antifemininity, subordination to women, and sexual dominance in men's perpetration of sexual aggression. *Psychology of Men & Masculinities, 16*(2), 160–169.

The Learning Network. (2022, March 31). What students are saying about how social media affects their body image. *The New York Times*. https://www.nytimes.com/2022/03/31/learning/what-students-are-saying-about-how-social-media-affects-their-body-image.html

Wallace, J., Covassin, T., & Beidler, E. (2017). Sex differences in high school athletes' knowledge of sport-related concussion symptoms and reporting behaviors. *Journal of Athletic Training, 52*(7), 682–688.

Wilhelm, J. D. (2008). *"You gotta be the book": Teaching engaged and reflective reading with adolescents* (2nd ed.). Teachers College Press.

Williams, B. (2019, April 15). The Mountain confirms previous steroid use. *Men's Health*. https://www.menshealth.com/fitness/a27150995/thor-bjornsson-steroids/

Wolters, C. (2018, June 19). "Creed II" teaser poster released, trailer drops tomorrow. *The Philadelphia Inquirer*. https://www.inquirer.com/philly/entertainment/creed-ii-teaser-poster-released-trailer-drops-tomorrow-20180619.html

11 Reckoning with Drug Abuse among Athletes and Everyday People

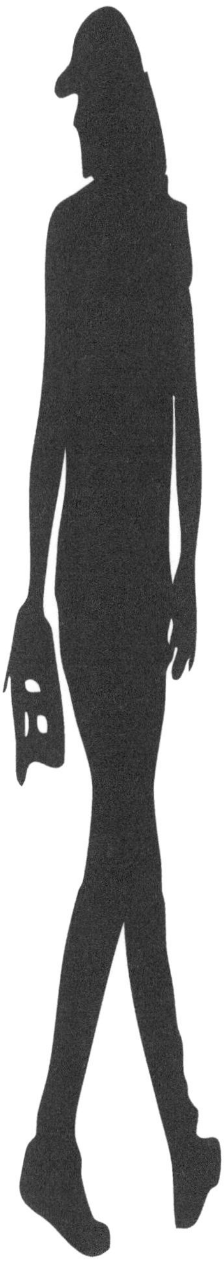

My goal has always been to drop the pills as soon as possible, and right now, it's not possible.

—*Mickey Catalan,* HEROINE *(McGinnis, 2019, p. 181)*

Drug abuse has taken an indelible toll in the United States, touching many lives, including those of people involved in sports culture. Time has shown that drug abuse can take the life of an athlete at any level, be it professional, college, or high school. Consider, for example, the following stories:

- A toxicology report revealed that ethanol, fentanyl, and oxycodone intoxication contributed to the July 2019 death of Tyler Skaggs, a pitcher for Major League Baseball's Los Angeles Angels (Bogage, 2019).
- Medical examiners ruled that the death of Jaylon Ferguson, a linebacker for the NFL's Baltimore Ravens, was accidental, resulting from the combined effects of fentanyl and cocaine (Oxenden, 2022).
- Jake Ehlinger, a University of Texas football player, reportedly died from an accidental overdose of Xanax and fentanyl in May of 2021 (Coleman, 2021).
- In December of 2020, a teenage soccer and track athlete died of fentanyl poisoning in California (Heap, 2021).

In light of such disheartening stories, this chapter is designed to aid teachers in using sports and young adult literature to facilitate literacy learning while supporting students as they make sense of the opioid crisis that continues to ravage our nation.

THE SOCIAL CONCERN OF DRUG ABUSE

Nearly 107,000 drug overdose deaths occurred in the United States in 2021, and approximately 75 percent of those deaths involved the use of opioids (Centers for Disease Control and Prevention, 2023), "a class of drugs that include the illegal drug heroin, synthetic opioids such as fentanyl, and pain relievers available legally by prescription" (National Institute on Drug Abuse, n.d.). In the US, opioid abuse as an ongoing public health crisis can be traced back to the 1990s, when opioid prescriptions began rising and the number of overdoses and deaths tied to prescription opioids climbed with it.

In addition to the tragedy that is a life lost prematurely, the opioid crisis undermines communities in other ways. For instance, there are economic costs for residents in regions marred by drug overdose deaths. Examining the northwest region of Ohio, which has seen an increase in opioid-related deaths since the late 2000s, Smirnov (2019) emphasized the indirect economic costs that follow the unexpected loss of locally spent income. A household's loss of income reverberates through a community, for when an individual dies prematurely, so does their stream of local expenditures, which is problematic for local businesses. When demand for a local business's goods or services dries up, so do the employment opportunities they can offer people in the community. Then, with employees losing jobs, their households spend less money locally as well, and the spiral of community suffering continues.

Non-fatal opioid abuse has repercussions, too. For instance, Feder et al. (2019) noted several problems stemming from a parent/guardian's opioid use that could affect a child's well-being. These include a child's poisoning or overdose from intentional misuse or accidental ingestion of prescription drugs; impaired parenting; material deprivation after money is spent on drugs; and an extended separation from parents due to a child's removal from the home or a parent's opioid-related incarceration, residential treatment, or death. Such problems underscore the fact that, while premature death is undoubtedly tragic, a family and community's suffering is not limited to instances of an untimely, opioid-fueled death.

The grip of the opioid crisis is far reaching, with studies indicating that it affects youth and young adults in the US. Presenting an analysis of responses provided by adolescents (aged 12–17) and young adults (aged 18–25) completing the National Survey on Drug Use and Health (NSDUH), Hudgins et al. (2019) found that nearly 28 percent of respondents reported using prescription opioids within the past year, and nearly 12 percent of respondents reported misusing opioids. Teenagers using (or misusing) prescription opioids is concerning because it may lead to the abuse of nonprescription opioids. For instance, Cicero et al.

(2014) found that, among participants seeking treatment for heroin addiction who began abusing opioids in the 2000s, 75 percent reported a prescription drug as their introduction to opioids. Such findings underscore the risks that come with prescribing opioids to youth and young adults.

As dire as the opioid crisis is, drug use among youth is not limited to opioids. It involves various other substances, including alcohol, cigarettes, and hallucinogens. Use of these and other illicit substances undermines outcomes for youth in numerous ways. For instance, consider academic engagement and performance. Examining the association between abstinence from all substances and academic achievement, Bugbee et al. (2019) found that high school seniors who used substances within the previous year had significantly greater odds of skipping school during the past month than lifetime non-users. They also found that the odds of past-year substance users earning grades at or below a C+ were significantly higher than the odds of lifetime non-users getting low grades. Moreover, even when adjusting for demographic variables, Bugbee et al. found that lifetime non-users of substances had greater self-efficacy regarding their academic abilities and more positive feelings about education compared to past-year substance users. Therefore, when thinking about youth outcomes, the social concern of drug abuse ought not be limited to opioids alone.

DRUG ABUSE IN SPORTS CULTURE

In light of the US prescription drug epidemic, researchers have worked to identify populations that face an increased risk of non-medical use of prescription drugs or, in other words, the use of prescription medications that have not been prescribed. Some studies indicate that competitive sports participation is significantly associated with non-medical use of prescription drugs. For example, when investigating the relationship between athlete status, injury history, and non-medical use of prescription opioids among college students, Ford et al. (2017) reported that healthy male athletes, athletes with injuries, and male athletes with injuries were at the greatest risk of non-medical use of prescription opioids.

Research offers possible explanations for why youth and young adults who participate in competitive sports are more likely to report non-medical use of prescription drugs. For instance, the severe injury rate of specific sports may be a factor. Conducting a cross-sectional study, Veliz et al. (2013) found that adolescents who participated in high-injury sports such as football and wrestling had 50 percent higher odds of non-medical use of prescription opioids than those who did not. US high school athletes competing in football and wrestling suffer severe injuries at rates higher than their peers competing in other sports (Darrow et al., 2009), a fact that may inform those heightened odds, as athletes seek to relieve the pain they suffer during competition. High rates of severe injury are also notable considering that leftovers from previous prescriptions have been established as a major source of the opioids taken by high school seniors for non-medical purposes (McCabe et al., 2013). Compared to their peers who do not participate in organized athletics, the youth and young adults competing in football and wrestling may have more opportunities to get prescription opioids from teammates who divert the drugs they were prescribed for medical purposes.

It is also worth noting that drug use among high school athletes is not limited to opioids. In a nationwide study investigating the impact of sports participation on alcohol, tobacco, marijuana, and other illicit drug use, Veliz et al. (2015) reported that adolescents who played high-contact sports (e.g., football, hockey, lacrosse, and wrestling) had higher odds of using substances during the previous thirty days than those who did not. Research has also shown that adolescents who participated in baseball, football, and weightlifting had higher levels of alcohol consumption than their peers (Denham, 2011). Looking beyond recreational drugs, researchers have documented the use of anabolic steroids and other performance-enhancing drugs among teenage athletes as well. For example, in a survey of high school students, Lorang et al. (2011) found that overall rates of steroid use were low yet higher among male students and those competing in at least one school-sponsored sport. In fact, the odds of current or previous steroid use increased by 91 percent if a student participated in at least one sport, and participation in football, wrestling, and soccer were the strongest predictors of steroid use (p. 363). So, while the opioid epidemic is of grave concern, opioids are not the only drugs abused by high school athletes.

FOCAL YA TEXT: *HEROINE* BY MINDY MCGINNIS

In *Heroine* (McGinnis, 2019), the tandem of seventeen-year-old Mickey Catalan, the story's narrator, and her best friend Carolina Galarza is the battery that makes their Ohio high school softball team hum. Mickey is the team's star catcher and Carolina is the team's pitching ace. However, their dreams for the upcoming season may be dashed when they both suffer significant injuries in a severe car accident. Following surgery and with the support of their respective families—Mickey's divorced parents and Carolina's close-knit crew—both players strive to recover in time to participate in the softball conditioning drills that are just months away. Recovery is a grueling process for both the catcher and the pitcher, but only Mickey relies on prescribed opioids to relieve her excruciating pain.

Mickey enjoys how the prescribed drugs make her feel, and her legitimate opioid use rapidly devolves into an unhealthy opioid addiction. Along the way, she finds herself immersed in a new social group, a mix of individuals who share the same illicit habits, which only accelerates her downward trajectory. Perpetually in pursuit of the next high, Mickey engages in uncharacteristic behavior: she lies, steals, and, for the sake of keeping her drug use a secret, shuts out those who were once closest to her, including Carolina. As she spirals into addiction, Mickey risks losing not only the dreams she held for herself and her softball team but also her life.

Critics have recognized *Heroine* as a high-quality work of fiction that appeals to teenage readers. Prior to its release in March of 2019, the book received starred reviews from numerous outlets, including *Booklist*, *Kirkus Reviews*, *Publishers Weekly*, *School Library Journal*, and *Voice of Youth Advocates* (VOYA). Additionally, *Heroine* was recognized as a Junior Library Guild selection in the "Sports High" category and included in CCBC Choices 2020, the Cooperative Children's Book Center's annual listing of the best books for children and teenagers. McGinnis's (2019) novel has also been celebrated among YALSA's 2020 Top Ten Best Fiction for Young Adults and YALSA's 2020 Top Ten Quick Picks for Reluctant Young Adult Readers. These distinctions stand to advance any argument for incorporating *Heroine* in the secondary ELA classroom.

INCORPORATING *HEROINE* INTO THE SECONDARY ELA CLASSROOM

With McGinnis's (2019) novel presenting the story of high school softball star Mickey Catalan's tragic descent into drug addiction, the following activities are intended to support students' exploration of two overarching essential questions:

- How does drug abuse affect individuals and communities?
- How do we respond to people in need?

Students can consider these questions and others as they read *Heroine* and related texts.

Prior to Teaching the Novel

There are various activities teachers can incorporate to aid students before they begin reading *Heroine*. Among those we suggest are facilitating the completion and discussion of a survey to spark students' thinking about issues relevant to McGinnis's (2019) novel; hosting a counselor to enhance students' understandings about addiction, opioids, and the ongoing prescription drug epidemic; or otherwise incorporating online materials to help students build background knowledge relevant to the topic and the text at hand.

Completing and Discussing a Survey

As a prereading activity, completing and discussing a survey can be useful for helping students think about issues relevant to the text at hand (Milner et al., 2017; Smagorinsky, 2008). Effective surveys include prompts in the form of declarative statements that are likely to invite disparate responses from students, which can then fuel discussion. In our own respective classrooms, we have invited students to first complete a survey independently, to then share their thinking with a partner or in small groups, and, finally, to discuss each prompt in a whole-class discussion.

Figure 11.1 includes an example of a survey that could be used with students prior to reading *Heroine*. Given the issue central to the novel, each prompt included in Figure 11.1 pertains in some way to drug addiction or the opioid crisis. If using prompts like these, we advise teachers to address students' misconceptions. For example, consider a statement such as "Drug addiction is a result of moral weakness." This statement reflects a stigma commonly placed on drug addicts, but the medical field has long established that drug addiction is not simply a behavior problem or the product of poor choices; rather, it is a disease. Therefore, it would be a mistake to affirm the idea that drug addiction is simply an individual's moral failing.

Share your thoughts by rating each statement from 1 (strongly agree) to 5 (strongly disagree).

1. Drug addiction is a result of moral weakness.
2. Drug abuse can lead to problems at school, health issues, and changes in behavior.
3. Drug abuse is an individual problem, not a community problem.
4. The abuse of opioids has reached a crisis level in the United States.
5. Young age is a risk factor for opioid misuse and addiction.
6. "To relieve physical pain" is a common reason for misusing prescription drugs.
7. People who participate in sports are unlikely to use drugs.
8. Athletes are less likely than most people to develop a drug addiction.
9. Administering anti-overdose medications only perpetuates the cycle of drug addiction.
10. Drug addiction is treatable and can be managed.

FIGURE 11.1: Example Prereading Survey

Hosting a Counselor to Address Drug Addiction

When literature creeps into an area beyond a teacher's expertise, it can be helpful to lean on the knowledge and experience accrued by professionals in that field. For example, when engaging high school juniors and seniors in the study of Ken Kesey's (1962) *One Flew Over the Cuckoo's Nest*, a novel set in an Oregon psychiatric hospital, Luke Rodesiler, one of the authors of this book, invited a psychiatric social worker with expertise in cognitive behavioral therapy and clinical supervision into the classroom to discuss the context of a psychiatric facility, to share his experiences as a professional in the field, and to answer students' questions. In a similar fashion, given the gravity of opioid addiction, the issue central to *Heroine*, we encourage teachers to consider bringing a counselor into the classroom to share with students their expertise on addiction, opioids, and the prescription drug epidemic.

As readers, students stand to benefit when they have prior knowledge regarding the issues and topics they are reading about. A counselor with expertise on drug addiction can help students build knowledge relevant to *Heroine* and field any questions they may have going into the novel. For instance, a counselor can help students understand the scope of the opioid crisis, the causes and effects of drug addiction, and the stigma that comes with it. Further, students may have questions of their own about drug abuse. They may wonder about the symptoms of abusing opioids, the timeframe for addiction, preventative measures, treatment, or numerous other aspects of the issue that a counselor is equipped to address. Accordingly, we suggest hosting a counselor to help students construct new knowledge as they prepare to read *Heroine*.

Building Background Knowledge about the Prescription Drug Crisis

If counseling professionals are not available or if bringing a guest into the classroom is simply not viable, there are other avenues for helping students build background knowledge about opioids, drug addiction, and the prescription drug crisis that has been devastating the US. For instance, teachers might present students with information from the Centers for Disease Control and Prevention (CDC, 2022). The CDC provides details about the history of the crisis, efforts made to combat it, and more. Given the story that unfolds in McGinnis's (2019) novel, teachers are likely to find the "Prescription Opioids" page of the CDC website especially relevant. The page provides readers with information about the prevalence of addiction that stems from prescribed opioids, which is what Mickey Catalan, the novel's central character, experiences. The page also details side effects that come with taking prescription opioids, which readers will then recognize as opioids are introduced into Mickey's life.

Teachers can also use relevant educational videos to aid students in building knowledge to support them as they read *Heroine*. For example, TED-Ed's (2020) "What Causes Opioid Addiction, and Why Is It so Tough to Combat?" is an animation featuring Mike Davis, who defines opioids and their addictive properties, briefly explains the growth of opioid prescriptions and addictions, and details what can be done to combat overdoses. "How America Got Hooked on Opioids" (VICE, 2020) offers a grittier look at the prescription drug epidemic through accounts shared by drug addicts and police officers and considers how the war on drugs has contributed to the problem. Such resources can help students understand the unthinkable scope of the prescription drug crisis and see how an otherwise successful student athlete like Mickey Catalan could succumb to drug addiction.

Voices from the Field
Grounding Escape in Empathy: An Approach to Addressing Addiction with Students

Kate Youngblood
English Teacher and Department Chair,
Orleans Parish, Louisiana

My junior English class has centered on the idea of escape for the past three years. I start my classes with an excerpt from John Green's *Looking for Alaska* (2005), where Alaska and Miles are discussing the "labyrinth." After Alaska's death, Miles's teacher assigns the question, "How will we ever get out of this labyrinth of suffering?" (Green, 2005, p. 158). Throughout the year, we view texts through the lens of labyrinths—physical, emotional, societal—that trap characters. How do characters try to escape those labyrinths? Is escape possible? If so, how and what awaits a character who has left whatever has been trapping them? I like to start with this idea of escape because it is incredibly universal; all of my students can relate to the idea of feeling stuck, of seeking out change. This universality allows students to build a relationship with the characters they encounter, to approach those characters with a seed of empathy.

Invariably, however, we end up reading about characters who attempt to escape societal pressures or expectations through less than healthy means: lying, cheating, and numbing themselves with drugs and alcohol. When we approach the latter, escape through drug abuse, I find that an important step to keeping students grounded in empathy is by making addiction seem concrete, starting with details, definitions, and facts. Students must understand the reality behind addiction to begin comprehending why a character would turn to alcohol or drugs as a coping mechanism in order to try to escape the struggles that keep them grounded.

When tackling a story of drug abuse like *Heroine* (McGinnis, 2019), it is important not only to make sure students understand the crisis of addiction but also that they leave their reading understanding that this coping mechanism isn't a healthy one. One way to do that is by incorporating resources about addiction in contemporary society. I recommend that students read the two-pager "Facing Addiction in America, the Surgeon General's

Report on Alcohol, Drugs, and Health" (Substance Abuse and Mental Health Services Administration, 2016). This fact sheet is extremely concrete and lends itself to building empathy, starting with truths about how pervasive substance abuse is in America. This sheet is also helpful in that it does not doom people who suffer from addiction; rather, it plainly spells out paths to recovery, both on the individual level (e.g., offering support instead of judgment) and the systemic level (e.g., through community outreach programs). A nice complement to this fact sheet is the CDC's Campaign for Rx Awareness: Real Stories (Centers for Disease Control and Prevention, 2020). These stories offer videos and transcripts of real people who suffer from addiction. They explain what made people turn to drugs and what struggles came after. Among the videos, Mike's story pairs well with *Heroine* in particular because, like Mickey, Mike struggles with opioid addiction after a sports injury.

After unpacking Mike's story, students can begin reading *Heroine* (McGinnis, 2019) or related stories about athletes suffering drug addiction. As students read, I recommend nudging them to try to understand the athlete's *why*, reminding them especially of the Surgeon General's recommendation to "be supportive (not judgmental)" and to focus on the "changes needed in the community" (Substance Abuse and Mental Health Services Administration, 2016), whether that community is a team, a school, or a city that will help people recover from addiction or attempt to prevent addiction in the first place. By keeping their focus on how addiction impacts real people around them and in their communities, students can foster empathy, learning that addicts are people just like them, often seeking a way to escape their labyrinths.

References

Centers for Disease Control and Prevention. (2020). *Real stories.* https://www .cdc.gov/rxawareness/stories/index.html

Green, J. (2005). *Looking for Alaska.* Dutton Books.

McGinnis, M. (2019). *Heroine.* Katherine Tegen Books.

Substance Abuse and Mental Health Services Administration. (2016). *Facing addiction in America: The surgeon general's report on alcohol, drugs, and health.* https://addiction.surgeongeneral.gov/sites/default/files/fact-sheet-individuals.pdf

Kate Youngblood has been teaching ninth- and eleventh-grade English at Benjamin Franklin High School in New Orleans, Louisiana, for the past nine years. She graduated from Louisiana State University with a BA in English, secondary education. She later earned her M.A.Ed. from Wake Forest University. She has presented at the National Council of Teachers of English Annual Convention five times and has been published as a coauthor in Signal Journal *and* English in Education. *Kate was selected as the Louisiana State High School Teacher of the Year in 2021.*

As Students Read the Novel

As students read *Heroine*, teachers can facilitate various activities to deepen students' engagement with the aforementioned essential questions and the novel itself. Graphing the lives of Mickey and Carolina over the course of the novel, discussing Mickey's experience via a concentric circles protocol, and considering Mickey's struggles in light of athletes' lived experiences are viable activities for teachers to facilitate as students work their way through the story.

Constructing a Life Graph

When teaching sophomores in an American literature class, Luke once facilitated a "life graph" activity (Rief, 1992) early in the school year. Essentially, the activity involved students graphing positive and negative experiences they had in their lifetimes that they felt comfortable writing about and sharing with others. It served as both a way for students to get to know one another and a way for them to generate various topics they might choose to write about during the year. However, life-graphing can also be adapted to support literature study, for it helps students see the trajectory—the ups and the downs—of characters' lives over the course of a story. When studying *Heroine*, charting Mickey's life and Carolina's life on the same graph can help students see the different trajectories their lives take and can facilitate discussion about the factors at play for each character.

To help students begin graphing characters' lives, teachers can distribute a premade template or graph paper on which students can draw the x-axis and the y-axis (see Figure 11.2). As shown in the example provided, the x-axis marks the passage of time in the novel. In the case of *Heroine*, using months as the unit of time would be appropriate, for the bulk of the story unfolds from the car accident in December to the end of the following softball season, or approximately six months. The y-axis, then, offers an indication of how positive or negative each development in the novel was for a given character. While reading, students should mark new developments involving Mickey and/or Carolina as they arise and graph them accordingly.

As shown in Figure 11.2, the first meaningful event in the story for Mickey is the car accident in the book's opening chapter. Given the severity of the injuries Mickey and Carolina suffer, some students might be inclined to place the accident at the very bottom of the graph's y-axis. Yet we know that things will actually get worse for Mickey as the novel progresses and her addiction takes hold, so students will need room on the graph to drop lower still. Therefore, it may be helpful to frame the bottom of the y-axis as, say, the character's death. That should give students a point of reference as they think about where to plot various developments on the graph as they unfold in the novel.

When graphing, students will begin to see Mickey and Carolina's lives trending in different directions. At that point, it can be helpful to discuss how each character got where they are. For example, teachers might invite students to discuss how Mickey ended up in her situation and how Carolina avoided those same circumstances. It is a pertinent topic of discussion, for it is one Carolina and Mickey take up in Chapter 55. Teachers might also invite students to consider how Mickey could possibly climb out of the hole she finds herself in at various low points in her life, such as when she begins stealing and lying to feed her addiction.

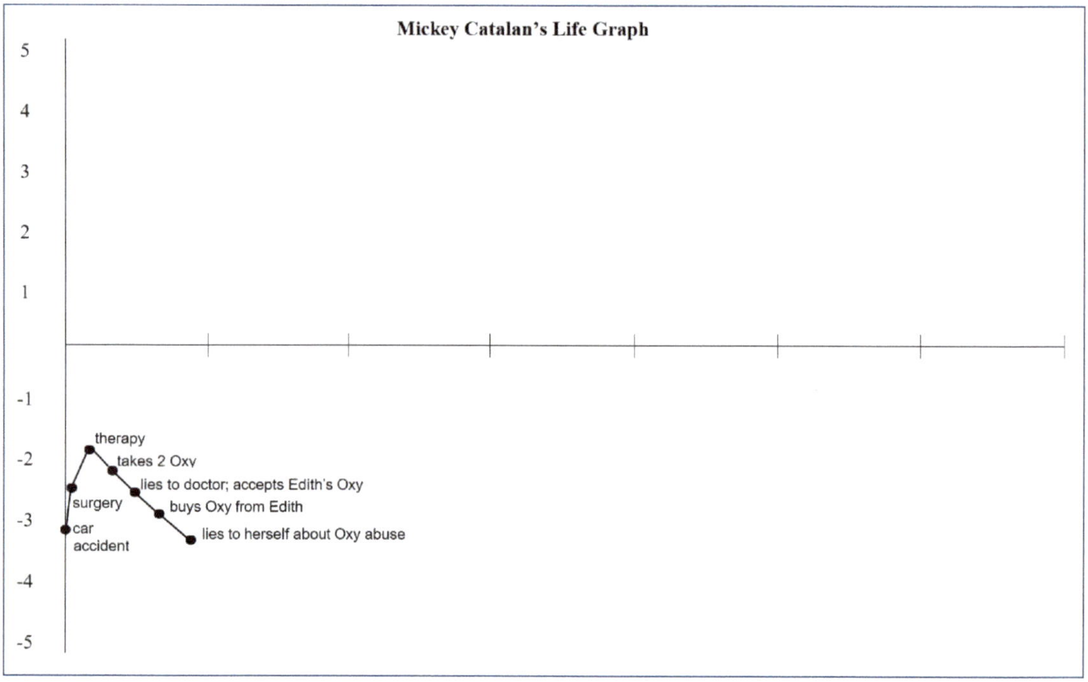

FIGURE 11.2: Example Life Graph for Mickey Catalan, Chapters 1–10

Discussing Mickey's Experience via Concentric Circles

Discussing Mickey's experience with drug use, abuse, and addiction is time well spent when reading *Heroine*. There are many valuable protocols a teacher could use to generate such a discussion, but the concentric circles protocol is especially helpful when teachers aim to get students talking more frequently during the class period. Fishbowls and Socractic seminars are time-tested structures for discussion, but they only allow for one student to speak at a time. The concentric circles protocol, however, allows for half of the class to speak at the same time.

When employing concentric circles, Luke begins by first having students count off. After all students have called out a number, he directs the students with an odd number to form a circle in the center of the room and face outward. Next, he asks students with an even number to form a circle outside the odds and face inward. Each pair of students across from one another in the concentric circles are partners for the first round of discussion. Luke then reads aloud a projected prompt and invites students to discuss it. After a given amount of time, he signals that it is time to end the discussion, and students in the outer circle are to rotate clockwise so that everyone has a new partner for the next round. Then, Luke reads aloud a new prompt that is projected in the room for students to discuss. The process continues in that manner until all prompts have been discussed. Time permitting, teachers might also consider inviting some pairs to report out and share what they discussed before prompting the rotations.

Figure 11.3 presents a series of example discussion prompts a teacher might use when facilitating the exploration of Mickey's experience during the first quarter of McGinnis's (2019) novel, whether using concentric circles or another discussion protocol. The prompts provided account for significant topics that arise in the first 100 pages or so of *Heroine*. These topics include Mickey's relationships with her family and her classmates, the identity she has built for herself as a star softball player, her drug use (and abuse), and the rationales she crafts to justify seeking drugs from Edith after her own prescription medication has run out. Through discussion, students can develop and begin to articulate their thinking about Mickey's experiences while learning from their peers' perspectives as well. Depending on students' needs, teachers might opt to use concentric circles to facilitate discussion at each of the book's four quarters.

Topic	Questions to Discuss
Mickey's relationships	What do we know about Mickey's relationships? How, if at all, might the relationships she has at school and at home make her feel disconnected from others? What makes you say so?
Mickey's recovery	When asked about her timeline for recovery, Mickey lies to her teammates. Why do you think she lies? How, if at all, might that lie become problematic for her down the road?
Mickey's identity	How does Mickey define herself? That is, what is her primary identity, and how do you know? What danger, if any, do you see in people defining themselves in such a narrow way?
Mickey's drug use	How does Mickey's drug use progress in the first several chapters of the book? What do the drugs do for Mickey? How, if at all, could this be problematic for her in the long run?
Mickey's rationales	After visiting Edith for the first time, how does Mickey rationalize her drug use? To what degree, if any, are her rationales reasonable? What makes you say so?
Mickey's altruism	As Chapter 13 ends, Mickey describes her drug use in altruistic terms, claiming, "I'm taking [Oxy] for other people" (p. 91). How truthful do you find that statement to be, if at all? What makes you say so?

FIGURE 11.3: Example Prompts for Discussing Mickey's Experience in the First Quarter of *Heroine*

Considering Mickey's Struggles in Comparison to Those of Real Athletes

After students have covered considerable ground in *Heroine* and developed a clear sense for Mickey's struggles with drug addiction, including how it is affecting her relationships, her health, and her performance on the softball diamond, it may be beneficial to consider her story in light of the lived experiences of a real athlete. One way to do that is by pairing the novel with texts that tell the stories of athletes who are on record as having engaged in drug abuse or having suffered from drug addiction. *The Players' Tribune* has published essays attributed to athletes detailing their battles with substance abuse and addiction. These include pieces by hall-of-fame boxer Sugar Ray Leonard (2020), retired MLB players Tyler Cravy (2020), Bobby Jenks (2019) and CC Sabathia (2016), former NBA player Lamar Odom (2017), and former NHL player Rich Clune (2015). Essays like these can help to further humanize those who suffer from drug addiction and to ground in reality Mickey's struggles with opioids.

Beyond essays, teachers can also bring documentary films into the classroom to share the stories of real athletes who have battled drug addiction. For example, teachers can show a film such as *Unguarded* (Hock, 2011), which focuses on the experience of former NBA player Chris Herren. After starring on the hardwood as a basketball prodigy in Fall River, Massachusetts, during the 1990s, Herron would go on to fail drug tests at two different stops in college and never truly fulfill his promise as a professional basketball player because he was in the clutches of drug addiction. Fortunately, Herren would fight to find redemption and share with today's youth his experiences with drug abuse and addiction. Jonathan Hock, an award-winning filmmaker, told Herren's story in the ESPN Films documentary, which offers a promising companion to *Heroine*. Alternatively, teachers might opt to share Herren's story through excerpts of *Basketball Junkie: A Memoir* (Herren & Reynolds, 2011), which relays Herren's harrowing experience in his own words.

No matter which of the aforementioned texts teachers opt to share as a companion to *Heroine*, students can use a graphic organizer like the one featured in Figure 11.4 for support as they compare and contrast the fictional experiences of Mickey Catalan with those of a real-life athlete who has acknowledged their struggles battling substance abuse and drug addiction. As described in the next section, the notes students take while using the organizer can prove helpful when generating a comparison-and-contrast essay as a culminating task.

Points of Comparison	Mickey Catalan (*Heroine*)	Chris Herren (*Unguarded*)
What factor(s) prompted the athlete's drug use?		
What effect(s) did drug use have on the athlete's relationships with others?		
How, if at all, did the athlete's drug use affect their health?		
How, if at all, did the athlete's drug use affect their performance?		
What brushes with death, if any, did the athlete have as a result of drug use?		
How did people in the athlete's communities respond to their addiction?		
What future plans, if any, were derailed by the athlete's drug addiction?		
Who, if anyone, intervened on the athlete's behalf to help them get clean?		
How willing, if at all, was the athlete to get help for their drug addiction?		
What support, if any, did the athlete receive to support their recovery?		

FIGURE 11.4: A Graphic Organizer for Comparing Mickey's Struggles with Those of a Real Athlete

Culminating Tasks after Reading the Novel

In light of the essential questions and the preceding activities, teachers might invite students to write comparison-and-contrast essays or to take up a poetic response to McGinnis's (2019) novel as described in the following sections.

Writing Comparison-and-Contrast Essays

With students having read *Heroine* and explored the story of a real-life athlete who has publicly addressed their history of substance abuse and drug addiction, teachers can build on that work by facilitating the writing of comparison-and-contrast essays. Students can draw information from their graphic organizers (see Figure 11.4) to support them in writing an essay that compares Mickey Catalan's struggles with drug addiction to those of a real-life athlete whose experience they learned about during the unit of study. For example, teachers might provide students with a prompt like the following:

> *Heroine* (McGinnis, 2019) is a work of fiction, but just how realistic is it? Considering what you have learned about how drug abuse affects individuals and communities, write an essay in which you compare and contrast Mickey Catalan's struggles as an athlete battling drug addiction to those of Chris Herren, the subject of *Unguarded* (Hock, 2011), to make a case that McGinnis's novel is or is not a realistic depiction of an athlete's struggles with drug addiction.

Alternatively, teachers might nudge students to use the book's title as a springboard into a comparison and contrast essay that explores the fine line between an athlete's celebration and condemnation using a prompt like the following:

> The title of McGinnis's (2019) novel *Heroine* plays on a pair of homophones: *heroine*, a woman who is admired for her achievements and/or exceptional qualities, and *heroin*, the highly addictive opioid. The play on words is apt, for Mickey's journey from being celebrated for her accomplishments on the diamond (i.e., "heroine") to being condemned for her abuse of opioids (i.e., "heroin") is short. Unfortunately, Mickey's not alone in falling from grace; numerous real-life athletes have fallen from great heights due to the abuse of drugs and/or alcohol. With that in mind, explore the fleeting nature of heroism and/or the precariousness of humanity in an essay that compares Mickey's experience with that of a real-life athlete whose drug abuse facilitated a considerable fall from grace.

No matter the prompt, we do recommend that teachers provide mini-lessons, engage students in one-to-one conferences, and offer other necessary support to aid students as they develop their essays. For instance, as students begin prewriting, teachers might provide a think-aloud in which they model how to go about determining the points of comparison around which they could develop an essay.

Crafting Responses via Found Poetry

The second essential question presented in this chapter invites students to consider how we respond to people in need. One way students can revisit and respond to that question after reading *Heroine* is by crafting found poetry, which involves the process of excerpting selected words and phrases from an existing text and arranging them to form an original poem. In the classroom, writing found poetry in response to literature is a worthwhile venture because it requires students to return to the book in question, reread sections closely, and locate specific words and phrases they can use to express a particular idea or feeling. In line with the second essential question, we suggest tasking students with writing found poetry to convey how people in Mickey's life respond to her and her needs.

When introducing the concept of found poetry to prospective teachers, Luke has shared excerpts from *Bowietry* (2016), a special issue of *The Found Poetry Review* featuring poems sourced from and inspired by texts associated with musician David Bowie, including album lyrics, screenplays, tweets, and biographies. A sports-specific found poem like "Climbing" by Christina Burress (2011) can also help students see that a found poem consists of content drawn from another source, for it is rich with unique rock-climbing terminology pulled from the 1997 book *Sport Climbing* by John Long. Teachers can even share a model like the multivoiced found poem presented in Figure 11.5 to help students imagine how they might develop an original found poem sourced from McGinnis's novel.

We encourage teachers who facilitate the writing of found poetry to think through the kinds of mini-lessons they can provide to support students in completing the task. For example, recognizing how form serves as an extension of content in poetry, teachers might present students with poems that take different forms and, using a gradual release of responsibility model (Fisher & Frey, 2013), help students analyze how each poem's form contributes to the meaning one makes when reading it. In such a scenario, a teacher might invite students to join in when considering how the content of Walt Whitman's (1855/1977) "Song of Myself" is advanced through the poem's sprawling lines or how, in contrast, John Haines (1966) uses tight, narrow lines in a poem like "Snowy Night" to extend its content. Such work stands to help students see line length as a point of consideration when writing poetry. Students can then apply ideas gleaned through such mini-lessons as they write found poems sourced from *Heroine*.

Taking a step toward social action, teachers can work to ensure that students' poems reach an audience beyond their classmates alone. Promoting and hosting a public poetry reading as Schwalb (2006) described is one way to get students' words out into the world. Alternatively, as Skelton (2006) detailed, students can put their poems on display in a common area within the school, such as a gymnasium. Or, as Buchanan (2012) suggested, students can publish their poems in zines for widespread distribution. Of course, publishing in online venues is a possibility as well. When teaching sophomores from southeast Michigan in an American literature class, Luke positioned them to write for an authentic audience by creating opportunities to publish their poems online. Regardless of the method, we encourage teachers to consider putting into the world students' poetic messages about responding to people in need.

To close this culminating task, teachers can prompt students to submit a reflection with their original found poem. Through reflection, students can

Why would anyone stick
a needle in
their arm?

How many
you need?

Don't
overdo it.

You know
you can talk to me.

You're a goddamn
idiot,
that's what's wrong
with you.

I went through therapy
and took Oxy
just like you.
Why you
and not
me?

I'm calling bullshit
on that.

The drugs were more
important
to you
than everyone; now everyone
has found
more important things
than you.

I need
that relief.

I want to feel
good.

I'm exhausted.

Too tired for words.

I'm not
worried.

I don't know.

That's what I feel like.

Don't go.
Don't
go.

FIGURE 11.5: An Example Found Poem Using *Heroine* as a Source to Convey Responses to Addiction

explain the thinking that went into the piece they created. What were they trying to convey about how people in Mickey's life responded to her and her needs? How do the words and phrases they chose support their intended message? How does the form of their poem extend the content? Answering questions like these in reflection positions students to engage in important metacognitive work, plus it ensures teachers will not be left to simply guess what students had in mind when crafting their found poems.

CONCLUSION

Considering the gravity of the opioid epidemic in the United States, *Heroine* (McGinnis, 2019) is an incredibly important work of contemporary literature—sports-related or otherwise. The compelling story of softball star Mickey Catalan's freefall into opioid addiction creates valuable opportunities for students to build new understandings about the devastating toll drug abuse takes on individuals and communities and to contemplate how we as a society respond to people in need. Making room in the ELA curriculum for McGinnis's distinguished novel stands to help students reckon with the devastation that drug abuse continues to inflict on people from all walks of life. The gripping story is one that students will not soon forget.

Options for Book Clubs

Teachers who prefer to facilitate book clubs as students reckon with drug abuse in sports culture and beyond can present *Heroine* alongside titles that include the following:

Leverage (Cohen, 2011)
Students can read this novel, also a suggested book-club option in Chapter 9, as they reckon with drug abuse among teen athletes. There are many problems with the culture surrounding the football program at fictional Oregrove High School, and steroid use is one of them.

Gym Candy (Deuker, 2007)
Running back Mick Johnson wants to bulk up to improve his game. To gain that edge, he hits the weights and takes supplements, but progress is slow for the eager teen, making a quick-fix via steroids all the more alluring. The shortcut produces results, but at what cost?

Crank (Hopkins, 2004)
This popular novel written in verse features high school junior Kristina Snow, a sixteen-year-old whose life is upended when her introduction to crank (methamphetamine) turns into addiction. This selection provides an option that is not sports-related.

Raiders Night (Lipsyte, 2006)
As the star running back in a football-crazed town, Matt seeks every edge to win. With his football coaches looking the other way, Matt even goes so far as to take drugs that enhance his performance.

Manning Up (Walsh, 2019)
This verse novel, recommended as a book-club option in Chapter 10, can also be incorporated as students explore drug abuse in high school sports. Jack, struggling with body dysmorphia and an eating disorder, begins taking steroids to boost his performance on the football field.

Options for Film Study

Teachers looking to use film study to help students reckon with drug abuse among athletes and everyday people could screen one of the following documentary films:

Doc & Darryl (Apatow & Bonfiglio, 2016)
This film from ESPN's 30 for 30 series revisits the highs and lows experienced by Doc Gooden and Darryl Strawberry, former teammates on MLB's New York Mets in the mid-1980s. The highs involved winning a World Series; the lows involved drug addiction.

Without Bias (Fraser, 2009)
Another film from ESPN's 30 for 30 series, this documentary accounts for the life and tragic death of Len Bias. Though drafted by the Boston Celtics with the second pick of the 1986 NBA Draft, Bias died from cocaine intoxication less than two days later.

Unguarded (Hock, 2011)
This documentary examines the toll drug addiction took on the life and career of Chris Herren, who played professional basketball in the late 1990s and early 2000s, as well as the struggles he endured to get his life back on track.

The Marinovich Project (Stephan & Dorsey, 2011)
This film documents the life of Todd Marinovich, whose father, a strength and conditioning coach, raised him to excel on the gridiron. The vision became reality, as Marinovich played in the NFL, but his life and career were derailed by drug abuse.

Young Adult Literature

Cohen, J. (2011). *Leverage*. Dutton Books for Young Readers.

Deuker, C. (2007). *Gym candy*. Houghton Mifflin.

Hopkins, E. (2004). *Crank*. Simon Pulse.

Lipsyte, R. (2006). *Raiders night*. HarperTempest.

McGinnis, M. (2019). *Heroine*. Katherine Tegen Books.

Walsh, B. (2019). *Manning up*. West 44 Books.

Other Texts for Classroom Use

Apatow, J., & Bonfiglio, M. (Directors). (2016). *Doc & Darryl* [Film]. ESPN Films.

Bowietry. (2016). The Found Poetry Review. https://bowietry.foundpoetryreview.com

Burress, C. (2011, July 3). *Climbing*. The Found Poetry Review: Volume One. https://foundpoetryreview.com/summer-2011/climbing-christina-burress

Centers for Disease Control and Prevention. (2022). *Opioids*. https://www.cdc.gov/opioids/index.html

Clune, R. (2015, July 2). *The battle*. The Players' Tribune. https://www.theplayerstribune.com/articles/rich-clune-hockey-nhl

Cravy, T. (2020, July 22). *Maybe you can help me*. The Players' Tribune. https://www.theplayerstribune.com/articles/tyler-cravy-mlb-milwaukee-brewers-anxiety

Fraser, K. (Director). (2009). *Without Bias* [Film]. ESPN Films.

Haines, J. (1966). *Winter news*. Wesleyan University Press.

Herren, C., & Reynolds, B. (2011). *Basketball junkie: A memoir*. St. Martin's Press.

Hock, J. (Director). (2011). *Unguarded* [Film]. ESPN Films.

Jenks, B. (2019, December 5). *Scar tissue*. The Players' Tribune. https://www.theplayerstribune.com/articles/bobby-jenks-baseball-scar-tissue

Kesey, K. (1962). *One flew over the cuckoo's nest*. Viking Press.

Leonard, S. R. (2020, April 16). *What we need now, more than ever*. The Players' Tribune. https://www.theplayerstribune.com/articles/sugar-ray-leonard-boxing-covid-19-addiction-alcoholics-anonymous

Odom, L. (2017, July 28). *Done in the dark*. The Players' Tribune. https://www.theplayerstribune.com/articles/lamar-odom-done-in-the-dark

Sabathia, C. C. (2016, March 8). *My toughest out*. The Players' Tribune. https://www.theplayerstribune.com/articles/cc-sabathia-yankees-alcohol-addiction-recovery

Stephan, A., & Dorsey, J. (Directors). (2011). *The Marinovich project* [Film]. ESPN Films; TEN100.

TED-Ed. (2020, May 7). *What causes opioid addiction, and why is it so tough to combat?* [Video]. YouTube. https://www.youtube.com/watch?v=V0CdS128-q4

VICE. (2020, October 20). *How America got hooked on opioids* [Video]. YouTube. https://www.youtube.com/watch?v=GJc-YI7OWfY

Whitman, W. (1977). *Leaves of grass* (M. Cowley, Ed.). Penguin Books. (Original work published 1855)

REFERENCES

Ahmad, F. B., Rossen, L. M., & Sutton, P. (2021). *Provisional drug overdose death counts.* National Center for Health Statistics. https://www.cdc.gov/nchs/nvss/vsrr/drug-overdose-data.htm

Bogage, J. (2019, August 30). Angels pitcher Tyler Skaggs had opioids, alcohol in his system at time of death. *The Washington Post.* https://www.washingtonpost.com/sports/2019/08/30/angels-pitcher-tyler-skaggs-had-opioids-alcohol-his-system-time-his-death/?outputType=amp

Buchanan, R. (2012). Zines in the classroom: Reading culture. *English Journal, 102*(2), 71-77.

Bugbee, B. A., Beck, K. H., Fryer, C. S., & Arria, A. M. (2019). Substance use, academic performance, and academic engagement among high school seniors. *Journal of School Health, 89*(2), 145–156.

Centers for Disease Control and Prevention. (2023, August 22). *Drug overdose deaths.* https://www.cdc.gov/drugoverdose/deaths/index.html

Cicero, T. J., Ellis, M. S., Surratt, H. L., & Kurtz, S. P. (2014). The changing face of heroin use in the United States: A retrospective analysis of the past 50 years. *JAMA Psychiatry, 71*(7), 821–826.

Coleman, M. (2021, October 21). Texas LB Jake Ehlinger died of "accidental overdose," family says in statement. *Sports Illustrated.* https://www.si.com/college/2021/10/21/jake-ehlinger-family-says-son-died-accidental-overdose-texas-longhorns-football

Darrow, C. J., Collins, C. L., Yard, E. E., & Comstock, R. D. (2009). Epidemiology of severe injuries among United States high school athletes: 2005–2007. *American Journal of Sports Medicine, 37*(9), 1798–1805.

Denham, B. (2011). Alcohol and marijuana use among American high school seniors: Empirical associations with competitive sports participation. *Sociology of Sport Journal, 28*(3), 362–379.

Feder, K. A., Letourneau, E. J., & Brook, J. (2019). Children in the opioid epidemic: Addressing the next generation's public health crisis. *Pediatrics, 143*(1), 1–3.

Fisher, D., & Frey, N. (2013). *Better learning through structured teaching: A framework for the gradual release of responsibility* (2nd ed.). ASCD.

Ford, J. A., Pomykacz, C., Veliz, P., McCabe, S. E., & Boyd, C. J. (2017). Sports involvement, injury history, and non-medical use of prescription opioids among college students: An analysis with a national sample. *The American Journal on Addictions, 27*(1), 15–22.

Heap, B. (2021, February 28). *"We need to talk about this": Parents warn of fentanyl danger from fake pills after Rocklin teen's heartbreaking death.* KCRA. https://www.kcra.com/article/fentanyl-danger-fake-pills-rocklin-teen-death-kcra/35635277

Hudgins, J. D., Porter, J. J., Monuteaux, M. C., & Bourgeois, F. T. (2019). Prescription opioid use and misuse among adolescents and young adults in the United States: A national survey study. *PLOS Medicine, 16*(11), 1–15.

Lorang, M., Callahan, B., Cummins, K. M., Achar, S., & Brown, S. A. (2011). Anabolic androgenic steroid use in teens: Prevalence, demographics, and perception of effects. *Journal of Child & Adolescent Substance Abuse*, *20*(4), 358–369.

McCabe, S. E., West, B. T., & Boyd, C. J. (2013). Leftover prescription opioids and non-medical use among high school seniors: A multi-cohort national study. *Journal of Adolescent Health*, *52*(4), 480–485.

Milner, J. O., Milner, L. M., & Mitchell, J. F. (2017). *Bridging English* (6th ed.). Pearson.

National Institute on Drug Abuse. (n.d.). *Opioids*. https://www.drugabuse.gov/drug-topics/opioids

Oxenden, M. (2022, July 1). Jaylon Ferguson, Baltimore Ravens linebacker, died from an overdose. *The New York Times*. https://www.nytimes.com/2022/07/01/sports/football/ravens-jaylon-ferguson-fatal-overdose.html

Rief, L. (1992). *Seeking diversity: Language arts with adolescents*. Heinemann.

Schwalb, N. (2006). East of the river: Crossing borders through poetry in middle school. *English Journal*, *96*(1), 40–45.

Skelton, S. (2006). Finding a place for poetry in the classroom every day. *English Journal*, *96*(1), 25–29.

Smagorinsky, P. (2008). *Teaching English by design: How to create and carry out instructional units*. Heinemann.

Smirnov, O. A. (2019). *The economic impact of the opioid epidemic in Northwest Ohio*. The University of Toledo.

Veliz, P. T., Boyd, C., & McCabe, S. E. (2013). Playing through pain: Sports participation and nonmedical use of opioid medications among adolescents. *American Journal of Public Health*, *103*(5), e28–e30.

———. (2015). Competitive sport involvement and substance use among adolescents: A nationwide study. *Substance Use & Misuse*, *50*(2), 156–165.

12 Sports and Sociopolitical Issues: There Is More to Be Done

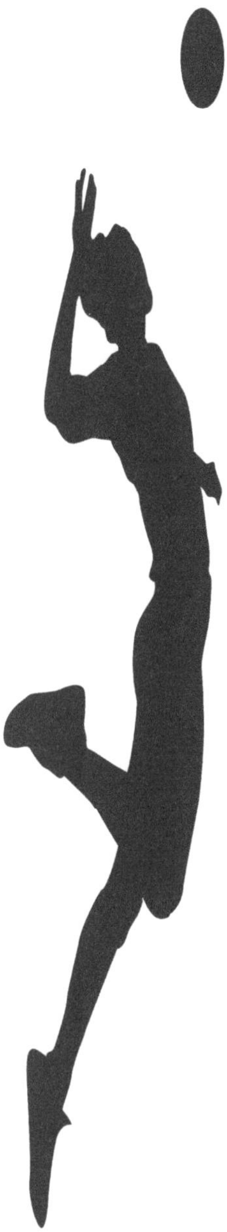

While the preceding chapters stand to support teachers in facilitating the exploration of sociopolitical issues via sports-related young adult literature and other texts from sports culture, the possibilities for such work extend beyond what we are able to include in the pages of this book. No doubt, teachers and students are likely to recognize additional issues that have emerged as matters of concern in the sports world. For instance, the 2022 Beijing Winter Olympic Games raised the specter of climate change and its effects in all our lives, anti-trans legislators have increased resistance to transgender youth's participation in interscholastic sports, and the complicated relationship between sport and religion continues in the United States.

The 2022 United Nations's Intergovernmental Panel on Climate Change Report (IPCC) made it clear that the planet is getting warmer and that the effects of this change in climate will have major repercussions for global communities and events. The environmental circumstances surrounding the 2022 Beijing Winter Olympic Games exemplify the claims made in the IPCC's report. It was the first Winter Olympics to rely completely on artificial snow to host the competitions. In fact, the Chinese government used approximately 49 million gallons of water, at a cost of $4 billion, to provide enough snowpack to ensure safe conditions for the athletes to compete (Moore, 2022). While the International Olympic Committee (2022) made continual claims that they worked with China to minimize the environmental impact of the snowmaking process and that they want both the Summer and Winter Games to become carbon neutral, the environmental impact of such decisions related to hosting large sporting events cannot be ignored. Scientific studies have shown that a vast majority of cities in the Northern Hemisphere will not have safe environmental conditions to host either the Summer or Winter Olympic Games within the next 50 years (Scott et al., 2018; Smith et al., 2016) and that athletes are very concerned about the future sustainability of winter sports (Scott et al., 2023). Discussing with youth the realities of global climate change should be part of any English language arts curriculum (Beach et al., 2017), and using sports-related YAL is one way to engage students with the issue. For example, Alina Chau's (2021) *Marshmallow*

& Jordan tells the fantastical story of Jordan, an Indonesian girl who joins a water polo team after being paralyzed from the waist down in an accident, and Marshmallow, her elephant friend. Her experiences on the water polo team are paired with how her island community is responding to the effects of long-term drought caused by climate change. Reading this graphic novel in conjunction with an exploration of climate change can provide an opportunity for students to think about how the future of sports and environmentalism are intertwined.

In recent years, anti-trans legislators across the US have worked to erase transgender athletes from sports culture. The efforts first took hold in 2020, when Idaho became the first state to pass legislation prohibiting transgender girls and women who attend public schools, colleges, or universities from competing on school-sponsored sports teams that align with their gender identity (Minsberg, 2020). Since then, the number of states that have established laws to prevent transgender athletes from competing in sports alongside others who share their gender identity has exploded. As of this writing, twenty-three states have established such laws (Movement Advancement Project, 2023)—and such anti-trans measures do not stop at the state level. In April of 2023, the US House of Representatives voted to pass a bill aimed at banning transgender athletes from women's and girls' sports at schools and educational institutions that receive federal funding (Karni, 2023). Though not presently taken up by the Senate, this bill and others like it further marginalize youth who are already less likely to participate in team sports for fear of bullying (Ramirez, 2021). The increased marginalization of transgender athletes warrants exploring their stories. With that aim, teachers might account for the story of swimmer Lia Thomas, the first known transgender athlete to win a Division I national championship (Carpenter, 2022). Thomas's experiences invite students to think about matters such as inclusion and fairness, as well as whether both goals can truly be achieved (Barnes, 2022). Incorporating *The Passing Playbook* (Fitzsimons, 2021), a YA novel introduced in Chapter 4, can also be beneficial, for it invites students to reconsider the policies that restrict one's participation in sports and shows what inclusion within team sports can look like for transgender athletes.

The relationship between sport and religion has also received increased attention in recent years, making it a viable topic for exploration. Incidents in which high school athletes were disqualified from competitions in Ohio and Tennessee for wearing a hijab (Stack, 2019; West, 2020) and the Supreme Court's June 2022 ruling that a high school football coach has the right to engage in post-game prayer at the 50-yard line (Liptak, 2022) reveal the intersections of sport and religion. Stories like these invite students to ponder their right to live and take up athletic endeavors in ways that align with their faith, whatever it may be. Moreover, they nudge students to consider how some individuals and not others are marginalized for practicing their faith and to contemplate the measures they are willing to take to fight for religious freedom. And when it comes to YA literature, *Box Out* (Coy, 2008) supports exploring the intersections of religion and sport. In the novel, Liam, a sophomore on his public school's varsity basketball team, is troubled by his coach's insistence on players engaging in team prayers. His discomfort forces him to make difficult decisions and positions him to find out if he can remain true to himself. In that way, the novel invites students to critically consider the popular notion that athletes must sacrifice their identity for team success.

The impact of climate change on sports, the resistance to transgender youth participating in interscholastic sports, and the relationship between sport and religion are but three examples of sociopolitical issues that, while viable for exploration via YAL and other sports-related texts, have gone unaddressed in this book. We encourage readers to consider other possibilities and the shape a full unit of study might take for each.

WORKING IN CHALLENGING TIMES

In Chapter 1, we acknowledged that many of the titles featured in this book may be considered "challenging texts." It is also true that teachers across the US find themselves working in challenging times. Beyond the typical stressors that come with the incredible responsibility of educating our nation's youth, teachers have had to contend with the ongoing threat of gun violence (Taichman, 2023), the burden of sacrificing prep periods to cover unstaffed classes (Superville, 2022), and the weight of morale sinking further and further for various reasons, including insufficient compensation and the de-professionalization of teaching, which has been accelerated as states lower the education requirements for teacher licensing (Will, 2022). Making these times still more challenging for teachers is the pressure external forces, including legislators and conservative advocacy groups, are applying to remove books and snuff out classroom discussions about contemporary sociopolitical issues, including sexual orientation, gender identity, and racism (Pendharkar, 2023). This unique challenge is particularly relevant considering the texts and topics we have suggested taking up in the preceding pages.

We are sympathetic to the concerns we hear from teachers—usually from prospective and early career teachers—about receiving pushback from parents or administrators if they invite students to contemplate what could be perceived as "hot-button" issues. Still, we caution against self-censorship, the avoidance of incorporating into the classroom select texts or topics for fear of the headaches that could follow. The end result of self-censorship is no different than that of book bans or the censorship of particular topics imposed by forces beyond the walls of the classroom: it infringes upon students' right to read and stands to inhibit their understanding of the topics in question. Could an administrator challenge a teacher's decision to facilitate the critical reading of traditional masculinity ideology in *The New David Espinoza* (Aceves, 2020)? Could a parent push back against a teacher choosing to prompt the exploration of LGBTQ+ experiences in sports and society through a unit of study anchored by *Spinning* (Walden, 2017)? Sure. Such scenarios are possible. But it is also true that "any text is potentially open to attack by someone, somewhere, sometime, for some reason" (National Council of Teachers of English, 2018). Recognizing that, we encourage teachers to be wary of self-censorship, to use professional judgment when selecting texts and topics for their instructional units, and to honor the realities of students' lives. Doing the latter requires first recognizing that the world students live in cannot be separated from the sociopolitical issues that make people uncomfortable and then inviting students into honest, open discussions about the world they inhabit, warts and all.

Being prepared to rationalize the classroom use of selected materials can also help when teaching during these challenging times. In this book, the information provided in each core chapter about the featured work of sports-related YAL is intended to help teachers rationalize the title's inclusion in the secondary ELA curriculum. Additionally, teachers may find a resource such as NCTE's This Story Matters helpful when justifying the selection of a particular text. Launched in 2022 with support from Penguin Random House Education, This Story Matters is an online database of rationales for books teachers might use in the classroom. Rationales in the database include various elements, including a summary, grade-level suggestions, the titles of texts that could be provided as alternatives, and more. So, teachers can bolster their justifications for using select texts by tapping into that database, a move that is sure to support their work in these challenging times.

SOCIAL JUSTICE: ACTION & ADVOCACY

In Chapter 1, we drew from Morrell (2005) and Vasquez et al. (2019) to stress that teaching for critical literacy involves not only facilitating the examination of sociopolitical issues in ways that scrutinize the status quo and challenge inequities but also working to redesign a better world. Now, all these chapters later, we reiterate that point to stress the important role social action plays in enacting critical literacy. Reading about and discussing sociopolitical issues is necessary work, but change also requires action that pushes beyond the classroom alone.

Some of the preceding chapters include more ideas for social action than others, but we hope that readers see the malleability of those projects. For example, in Chapter 4 we recommended that teachers support students in developing and distributing public service announcements (PSAs) about sexual violence in sports culture. Creating and administering original PSAs to improve communities is work students and teachers could take up when exploring other sociopolitical issues addressed in this book, including hazing and bullying, sport-induced brain trauma, and drug abuse. As well, we encourage teachers to consider the social action of students sharing their words—either written or spoken—with an audience beyond their peers in the classroom. For instance, in Chapter 9 we suggested that teachers engage students in developing and delivering "here to stay" speeches. Whether shared virtually in online spaces, broadcast on local TV, or delivered to an in-person audience, the celebration of qualities that make students who they are could stand as a powerful form of social action, a step toward fostering a community of acceptance. With that model in mind, we encourage teachers to contemplate how, in the spirit of social action, they can help students share with a wider audience their writings about contemporary sociopolitical issues.

When writing about or otherwise digging deeply into issues at the heart of the stories featured in this book, some students may find themselves looking to take action beyond that which teachers are able to facilitate with an entire class. We hope that, in such instances, teachers will embrace the role of ally and aid students in carrying out responsible actions that promote social justice. In *The Running Dream* (Van Draanen, 2011), the novel anchoring Chapter 5, Coach Kyro goes the extra mile to help student-athlete Jessica Carlisle not only run again but do so while promoting inclusion and treating her friend Rosa to the thrill of a race for the very first time. Kyro's efforts stand as a model for the kind of allyship and advocacy that teachers, coaches, and other figures in students' lives can provide to lift them up as they strive to make a difference in the world they inhabit.

SPORT, LITERACY, AND SOCIETY

Throughout contemporary US history, stories about sports and sport culture have stood alongside other headlines on the "front page" of news and social media outlets. For example, in late summer 2022, headlines across major media outlets—NBC News, Fox News, and CNN—encouraged readers to learn more about the war in the Ukraine, how the US Senate planned to address economic inflation, and the continuing investigation into the January 6 insurrection. Among those headlines reflecting current social and political concerns, readers would have also found headlines directing them to learn more about Brittney Griner, Deshaun Watson, Alexander Trent-Arnold, Rolando McClain, and the start of a new NFL season. These latter stories are not relegated to the "sports" section but can be found on the homepages of these media outlets. Some of the stories did fade—such as the piece about the family-focused life of Trent-Arnold (Lewis & Morse, 2022) and the one about criminal charges against McClain (Dedaj, 2022)—but some of them endured. For example, Griner's complicated story (Da Silva, 2022) of her arrest by Russian officials for drug possession, whether she was being exploited as a "political pawn" and the use of her sports-celebrity status to raise awareness about all Americans unjustly imprisoned across the world, was the focus of popular media beginning with her detainment in February 2022 and continuing long into 2023. As well, arguments about the appropriate punishment—at the criminal, civic, and professional levels—for Watson's serial sexual misconduct remained the center of popular media discussions from the filing of the first lawsuit against him in March 2021 into the 2023 NFL preseason (Coleman & Perez 2022; Leitch 2022; Maaddi 2023). The presence of these sports-related stories mixed with other social and political content demonstrates that sports are inextricable from contemporary society, as we have repeatedly illustrated across the preceding chapters. Moreover, these stories reveal that sports are not immune to social, cultural, and political concerns and movements rippling through society and that they often play central roles in those concerns and movements.

As we argued throughout this book, interest in sports is a useful way to engage secondary students with literacy processes and practices. Students who are highly connected to sports most likely already read sports-related news, follow favorite athletes on social media, and view sports-related television and films. Even youth who are not highly intrigued by sports-related entertainment often attend interscholastic sporting events as part of their social lives or might follow other sports-related news stories, such as ones that include many of the sociopolitical concerns the chapters in this book discuss. This engagement, at any level, not only supports the enrichment of traditional literacy practices but also critical literacy practices as youth contemplate and critique the role of sports in their lives and in society.

So, sports matter. Not in the way that Black lives matter or LGBTQ+ rights matter. But in the way that they are not just simply entertainment or distraction; sports matter because they both reflect society and influence how people view sociopolitical issues. Audiences can witness the joy of community as a local team rallies together not just to win on the field but to support struggling members living in their neighborhoods and schools. Audiences see the special treatment some famous athletes receive—similar to the privilege other famous and/or wealthy people in our society receive—when they act criminally or egregiously. Yet audiences can also recognize athletes who use their fame to advocate for change and who proudly put their own human faces on abstract social ills. As educators, it is possible to ignore sports when discussing sociopolitical concerns with youth, but we argue that decision unnecessarily limits the opportunities to engage youth with various issues, to show them how those concerns permeate all aspects of our lives, and to help them think about using their personal passions to advance social justice and effect productive change. The stories shared in the young adult literature presented throughout this book teach readers much about sport but, more important, they also teach readers much about life.

Young Adult Literature

Aceves, F. (2020). *The new David Espinoza*. HarperTeen.

Chau, A. (2021). *Marshmallow & Jordan*. First Second.

Coy, J. (2008). *Box out*. Scholastic Press.

Fitzsimons, I. (2021). *The passing playbook*. Dial Books.

Van Draanen, W. (2011). *The running dream*. Knopf Books for Young Readers.

Walden, T. (2017). *Spinning*. First Second.

REFERENCES

Barnes, K. (2022, February 20). *Penn swimmer Lia Thomas leaves Ivy League meet a four-time champion, but questions remain.* ESPN. https://www.espn.com/college-sports/story/_/id/33332856/penn-swimmer-lia-thomas-leaves-ivy-league-meet-four-champion-questions-remain

Beach, R., Share, J., & Webb, A. (2017). *Teaching climate change to adolescents: Reading, writing, and making a difference.* Routledge.

Carpenter, L. (2022, March 20). Lia Thomas broke no records at the NCAA championships but left plenty of questions. *The Washington Post.* https://www.washingtonpost.com/sports/2022/03/20/lia-thomas-ncaa-swimming-championships-questions/

Coleman, M., & Perez, D. (2022, June 21). Deshaun Watson timeline: What has happened since first lawsuit filed. *Sports Illustrated.* https://www.si.com/nfl/2022/03/11/deshaun-watson-timeline-what-has-occurred-first-lawsuit-filed

Da Silva, C. (2022, August 5). *Russia says it's ready to discuss prisoner swap with U.S. after Griner gets 9 years in jail.* NBC News. https://www.nbcnews.com/news/world/russia-ready -discuss-prisoner-swap-us-griner-sentence-rcna41683

Dedaj, P. (2022, August 4). *Ex-Cowboys linebacker Rolando McClain arrested on gun, drug charges: Report.* Fox News. https://www.foxnews.com/sports/ex-cowboys-linebacker-rolando-mcclain-arrested-gun-drug-charges-report

Intergovernmental Panel on Climate Change. (2022). *Climate change 2022: Impacts, adaptation and vulnerability.* https://report.ipcc.ch/ar6/wg2/IPCC_AR6_WGII_FullReport.pdf

International Olympic Committee. (2022, February 9). *Sustainability in the spotlight at Beijing 2022.* https://olympics.com/ioc/news/sustainability-in-the-spotlight-at-beijing-2022

Karni, A. (2023, April 20). House passes bill to bar transgender athletes from female sports teams. *The New York Times.* https://www.nytimes.com/2023/04/20/us/politics/transgender-athlete-ban-bill.html

Leitch, W. (2022, August 2). *How not to talk about Deshaun Watson's six-game NFL suspension.* NBC News. https://www.nbcnews.com/think/opinion/nfl-suspends-clevelands-deshaun-watson-six-games-nice-try-rcna41056

Lewis, D., & Morse, B. (2022, August 4). *Trent Alexander-Arnold: The Premier League winner who still lives at home and helps his parents with the dishes.* CNN. https://www.cnn.com/2022/08/04/football/trent-alexander-arnold-liverpool-premier-league-spt-intl/index.html

Liptak, A. (2022, June 27). Supreme Court sides with coach over prayers at the 50-yard line. *The New York Times.* https://www.nytimes.com/2022/06/27/us/politics/supreme-court-coach-prayers.html

Maaddi, R. (2023, August 4). *Deshaun Watson moving forward heading into his first full season since his suspension.* Associated Press. https://apnews.com/article/deshaun-watson-new-season-959ed3acda9aed3971e6fdcefa9250c3

Minsberg, T. (2020, April 1). "Boys are boys and girls are girls": Idaho is first state to bar some transgender athletes. *The New York Times.* https://www.nytimes.com/2020/04/01/sports/transgender-idaho-ban-sports.html

Moore, A. (2022, February 10). *Beijing Winter Olympics a cautionary climate tale, expert says.* NC State University College of Natural Resources News. https://cnr.ncsu.edu/news/2022/02/beijing-winter-olympics-a-cautionary-climate-tale-expert-says/

Morrell, E. (2005). Critical English education. *English Education, 37*(4), 312–321.

Movement Advancement Project. (2023). *Bans on transgender youth participation in sports.* https://www.lgbtmap.org/equality-maps/youth/sports_participation_bans

National Council of Teachers of English. (2018, October 25). *The students' right to read.* https://ncte.org/statement/righttoreadguideline

———. (2023). *This story matters.* https://ncte.org/book-rationales/this-story-matters/

Pendharkar, E. (2023, March 29). Book challenges doubled in 2022 and became more organized. *Education Week*. https://www.edweek.org/teaching-learning/book-challenges-doubled-in-2022-and-became-more-organized/2023/03

Ramirez, M. (2021, September 16). LGBTQ youths are less likely to play sports because of bullying—and advocates fear they're missing out. *USA Today*. https://www.usatoday.com/story/news/2021/09/16/lgbtq-youth-mostly-avoid-sports-citing-bullying-and-discrimination/8347727002/

Scott, D., Knowles, N. L. B., Ma, S., Rutty, M., & Steiger, R. (2023). Climate change and the future of the Olympic Winter Games: Athlete and coach perspectives. *Current Issues in Tourism, 26*(3), 480–495. https://www.tandfonline.com/doi/pdf/10.1080/13683500.2021.2023480?needAccess=true

Scott, D., Steiger, R., Rutty, M., & Fang, Y. (2018). The changing geography of the Winter Olympic and Paralympic Games in a warmer world. *Current Issues in Tourism, 22*(11), 1301–1311.

Smith, K. R., Woodward, A., Lemke, B., Otto, M., Chang, C. J., Mance, A. A., Balmes, J., & Kjellstrom, T. (2016). The last Summer Olympics? Climate change, health, and work outdoors. *The Lancet, 388*(10045), 642–644.

Stack, L. (2019, October 24). Muslim student athlete disqualified from race for wearing hijab. *The New York Times*. https://www.nytimes.com/2019/10/24/us/Ohio-hijab-runner.html

Superville, D. R. (2022, October 13). Schools are still understaffed. Here's how hard-pressed principals are responding. *Education Week*. https://www.edweek.org/leadership/schools-are-still-understaffed-heres-how-hard-pressed-principals-are-responding/2022/10

Taichman, M. G. (2023). What I learned in school today. *The New England Journal of Medicine*, *389*(9).

Vasquez, V. M., Janks, H., & Comber, B. (2019). Critical literacy as a way of being and doing. *Language Arts*, *96*(5), 300–311.

West, J. (2020, September 28). Muslim athlete disqualified from high school volleyball game for wearing hijab. *Sports Illustrated*. https://www.si.com/high-school/2020/09/28/muslim-athlete-disqualified-high-school-volleyball-game-hijab

Will, M. (2022, June 28). States relax teacher certification rules to combat shortages. *Education Week*. https://www.edweek.org/teaching-learning/states-relax-teacher-certification-rules-to-combat-shortages/2022/06

Index

The letter *f* following a page locator denotes a figure.

Authors

Luke Rodesiler is associate professor of secondary education and chair of the Department of Teacher Education at Purdue University Fort Wayne. He previously worked as a high school English teacher and coach in Michigan. His research interests include the use of popular cultural texts in the secondary English language arts classroom, nontraditional forms of teacher professional development, and media literacy education. His work has appeared in various book chapters and in refereed journals that include *English Education, English Journal, Journal of Adolescent & Adult Literacy, English Teaching: Practice and Critique,* and *The ALAN Review*. He is also a coeditor of *Developing Contemporary Literacies through Sports* (NCTE Press) and the author of *Bringing Sports Culture to the English Classroom* (Teachers College Press).

Mark A. Lewis is professor of literacy education at James Madison University. His research interests include examining and critiquing representations of adolescence and youth in young adult and adult literature, defining the multifaceted literary competence of secondary students, and identifying effective ways to support linguistically diverse learners. Prior to coming to JMU, he taught middle school English and En-glish as a second language in Arizona and worked with Indigenous high school students in Colorado. Dr. Lewis has over 30 publications, including multiple book chapters and in scholarly journals such as *English Education, English Journal, Middle Grades Research Journal, Study & Scrutiny, The ALAN Review, Journal of Literacy Research,* and *Reading Research Quarterly*. He is also a coauthor of *Rethinking the "Adolescent" in Adolescent Literacy* (NCTE Press).

Alan Brown is associate professor of English education and chair of the Department of Education at Wake Forest University. A former high school English teacher and basketball coach, he is the inaugural director for the Wake Forest Center for Literacy Education and a leadership team member for the Skip Prosser Literacy Program and Winston-Salem TEACH. Dr. Brown teaches undergraduate and graduate courses on topics including action research, adolescent literacy, arts integration, secondary education, and young adult literature. His scholarly interests include critically examining the culture of sports in schools and society while connecting contemporary literacies to students' extracurricular interests. He is the coeditor of *Developing Contemporary Literacies through Sports* (NCTE Press) and has published in numerous journals related to education, sport, and young adult literature.

This book was typeset in Myriad Pro and Palatino by Barbara Frazier.

The typefaces used on the cover include ITC Franklin Gothic LT Demi, Franklin Gothic Medium, Egyptian Slate Pro, and Freeland.

The book was printed on 50 lb., white offset paper.

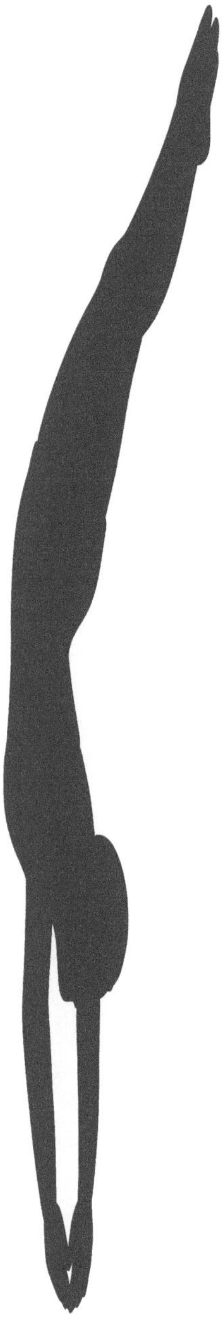